The Silencing of
Jesuit Figurist
Joseph de Prémare in
Eighteenth-Century China

The Silencing of Jesuit Figurist Joseph de Prémare in Eighteenth-Century China

D. E. Mungello

LEXINGTON BOOKS
Lanham • Boulder • New York • London

Published by Lexington Books
An imprint of The Rowman & Littlefield Publishing Group, Inc.
4501 Forbes Boulevard, Suite 200, Lanham, Maryland 20706
www.rowman.com

6 Tinworth Street, London SE11 5AL, United Kingdom

Copyright © 2019 by The Rowman & Littlefield Publishing Group, Inc.

Cover image: The Ruined Church of San Paulo. Macau, China. Universal Photo Art Co. Philadelphia: C. H. Graves, publisher, ca. 1904. Library of Congress Prints and Photographs Division, Washington, D.C.

All rights reserved. No part of this book may be reproduced in any form or by any electronic or mechanical means, including information storage and retrieval systems, without written permission from the publisher, except by a reviewer who may quote passages in a review.

British Library Cataloguing in Publication Information Available

Library of Congress Cataloging-in-Publication Data

Names: Mungello, D. E. (David Emil), 1943-, author.
Title: The silencing of Jesuit figurist Joseph de Premare in eighteenth-century China / D. E. Mungello.
Description: Lanham : Lexington Books, 2019. | Includes bibliographical references and index.
Identifiers: LCCN 2019012158| ISBN 9781498595643 (cloth) | ISBN 9781498595650 (electronic) | ISBN 9781498595667 (pbk) Subjects: LCSH: Premare, Joseph Henri, 1666-1736. | Jesuits—China—Biography. | Jesuits—China—Missions—History. | Christianity and other religions—Chinese.
Classification: LCC BX4705.P691676 M86 2019 | DDC 271/.5302 [B] —dc23
LC record available at https://lccn.loc.gov/2019012158

Contents

List of Illustrations	vii
Preface	ix
Introduction	1
1 Water	5
2 Drama versus History	25
3 The *Vestigia*	45
4 Daoism and Hieroglyphics in the *Vestigia*	67
5 Earth to Earth, Dust to Dust	87
Bibliography	105
Index	115
About the Author	123

List of Illustrations

Map 1. China ca. 1700.

Map 2. Seventeenth-Century Provinces of China. From Martino Martini's *De bello tartarico historia* (1654).

Figure 1.1. Han Tan's preface to Joachim Bouvet's *Tianxue benyi*. 1703. Bouvet, Joachim, SJ. *Gujin jing Tian jian Tianxue benyi* (An Examination of the original meaning of the Heavenly Teaching in the ancient and modern expression "revere Heaven"), Zikawei (Xujiahui) Library, Shanghai.

Figure 1.2. The first page of Prémare's Latin translation of Han Tan's preface to Bouvet's *Cuelestls disciplina vera notitia* (A Report on the true teaching of Heaven), Biblioteca Fabroniana, Pistoia, Ms. 53, 1703 (?), translated from *Gujin jing Tian jian Tianxue benyi*.

Figure 2.1. Prologue to Prémare's *Tchao Chi Con Ell [Zhao Shi Gu Er] ou Le Petit Orphelin de la Maison de Tchao. Tragedie Chinoise*. Paris, 1735.

Figure 2.2. The first page of Prémare's ancient history of the world according to the Chinese, published as *Discours Preliminaire* (composed 1730), published together with Antoine Gaubil's *Le Chou-king*. Paris, 1770.

Figure 3.1. First page of Joseph de Prémare's SJ. *Selecta quaedam Vestigia praecipuorum Christianae relligionis dogmatum ex antiquis Sinarum Libris Eruta* (Certain selected vestiges of principal Christian religious teachings extracted from ancient Chinese books). Canton, 1725.

Figure 3.2. Yellow River Chart and Luo River Book (*Hetu luoshu*) (*Vestiges*, p. 376).

Figure 3.3. An ancient image of the nonary chart on the back of a horse wading in the Yellow River (*Hetu*) and the nonary diagram on a tortoise shell emerging from the Luo River (*Luoshu*).

Figure 3.4. Title page of Prémare's *Vestiges des principaux dogmes chrétiens tirés des anciens livres chinois.*
Edited and translated by Augustin Bonnetty & Paul Perny. Paris, 1878.

Figure 3.5. Genealogical Table of Chinese Antiquity (*Vestigia*, f. 306v).

Figure 3.6. Jing 井 Diagram and Royal City Diagram (*Vestigia*, f. 97v).

Figure 4.1. The Kunlun Mountain Earthly Paradise, based on *Shanhaijing* (Classic of Mountains and Seas) (*Vestigia,* f. 65v)

Figure 4.2. The Kunlun Mountain Earthly Paradise and the Buzhou Mountain Celestial Palace, based on *Shanhaijing* (Classic of Mountains and Seas).
Adapted by Bonnetty and Perny in *Vestiges*, p. 132.

Figure 4.3. Title page of Prémare's *Notitia Linguae Sinicae* (An examination of the Chinese Language). Malacca, 1831.

Figure 4.4. Preface of Prémare's *Liu shu shiyi* 六書實意 (The true meaning of the six kinds of Chinese characters). 1720. Zikawei Library, Shanghai.

Figure 5.1. The Diagram of the Supreme Ultimate (*Taiji tushuo* 太極圖說) by Zhou Dunyi (1017–1073). In *Xingli jingyi* 性理精義 (The Essential Meaning of Neo-Confucianism), edited by Li Guangdi, 1715–1717.

Preface

My first encounter with the works of the China scholar-priest Joseph Henry-Marie de Prémare, SJ was in June of 1974 when I was returning from a year of teaching at Lingnan College in Hong Kong. On the way back to the United States, I stopped off at Rome in order to visit the Vatican Library. There I found a copy of the *Vestiges des principaux dogmes chrétiens tires des anciens livres chinois* (Vestiges of the principal Christian teachings extracted from ancient Chinese books), the 1878 French adaptation of Father Prémare's 1725 unpublished work. I was so fascinated by the book that I had it photocopied and carried the copy back to the U.S. where it remained in a file for forty-three years. The reason it remained untouched was because at that time, I lacked the ability to undertake this intimidating project. And yet it was too fascinating a work to discard. Finally, after teaching my last class in May 2017, I returned to this work.

In the intervening forty-three years since I obtained a copy of Prémare's work, I found that the *Vestiges* and the original manuscript on which it was based had remained practically untouched by scholars. The sole copy of *Selecta quaedam Vestigia praecipuorum Christianae relligionis dogmatum ex antiquis Sinarum Libris Eruta* (Certain selected vestiges of principal Christian religious teachings extracted from ancient Chinese books) was preserved at the Bibliothèque nationale Paris. The original reasons for its suppression had been removed by the passage of time, but the intellectual demands of undertaking a study of it remained considerable. The bilingual (Latin and Chinese) form of the handwritten manuscript combined two difficult languages that were rarely combined in the training of contemporary scholars. The extensive quotations in Chinese were drawn from a mixture of demanding Chinese texts that cross the lines of academic specializations (Sinology, history, etymology, mathematics, philosophy, and religion). Moreover, Prémare quoted Chinese texts using abbreviated bibliographical citations, following the traditional assumption of Chinese literati that readers were familiar with these canonical works. Also, Prémare used an arcane eighteenth-century Romanization with which few scholars were familiar. Finally, the subject matter of the *Vestigia* used an approach to hieroglyphic characters that is alien to modern linguistic theories.

In addition to all of the above impediments to the scholarly study of the *Vestigia*, there is the radical nature of Figurism itself. Condemned by clerics and intellectuals alike, Figurism seemed to have little relevance to modern scholarship. Unprepared to deal with as demanding a text as the *Vestigia*, I began by studying a more modest work by Prémare entitled *Essai sur le monothéisme de Chinois* (1728) which was edited and published by G. Pauthier in 1861. Thanks to the invitation of the late Professor Wm. Theodore de Bary (1919–2017), I was able to present the results of this early research to the Regional Seminar in Neo-Confucian Studies at Columbia University in 1975. This was followed by the publication of an article on this work by Prémare in *Philosophy East and West*.[1] Over the following four decades, I would return to Prémare again and again, but always in an indirect way.

In order to convey the Sinification of Prémare's mind and sensibility that occurred during the thirty-eight years of his residence in China, I have named each of the chapters in this book after one of the Chinese five elements (water, fire, wood, metal, and earth). The order of the five elements can be enumerated in different ways, but I have chosen to use the order in which the elements are given in the *Classic of History* (*Shujing* 書經 or *Shangshu* 尚書) because of Prémare's deep familiarity with this book. Having spent the first thirty-two years of his life in Europe, it is difficult to say that Prémare became fully Sinified, and yet his way of thinking had become alien to many Europeans. The challenge to readers today, three centuries later, is to read the same words from Chinese texts that he read and try to make the same connections that he made.

I am deeply indebted to great teachers and erudite colleagues. I was introduced to Chinese antiquity by Professor Ho Ping-ti (He Bingdi) (1917–2012) in a history course at University of California Berkeley in 1967. Professor Peter A. Boodberg (1903–1972) and his teaching assistant William G. Boltz introduced me to literary Chinese. Professor Joseph R. Levenson (1920–1969) introduced me to Confucianism. Professor Wing-tsit Chan (1901–1994) was a living link to the literati tradition and he kindly responded to my queries, including assistance in translating the Yongzheng emperor's memorial of 1727. Professor Jonathan Chaves was tireless in helping me translate difficult Chinese passages. Dr. Ad Dudink was always available to answer my numerous technical questions involving texts and Chinese terms in the history of Christianity of China. He and Professor Nicolas Standaert provided crucial assistance in helping with two of the illustrations. Professor Claudia von Collani was a rich and generous source of information on the Figurists. Dr. Giuliano Mori kindly shared his copy of the *Vestigia*. P. Professor Zbigniew Wesołowski, SVD provided crucial assistance in helping me obtain some Chinese articles.

Finally, I owe an enormous debt to my late friend and colleague Professor Knud Lundbæk (1912–1995). We shared a common interest in Prémare and he gave me great assistance through our correspondence. Lundbæk's 1991 book on Prémare was ground-breaking and has been of great value to me in composing this work.

I dedicate this book to the memory of my father, Donald Domenico Mungello (1913–1983).

D. E. M.
Waco, Texas, December 2018

NOTE

1. David E. Mungello, "The Reconciliation of Neo-Confucianism with Christianity in the Writings of Joseph de Prémare, SJ," *Philosophy East and West* 26 (4) (October 1976): 389–410.

Introduction

The antiquity of China is both its greatest glory and its greatest mystery. There is little doubt that it is the longest continuous civilization in the world, based in large part on the continuity of its written language. However, debate continues over whether China can lay claim, along with Sumeria and Egypt, to being one of the oldest civilizations in the world and to what extent its development was independent from the rest of the world. In 1975, the eminent historian Ho Ping-ti (He Bingdi 何炳棣) stirred debate on these topics in his controversial book *The Cradle of the East*.

Prof. Ho was born in 1917 and educated in the atmosphere of the Chinese Renaissance that combined admiration for the West with iconoclasm toward China's past. He migrated to the United States in 1945. In 1968 he realized that for decades he had been "an unknowing victim of certain forms of Western intellectual chauvinism."[1] This realization, combined with recent archeological advances in China, allowed him to make the bold claim that China had developed independently from other ancient civilizations and to push back the origins of Chinese civilization to 5000–1000 BC. He claimed that carbon-14 dating traced the development in China of dry-land farming based primarily on millet to around 5000 BC. He argued that continuities over three and a half millennia from an early phase of Yangshao culture to the late Shang period would push back the beginnings of Chinese writing to the first half of the fifth millennium BC. Such an early origin of Chinese writing would predate the earliest Sumerian cuneiform script dating from 3100 BC or 3200 BC and make China the oldest civilization in the world.

As the first Asian-born scholar to be elected president of the Association for Asian Studies, Prof. Ho was able to follow up his book with a widely publicized presidential address to the Association for Asian Studies annual meeting at Toronto in 1976.[2] He cited archeological findings of about twenty-two potsherds with incised word-signs found at the Yangshao cultural site of

Banpo (near Xi'an). He believed this provided evidence to support the claim that shortly after 5000 BC, proto-Chinese groups in the Wei River basin had reached a level of indigenous cultural development that produced a simple script which marked the beginning of Chinese civilization. The claims in Ho's book were controversial and one reviewer criticized him for allowing himself to be influenced by "national pride."[3] Another reviewer accused him of replacing "Western intellectual chauvinism" with "Greater Han chauvinism."[4]

The matter remains unresolved and the debate over China's antiquity has continued. In November of 2000 the Xia-Shang-Zhou Chronology Project sponsored by the Chinese government and involving 200 scholars announced that it had substantiated traditional claims for pushing back China's historical record 1,229 years—from 771 BC, that is, from the fall of the Western Zhou dynasty back to 2070 BC when the Xia dynasty is said to have begun.[5] The announcement was given a lot of publicity in Chinese media, but was criticized by numerous scholars both inside and outside of China for being tainted by political and nationalistic concerns.[6]

The dating of Chinese antiquity has a long history of scholarly debate within China. In the early eighteenth century, a small group of China Jesuits entered that great debate and developed a controversial new theory on dating China's antiquity. This new theory developed out of the earlier work of Jesuits in China. The origin of Jesuit accommodation around 1600 by Father Matteo Ricci (1552–1610) evolved a century later into the development of Figurism by the Jesuit Father Joachim Bouvet (1656–1730).[7] The Figurists drew from an ancient Christian interpretation of Scripture or hermeneutical method of Biblical exegesis.[8] According to this tradition, the coming of Christ and its significance was prefigured in the Old Testament. This knowledge was presented in symbolical, allegorical and archetypal forms of figura.

In the previous century there had been a vogue for these theories among notable scholars, such as Athanasius Kircher (1602–1680). He argued that the Ancient Theology (*prisca theologia*) texts ascribed to Hermes Trigmegistus, Pythagoras, and others anticipated the Christian cross and the Trinity. Although the scholarship of the Hermeticists was flawed, the basic ideas of their claims continued to live on and were adopted and modified to China by the Jesuit Figurists.[9] However, their theory was so radical that it was suppressed by both the Catholic Church and the secular thinkers of the Enlightenment. This book is an account of the silencing of one of the leading figures in that group who spent most of thirty-eight years in remote areas of China pouring over Chinese books and developing this theory.

Joseph Henry-Marie de Prémare, SJ (1666–1736) was a scholar and missionary in China whose extensive study of ancient Chinese texts led him to conclude that these texts were metaphorical rather than historical in nature. He claimed that when read metaphorically, the ancient Chinese texts contained evidence of a universal true religion and a direct Revelation of Christ's teaching years before Jesus had even lived. This interpretation led him to claim that these ancient texts were not historical records of the Xia, Shang and Western Zhou dynasties, but rather forms of symbolic theology. Ho Ping-ti claimed that the "earliest absolute date in Chinese history" was 841 BC when King Li 厲 of the Western Zhou was deposed and the He 和 regency under Lord Gong 共 was established. He said that the fall of the Zhou in 771 BC was an indisputable date.[10] Prémare, by comparison, claimed that the Chinese historical texts would support dating the beginning of Chinese history only from the eighth century BC (770 BC or 722 BC).

In the seventeenth century, numerous Europeans had formulated radical theories about China.[11] Prémare differed from those amateur proto-Sinologists in having a sophisticated knowledge of a wide range of Chinese ancient texts. Of the Figurists, he composed the most complete articulation of this theory. Although his theory conflicted with established eighteenth-century European religious and intellectual thinking, Father Prémare claimed that he was obliged by his faith to reveal to the Chinese a teaching buried in their ancient texts which they had lost in the intervening centuries.

The debate and acrimony over the radical nature of Figurist ideas has obscured the fact that the Figurists surpassed most of the Jesuit accommodationists who followed Matteo Ricci in their knowledge of Chinese texts. While the spirit of accommodation between European Christianity and Chinese culture continued into the eighteenth century, the greater knowledge of Figurists like Prémare led to a more nuanced understanding of the relationship between Christianity and other elements of Chinese culture, particularly Daoism. Because of their emphasis on the Five Classics (*Wu Jing*), the Figurists were sometimes called Jingists.[12]

There was enormous resistance to these so-called "Figurist" ideas, although the greatest resistance did not come from the Chinese. The resistance included not only most of Prémare's fellow China missionaries as well as Vatican clerics, but also most European savants, with some high-profile exceptions like the philosopher G. W. Leibniz (1646–1716) who was fascinated by Figurism and its implications for the universal nature of religious truths. Over the years, Prémare avoided the limelight and worked quietly mainly in isolated areas of China. However, the power of Figurist ideas eventually provoked such a negative reaction that his writings were forbidden by his superiors to be published or even circulated. Intellectuals in Europe refused his pleas to disseminate his ideas. He ended his life in exile and poverty. Most of his writings lay unread in manuscripts for many years. This is an account of their contents and the struggle of Father Prémare to bring them to light.

NOTES

1. Ho Ping-ti, *The Cradle of the East: An Inquiry into the Indigenous Origins of Techniques and Ideas of Neolithic and Early Historic China, 5000–1000 B.C.* (Hong Kong: Chinese University of Hong Kong Press; Chcago: University of Chicago Press, 1975), p. xvii.

2. Ho Ping-ti, "The Chinese Civilization: A Search for the Roots of Its Longevity," *Journal of Asian Studies* 35 (1976): 551.

3. E. G. Pulleyblank, review of Ho Ping-ti's *Cradle of the East, Journal of Asian Studies* 36 (1977): 715–17.

4. David N. Keightley, "Ping-ti Ho and the Origins of Chinese Civilization," *Harvard Journal of Asiatic Studies* 37 (1977): 397.

5. Erik Eckholm, "In China, Ancient History Kindles Modern Doubts," *New York Times*, November 10, 2000.

6. The politics of racial nationalism also plays a role in the debate over the paleoanthropological origins of the Chinese and whether the Chinese share a common human origin with the rest of the world. See Yinghong Cheng, "'Is Peking Man Still Our Ancestor?'—Genetics, Anthropology, and the Politics of Racial Nationalism in China," *Journal of Asian Studies* 76 (2017): 575–602.

7. D. E. Mungello, *Curious Land: Jesuit Accommodation and the Origins of Sinology* (Stuttgart: Steiner Verlag, 1985), p. 18–19.

8. Michael Lackner, "Jesuit Figurism." In *China and Europe: Images and Influences in Sixteenth to Eighteenth Centuiries*. Thomas H. C. Lee, ed. (Hong Kong: Chinese University Press, 1991), p. 130.

9. Mungello, *Curious Land*, p. 136–37.

10. Ping-ti Ho, *The Cradle of the East*, p. 1.

11. For a discussion of the theories about China developed by seventeenth-century European proto-Sinologists, see D. E. Mungello, *Curious Land: Jesuit Accommodation and the Origins of Sinology* (Stuttgart: Franz Steiner Verlag, 1985), p. 134–246.

12. Sebald Reil, *Kilian Stumpf 1655–1720. Ein Würzburger Jesuit am Kaiserhof zu Peking* (Münster Westfalen: Aschendorff, 1978), p. 160.

Chapter One

Water

Water is the first of the Five Elements

CROSSING THE GREAT STREAM

Water—for seven months he was surrounded by it, passing the Cape of Good Hope, Batavia, and Malacca. Years later when he studied the Classic of Changes (*Yijing*), he would read the prophetic passage from the *Tong Ren* 同仁 (Uniting People) hexagram: "It will be advantageous to cross the great stream."[1] When the Jesuit Joseph Henry-Marie de Prémare ended his long sea voyage from France to China and stepped ashore in the Portuguese colony of Macau on October 24, 1698, he was thirty-two years old. He was beginning a cycle that would end thirty-eight years later when he would be forced to return to Macau as one of the most accomplished Sinologists the world had ever known to die in poverty and obscurity.

Macau's 400-year history as a Portuguese enclave on the southern edge of China has transformed it today into a city "whose very name is a springboard for the imagination."[2] Until recently, it was an understated place situated on the periphery of a long-undeveloped countryside that gave little indication to travelers that they were approaching the border of one of the greatest civilizations in the world. In 1635, António Bocarro described the tiny dimensions of Macau in this way: "The peninsula is about a league [approximately three miles] round and four hundred paces across at its broadest part. The city is about half a league round, measuring fifty paces at its narrowest extremity and three hundred and fifty at its broadest, being washed by two seas on the east and west."[3] From these small physical beginnings, Macau has been enriched by the dimensions of history. In the process of becoming a trade emporium, it served as the primary port of arrival and departure for Catholic missionaries from Europe throughout the sixteenth, seventeenth and eighteenth centuries. It contained numerous churches and religious establishments. The Jesuits built the college and church of Madre de Deus (São Paulo) whose famous *façade* still stands (see cover). The Spanish Dominicans built a monastery and São Domingos church near the main market.[4] Tensions between them led to skirmishes between the brothers and the authorities in 1707.

Prémare arrived in Macau filled with hope, but he could not have known that his years in China would transform him into a scholar with a radically new interpretation of Chinese history. Applying his knowledge of Chinese texts, he would attempt to show that the Chinese had once known, but since lost, knowledge of the true religion. This is how he explained it:

> Adam, a degenerate son, became unworthy of the empire of the world. God repudiated him and transferred everything under Heaven (*Tianxia* 天下) to Christ. This is the figurative meaning of [the legendary emperor] Yao transferring the empire to [the legendary emperor] Shun, and of Shun passing it on to [the legendary emperor] Yu the Great. The devil, this abominable tyrant, held the world under his harsh servitude. Christ combatted him and expelled him. This is the figurative meaning of [the Shang dynasty founder] Tang overthrowing [the last Xia dynasty emperor] Jie and of [the Zhou dynasty founder] Wu overthrowing [the last Shang dynasty emperor] Zhou from the throne. In fact, Jie and Zhou, in the *Classic of History* (*Shujing*), signify the same evil as [the mythical god of water] Gonggong and [the ferocious god] Chiyou do in the ancient chronology.[5]

Prémare's reinterpretation of Chinese antiquity reads like a bizarre fantasy, but it is, in fact, the carefully-researched theory of a learned scholar-priest whose arguments are grounded in citations from a wide range of ancient Chinese texts.

Father Prémare was born on July 17, 1666, in the city of Cherbourg in the region of Normandy. Little is known of his obscure family or of his biographical details. As befit the humility of a priest, he rarely wrote about his personal life. In 1710 he wrote a short essay in Chinese on his early years and arrival in China and he introduced himself as a "western European." He said that for seven years he had studied at the elementary level in France before advancing to a higher level.[6] The Jesuits were good at spotting talent and the records indicate that they enrolled him in the novitiate in 1683 at seventeen years of age. He was an enthusiastic student who studied far into the night. He particularly liked writing essays and composing poems. He wrote that he entered into advanced studies at the age of twenty-five. He described these advanced studies as "the study of our transcendent nature" and presumably they took place in a seminary. For a while he taught grammar at Rennes.[7] At this point his call to serve God became very clear because he said his mind was no longer troubled by doubts.

He was recruited for the China mission by Joachim Bouvet (Bai Jin 白晉) (1656–1730), who was exactly ten years older than him. Bouvet served at the Chinese court and had been ordered by the Kangxi emperor to make a return trip to Europe in order to recruit additional Jesuits trained in mathematics and the natural sciences to serve at the Beijing court.[8] During his one-year stay in Europe, Bouvet recruited nine Jesuits, including Prémare, for the China mission. They embarked from La Rochelle aboard *l'Amphitrite* on March 7, 1698. Prémare wrote: "At the age of thirty-three I boarded a boat and crossed the sea going east, traveling 90,000 li [30,000 miles]."[9] He gave his age in Chinese style at thirty-three rather than the European style of thirty-two. The grossly exaggerated, rounded mileage estimate of his journey was probably made in the style of a Chinese literary conceit. He described the violent and frightening storms that inundated the boat with water and almost drove it onto the rocks. On the boat to China, Bouvet began instructing the Jesuits in Chinese. Before landing, they each chose an area of specialization. Prémare chose the Chinese language and poetry.[10] Nevertheless Prémare described arriving in a state of complete confusion because he could not yet understand what the Chinese were saying. Bouvet had probably instructed them in the northern dialect of Beijing which was not spoken by the common people in the south.

CONTACT WITH THE CHRISTIAN LITERATUS LIU NING

From his arrival in 1698 until 1714, Prémare worked mainly in the southern province of Jiangxi—at Jianchang 建昌, Nanchang 南昌, Jiujiang 九江, and other obscure mission stations (see maps 1 and 2). He was ordained at Raozhou in Jiangxi in 1699. He took his great vows at Wenzhou 溫州 in 1701.[11] In the style of a Chinese literatus, he used several names. Most commonly, he is known by the transliterated form of Ma Ruose 馬若瑟 (Ma for Prémare and Ruose for Joseph) and, less commonly, Ma Longyong 馬龍用.[12] However, he also used Wenguzi 溫古子 (Master Wengu) and Wenguzi 文古子 as literary names. Jiangxi was poorer than the surrounding provinces to the east and south that included Zhejiang, Fujian, and Guangdong. It is surrounded by mountains on three sides. Prémare was based in mission sites in the northern half of the province which was flatter than the hilly south. A major artery of north-south transit was the Gan River, which flows on the north into Lake Poyang, the largest freshwater lake in China and from there into the Yangzi River. The climate of Jiangxi is humid and subtropical, with hot, humid summers and brief, cool, and damp winters. The principal crop grown in Jiangxi was rice.

In the eighteenth-century, China was undergoing a cultural shift among literati in which the Song and Ming Neo-Confucian emphasis on the personal cultivation of sagehood was giving way to an emphasis on philological research (kaocheng 考證).[13] This movement was centered in the affluent and sophisticated Lower Yangzi River region (Jiangsu, Anhui, and Zhejiang provinces). However, there were isolated literati outside of this region who also participated in this movement. One of them was Liu Ning 劉凝 (zi Erzhi 二至) in Jiangxi province who exerted a great influence on Prémare's scholarship.

In the preface to his 1710 essay *Jing zhuan yilun* 經傳議論 (Discussion of the Classics and their Commentaries), Prémare said that Liu Ning's scholarship represented the finest Qing research in etymology and paleography.[14] This was an acknowledgement of Liu Ning's influence.[15] In this work, Prémare focused on the text and commentaries of the *Spring and Autumn Annals*. He also spoke of devoting ten years to studying the Thirteen Classics, the Twenty-one Dynastic Histories, the writings of the earliest literati, and the works of the Hundred Philosophers, relying on Xu Shen's *Shuowen jiezi* dictionary for assistance.[16] Such was his passion for learning that he sacrificed food and sleep in order to study relentlessly.

Liu Ning was a Christian although little is known of his conversion and baptism. He was born in 1620 in Nanfeng 南豐 in northern Jiangxi province. He became an annual tribute student (suigong 歲貢) in 1677.[17] He was named assistant instructor (xundao 訓導) of Chongyi 崇義 county in Nan'an 南安 prefecture and spent most of his life working as an educational officer in this remote mountainous area in the far south of Jiangxi.[18] He was baptized as Paulus sometime before 1690.[19] In 1702 he retired to his hometown of Nanfeng. Liu devoted most of his research to studying Chinese script (philology). He also wrote prefaces for the works of several Jesuits and Franciscans, including an unpublished preface for Matteo Ricci's *Jiaoyou lun* 交友論 (Treatise on Friendship).[20] He also wrote an apologetic collection of five essays entitled *Juesi lu* 覺斯錄 (A Record of Reflections) and was the probable compiler of a collection of 284 Christian and scientific texts dating from 1599–1679 and entitled *Tianxue jijie* 天學集解 (A Collection of Chinese Christian Texts).[21] The year of his death was probably 1710.[22]

The most likely time for meeting with Prémare would have been during Liu's retirement years in Nanfeng between 1702 and 1710 when Prémare was based in a mission station in Jianchang located about thirty km north of Liu in Nanfeng. In his brief biographical comments made in *Jing chuan yilun* (1710), Prémare seems to be eulogizing Liu.[23] He praised Liu as one of the finest etymologists since the end of the Qin and Han dynasties, and he lamented that Liu's outstanding body of works were "buried in a mountain cave" (*shanxue* 山穴), that is, inaccessible. He referred to "seventy years of labor" on Liu's part, an apparent reference to Liu's longevity of dying at the age of eighty-nine (90 *sui*).[24] While there is no indication in these comments that he had a personal relationship with Liu, the Chinese scholar Xiao Qinghe claims that Prémare and Liu Ning had a close working relationship.[25] Liu's death seems to have marked a shift in Prémare's Figurist research.

In November 1713 the Kangxi emperor called Prémare and Jean-Alexis de Gollet, SJ (1664–1741) to Beijing to help translate European books.[26] Prémare arrived on March 11, 1714. Although the emperor did not accept them as translators, Bouvet persuaded Prémare to stay in the capital and assist in Figurist research.[27] Foucquet was also in Beijing from 1711 to 1720 working with Bouvet on interpreting the *Yijing* (*Classic of Changes*).[28] While Foucquet focused on Daoist elements, Bouvet focused on numerical and geometrical progressions. Prémare and Gollet joined them in this Figurist research. The China Jesuits typically relied upon low-ranking literati converts to assist them in translating and composing texts and documents. These assistants were called *xianggong* 相公 and were referred to as "catechists," but their duties also required a sophisticated knowledge of the Chinese written language. The provincial graduate (*juren* 舉人) Lu Ruohan 陸若翰 was one of these *xianggong* who assisted Bouvet in Beijing.[29]

Then a rupture with Bouvet and Foucquet occurred in which Prémare briefly rejected Figurism and temporarily aligned with the views of Frs. Pierre Jartoux, Dominique Parennin, and Pierre de Tartre.[30] Prémare was still in Beijng in 1717 when Foucquet requested his own recall to France. However, Prémare's criticism was directed only at the particular theories of Bouvet and Foucquet, not with Figurism per se which he reembraced in 1718, though with an emphasis that differed from that of Bouvet and Foucquet. In 1720 he was based in Jiujiang, located at the northern point of Jiangxi where the Gan River flows into the Yangzi River.

Liu Ning's death and Prémare's time in Beijing seem to have altered his way of thinking. While he continued with the philological orientation that he had absorbed from Liu, he expanded the works on which he based his Figurist theories. Whereas Prémare's earlier efforts focused on the Five Classics, his later efforts expanded to include Daoist texts and the ethnographical work *Shanhaijing* (*Classic of Mountains and Seas*). Perhaps this new direction flowed from Prémare's research in Beijing and differences with fellow Figurists Bouvet and Foucquet. In any case, Prémare's voracious reading of ancient Chinese texts led to new insights.

The Chinese scholar Xiao Qinghe has focused on Prémare's early works in Chinese. These include the *Meng meidu ji* 夢美土記 (Dream of a Pilgrim)

(1709), *Tianxue zonglun* 天學總論 (Introduction to the Heavenly Teaching) (1710), *Jingchuan zhongshuo* 經傳眾說 (A Discussion of the Classics and their Commentaries) (1710), *Jingchuan lunyu* 驚傳論語 (A Discourse on the Classics and their Commentaries) (1710), *Rujiao shiyi* 儒教實意 (The True Meaning of the Literati Teaching) (1715–1718), *Liushu shiyi* 六書實意 (The True Meaning of the Six Classes of Characters) (1720–1721), and *Ru jiao xin* 儒交信 (Literati Correspondence) (1729?).

THE INFLUENCE OF JOACHIM BOUVET, SJ

Bouvet's work in Beijing in developing a new way of interpreting the Chinese Five Classics (*Jing* 經) stirred the imaginations of several fellow Jesuits. In his letter dated November 8, 1702, to the German philosopher and polymath Gottfried Leibniz, Bouvet wrote: "If I had at my disposal only four or five of our missionaries, who already were supportive of this way of thinking, and who wished to work with me, I would like to begin to make new commentaries on all of the canonical books of the Chinese, and on the first part of their history, and to make a new dictionary by means of the analysis of each character."[31]

The French Jesuits were the first to introduce the idea of a scientific academy to the China mission. New intellectual traditions were emerging in seventeenth-century Europe which added experimental knowledge to older Aristotelian traditions of rationalism and logic.[32] This new emphasis on experimentation led to the formation of societies of learning, the forerunner of which was the Accademia dei Lincei of Rome of which Galileo was a member. This was followed by the short-lived Accademia del Cimento of Florence (1657–1667) and the Royal Society of London founded in 1662. The Académie des Sciences of Paris was founded in 1666 and the Akademie der Wissenschaften of Berlin in 1700. This new emphasis on societies of learning had led to Louis XIV's sponsorship of a mission of six French Jesuits to China in 1685. One of these Jesuits was Bouvet who became one of the most important intermediaries in Sino-European relations of that time.

Bouvet had not only a synthetic mind that was Renaissance-like in encompassing mathematics, languages, and theology, but he also had politically-attuned and administrative skills. Although his ideas would generate great controversy, he was not a confrontational personality. Because of his abilities, the Kangxi emperor gave him remarkable access to the throne. He not only used Bouvet as a geometry tutor for himself and his sons, but he sent Bouvet to Europe on the diplomatic assignment in 1693–1699 in which he recruited Prémare. Bouvet also possessed the knack of survival which enabled him to remain at the Chinese court from 1699 until his death in 1730, serving not only the sympathetic Kangxi emperor, but also his hostile son, the Yongzheng emperor who needed his skills, but hated his religion. Unlike the other Jesuits, Bouvet and other court Jesuits were not exiled to Guangzhou (Canton) in 1724, but remained in Beijing.

The Kangxi emperor, who was fascinated by the *Classic of Changes* (*Yijing*), wanted to know more about Bouvet's research on this classical work. Because Bouvet's many commitments at court prevented him from devoting time to this research, the Emperor commanded Bouvet to bring other Jesuits to Beijing to assist him.[33] Bouvet chose those Jesuits who had already demonstrated an interest in his research. Foucquet came to Beijing in 1711 and Prémare came in 1714.[34] It was from this study of the *Classic of Changes* that the school of Figurism emerged.

Bouvet sought to adapt the European model of a society of learning in Beijing. His specific goal was to carry out research on ancient Chinese texts with the aim of substantiating his Figurist theories.[35] He gave fullest formulation to this proposal for a "petite Academie Apostolique" (small apostolic academy) in a long communication of September 15, 1704, to Jean-Paul Bignon.[36] Bignon was a prominent cleric, friendly to the Jesuits, who was a leading figure in French intellectual life—both in the Académie des Inscriptions et Belles-Lettres and the Académie des Sciences. He sent numerous scientific missions abroad and conducted an extensive literary correspondence. In 1702 he became the director of the scholarly *Journal des Sçavans* and after 1709 was a member of the Royal Society of London.

FIGURISM

Joachim Bouvet, SJ is usually regarded as the founder of Figurism. His letter to Bignon contains one of the earliest references to the name by which these theories became known. Bouvet wrote that rather than judging the basis of Chinese books and philosophy only by means of modern Chinese authors, if they were "judged by means of the symbolic meaning of the hieroglyphic characters, and by means of an inner and figurative (*figuré*) meaning of the canonical books [i.e., Chinese Classics] . . . it would be hard to form an idea that equals the excellence of this admirable system"[37]

Bouvet made a second reference to *figuré* (figurative) in his letter to Bignon in outlining the hieroglyphic or symbolic nature of the ancient wisdom of the Chinese. He proposed "an attempt of analysis of the hieroglyphs, made by a type of geometrical method based on the elements of symbolic science, in order to make visible, that the principal meaning of each character, which is usually figurative (*figuré*), is a mysterious meaning, sacred and appropriate to the faith of the Messiah."[38]

When Bouvet explained his Figurist theories to Leibniz in letters of 1701 and 1702 and to Bignon in 1704, the term *figuré* (figurative) was a merely descriptive term, empty of either positive or negative connotations. But during the next thirty years, it acquired pejorative connotations among many Europeans. In both Rome and China many Catholic clerics opposed the theory on theological grounds and Propaganda banned the publication of Figurist works.

In comparison with the China Jesuits, the Parisian intellectuals had a very limited knowledge of the Chinese language and culture, but their prominence in the intellectual vanguard of Europe made them gatekeepers who controlled the dissemination of information through a process of selection. This gave them the power to suppress the Figurists' analysis of hieroglyphs as intellectually outmoded. Such gatekeepers tend to make their reputation by cultivating the most creative and intellectually fashionable mode of thought. For them, the Figurists represented a throw-back to older hieroglyphic traditions. Consequently, they became critical of the China Jesuits' theory and sought to suppress it in the name of advancing knowledge. Turning the descriptive adjective *figuré* (figurative) into the pejorative term *figurisme* (figurism) and mocking it was one way of suppressing the theory.

The first to have done so seems to have been Nicholas Fréret, a lover of controversy, who wrote the following condescending letter to Fr. Prémare in December 1732: "I will acknowledge My Reverend Father with all candor which should extend to our correspondence that I see with sorrow that the author of the dissertation gives into the figurism which has done so much harm in Europe to Fr. [Jean-François] Foucquet. Is it possible that good minds allow themselves to be tainted by this malady and that it may become universal enough to infect equally the people at two ends of the earth who are as far removed in their feelings as in the places that they inhabit—the Jesuits and the Jansenists?"[39] In effect, Fréret reduced a debate over the Chinese language, of which he knew very little, to a parochial debate between French religious factions.

In their dismissal of the Jesuit Figurists as intellectually defective, Fréret and others relied instead on an opposing interpretation of another group of Jesuits which included Antoine Gaubil (1689–1759), Joseph de Mailla (1669–1748), and Joseph-Marie Amiot (1718–1793). This opposing group accepted the basic Chinese claim that the records of ancient China were historical and that Chinese history dated from ca. 2850 BC.[40] The Figurists, by contrast, believed that the ancient works of the Chinese needed to be interpreted as symbolic and figurative rather than historical. The leading Figurists were Bouvet, Prémare, and Jean-François Foucquet (1665–1741) although there were differences in their theories.[41] There were other Jesuits who were intrigued by the ideas of Figurism, but who withdrew their support in the face of opposition from confrères and superiors.[42] For the Figurists, reliable accounts of Chinese history did not begin until much later—for Fouquet 424 BC but for Prémare 770 or 722 BC at approximately the time of the beginning of the Eastern Zhou dynasty. In the face of fierce criticism from fellow clerics and religious superiors, the intellectual attraction of Figurism for less committed Jesuits withered. The focal point of debate between these opposing groups was the status (historical versus symbolical) of the ancient Three Sovereigns or *Sanhuang* 三皇 (Fu Xi, Shen Nong and Huangdi), the Five Emperors or *Wudi* 五帝 (Shao Hao, Zhuan Xu, Emperor Ku, Yao, and Shun), and the three dynasties (Xia, Shang, and Zhou).

Although Prémare preferred to work in provincial isolation, the demands of his research and book purchases required contacts with Chinese literati. He was also an active missionary. After spending two years in China he wrote a letter to the Jesuit Father Charles Le Gobien in France, expressing his pastoral concerns. He spoke of the situation in China where "the richest and most flourishing Empire of the world is nevertheless, the poorest and most miserable of all."[43] Because of vast inequalities in wealth, selfish attitudes, and a proliferation of thieves, frequent famines caused "millions of souls to perish by famine."[44] Mothers were driven to "kill, or expose several of their infants" and "parents sell their daughters for something small." This suffering occurred in spite of the fact that the poor of China were intensely hard-working. Prémare drew a sad portrait of these unfortunates: "A Chinese will pass the days working the earth by the strength of [his] arms; often he will be in water up to his knees, and at night he is fortunate to eat a small bowl of rice, and to drink insipid water that he has boiled."

What can missionaries do to help these Chinese? Prémare suggests, first, to use the Gospel "to teach them to sanctify their suffering."[45] This involves teaching and making conversions and establishing churches. He wrote that the subsistence allowance for a parish priest or rural vicar in France with only a hundred parishioners would support a missionary in China who could convert 500 or 600 neophytes in one year.[46]

Secondly, Prémare proposed helping abandoned children, and particularly girls. He did not condemn the Chinese for abandoning their small infant girls because he believed that "the misery of the parents obliges" them to do so. However, Prémare does say that Christians were obliged to collect abandoned infants to save them from being eaten by beasts and to baptize them, even when moribund. In addition, Prémare spoke of his desire, shared by other missionaries, to establish "hospitals for fostering these exposed children."[47] He recognized that these hospitals would be composed mainly of girls for whom poor parents "have less pity than for boys, because they fear they will have more trouble getting rid of [girls] and in placing them in a state of earning their living." Prémare proposed that these infant girls who survived be given religious instruction and be "taught the arts of the country, appropriate to their condition and their sex." At fourteen or fifteen years of age the girls either would be assigned as domestics in Christian families which often meant, in practice, that they eventually would be married to Christian men, or else they would enter religious life.[48] Finally, Prémare appealed to Fr. Le Gobien to seek support from wealthy patronesses in Europe for establishing these hospitals, orphanages and convents.

CHINESE RITES CONTROVERSY

Growing tensions within the China mission between accommodationist Jesuits and theological purists came to a head after the Kangxi emperor's Edict of Toleration of 1692. The edict was issued, in part, as a reward for service to the Emperor by Bouvet and other Jesuits, such as, Tomé Pereira, SJ (1645–1708) and Jean-François Gerbillon, SJ (1654–1707), for negotiating the Treaty of Nerchinsk (1689) with the Russians.[49] This edict marked the highpoint of Catholic fortunes in imperial China. However, this auspicious atmosphere was soon undone by the Rites Controversy.

Pope Innocent XII assigned Bishop Charles Maigrot (Yan Dang 顏璫) to investigate the issue of the Chinese rites.[50] Maigrot had been a bishop (technically vicar-apostolic) in Fujian since 1687.[51] He was fiercely opposed to the Jesuits permitting the practice of Chinese forms of ancestral reverence, which he regarded as idolatrous. He also opposed allowing certain indigenous Chinese terms like *Tian* 天 (Heaven) and *Shangdi* 上帝 (Lord on High) to be used as the name for God. With these and other objections in mind, he issued a seven-point mandate in 1693 that initiated the famous Chinese Rites Controversy.[52] Although Maigrot's authority was limited to his vicariate in Fujian province, he sent his friend Nicholas Charmot, M. E. P. to Rome to secure a universal condemnation which was achieved with a 1704 decree of the Inquisition, confirmed by Pope Clement XI. However, the public proclamation of this decree was deferred until the official embassy of the Papal Legate Tournon arrived in China in 1706. Maigrot's weaknesses in his knowledge of the Chinese language and culture were later exposed by the Kangxi emperor in a humiliating audience in August of 1706.[53] Maigrot's mandate unleashed a torrent of writings on the Chinese rites.

In 1701 in Beijing, ten Jesuits, including Bouvet, published a group-authored Brevis Relatio on the Chinese understanding of Heaven, Confucius, and ancestral rites which supported accommodation.[54] The Brevis Relatio was composed in three versions: Chinese, Manchu, and Latin. The original version in Chinese was translated into Manchu, which may have been used by the Jesuits for strategic purposes because Maigrot could not read Chinese.[55] A Latin translation was made from the Manchu version. Meanwhile, Bouvet, who was far more literate in Chinese than Maigrot, began writing an essay defending the Jesuits' position against Maigrot's 1693 mandate.[56] Over the years 1703–1707 Bouvet's essay evolved along with his increasing knowledge of Chinese texts. Since this essay was prohibited from being published by the Papal Legate Tournon in 1705, only hand-written copies of the work exist.[57]

Nine different versions of this work are extant, including four in the Bibliothèque Nationale France, two in the Biblioteca Apostolica Vaticana, and one in the Xujiahui Library Shanghai.[58] In addition, one copy is in the Beitang Library Beijing.[59] And one copy is in the Skackov collection of the Rumyancov (Rumyantsev) Museum in Moscow.[60] The versions vary in content and title, reflecting not only Bouvet's growing knowledge, but also the need to navigate political and religious obstacles. The earliest form of the essay was entitled *Tianxue benyi* 天學本意 (The fundamental meaning of the Heavenly Teaching) which first took form in November 1701. Bouvet described the work in two letters in 1704 as "a small Chinese work that I made here in three years and that Fr. Noël has carried to Rome with him . . . This small work contains all that is found in the canonical books of China concerning the celestial doctrine."[61]

This small work grew over time from twenty to eighty-five double sheets. However, a comparison of the subheadings of the various versions of the work shows that the structure of the *Gujin* remained fairly constant throughout its development.[62] Bouvet added different prefaces as well as an epilogue. The title evolved and around 1705 was expanded to *Gujin jing Tian jian Tianxue benyi* 古今敬天鑑天學本意 (An examination of the original meaning of the Heavenly Teaching in the ancient and modern expression "revere Heaven"). The term *"jing Tian"* (revere Heaven) was included in the title because the Jesuits were criticizing Maigrot's 1693 prohibition of the term and defending their use of a term that had been sanctioned by the Kangxi emperor.[63] When the Kangxi emperor visited the Jesuit Beijing residence on July 12, 1675, he had presented a gift of his personal inscription of the characters *jing Tian*.[64] His inscription was copied and placed in many Christian churches.

The *Gujin* is divided into two parts, the first of which quotes selected passages from ancient and modern Chinese texts that elucidate the meaning of the Heavenly Teaching. The second part is organized around forty-one theological points, followed by supporting statements from Chinese culture, including people's proverbs (*minsu* 民俗), scholars' maxims (*shisu* 士俗),

and classical texts (*jingwen* 經文). Both parts attempt to prove that there are fundamental similarities between ancient Chinese religious ideas and those of Christianity. This emphasis on these similarities was aimed at two different audiences; one audience included the Chinese court and literati while the other audience was composed of European critics of Jesuit accommodation.

The differences between the early and later versions of Bouvet's *Gujin* were, in part, due to Bouvet's evolving knowledge of Chinese culture and the classical texts. A second reason appears to have been the influence of a Chinese work by the Christian literatus Zhang Xingyao 張星耀 (1633—after 1711) of Hangzhou.[65] This is a striking phenomenon because it indicates an early instance of the cross-pollination that was occurring between Chinese and European cultures and religious beliefs.

Zhang Xingyao was baptized in 1678 and given the baptismal name of Ignatius. In the intellectually fluid atmosphere of the Ming-Qing transition period, Zhang was attracted to Christianity by the vibrant Christian intellectuals in Hangzhou. Two of the Three Pillars of the early Christian church—Yang Tingyun (1557–1627) and Li Zhizao (1565–1630)—resided there.[66] Zhang was influenced by notable Jesuits like Martino Martini, SJ (1614–1661) and Prospero Intorcetta, SJ (1642–1696) who resided in Hangzhou. Martini's stay was brief, but significant, arriving in 1659 and building a beautiful Baroque-style church there before dying in 1661. Intorcetta had a longer presence in Hangzhou from 1676 until his death in 1696. He left his imprint in establishing a Jesuit cemetery that is still preserved and in cultivating close relationships with literati like Zhang Xingyao.

Zhang was a participant in a Confucian-Christian tradition developed by certain Chinese literati that can be traced to Xu Guangqi and his defining phrase *bu Ru yi Fo* 補儒易佛 (Supplement the Literati and displace the Buddhists). Zhang in Hangzhou and Shang Huqing 尚祜卿 (b.1619) in Jinan in Shandong province were two of the leading voices in this Confucian-Christian tradition although neither were prominent literati.[67] Both men had close contacts with missionaries and both wrote works blending Confucianism and Christianity which influenced missionaries in this movement of cultural cross-pollination.

Zhang Xingyao's *Tian Ru tongyi kao* 天儒同異考 [An examination of the similarities and differences between the Heavenly Teaching (i.e., Christianity) and the Literati Teaching (i.e., Confucianism)] was written and revised over many years.[68] The earliest preface to part I is dated 1672 and later prefaces (1702 and 1715) are found in other copies. There are numerous parallels between the passages from classical texts cited by Zhang in part I of his work and those cited by Bouvet in part 1 of his *Gujin*.[69] Moreover, the likelihood of Bouvet's access to this work is supported by a hand-written copy of Zhang's work under the slightly variant title of *Tianzhujiao Rujiao tongyi kao* preserved in the former Beitang Library, a missionary collection of Chinese and European books in Beijing that dates from the seventeenth century.[70]

Since the earliest publication of books in Chinese by Matteo Ricci a century before, Jesuit authors had followed the literary practice of seeking prefaces from eminent Chinese scholars. When Bouvet wrote his *Tianxue benyi*, he sought a preface from Han Tan 翰菼 (1637–1704) (see figure 1.1). In 1697 Han had been recalled to Beijing from his retirement near Suzhou in Jiangsu province and was given leading positions in the Hanlin Academy and the Board of Rites (*Li Bu*).[71] Initially the Kangxi emperor favored him, but later was offended by Han's outspoken candor and criticism of others. He made enemies and drank to excess. However, he had a reputation as a fine scholar and was a famous essayist and it was a coup for Bouvet to have obtained his agreement to contribute a preface. Han was not a Christian, but he had a favorable attitude toward the Jesuits. Consequently, in 1703 he composed a brief two-page preface of about 250 characters filled with complimentary comments about the Jesuits who had come from so far away to "revere Heaven" (*jing Tian* 敬天).[72] This was the phrase that the Kangxi emperor had personally inscribed for the Christians in Beijing and which would give such offense to critics of Jesuit accommodation.[73]

THE EUROCENTRISM OF THE PAPAL LEGATE TOURNON

From 1705 until 1710 the China Jesuits were traumatized by the visit of the Papal Legate Charles Thomas Maillard de Tournon.[74] Tournon's hostility to the Jesuits, combined with his imperious and uncompromising manner toward the Chinese court, had the effect of reversing the favorable treatment that Christianity had enjoyed since the Kangxi emperor's Edict of Toleration. The fear of the collapse of the mission created a sense of urgency among the Jesuits that stimulated the work of the Figurists while arousing a reaction among other Jesuits that Figurism needed to be suppressed because it was endangering the mission.

In April of 1705 the Papal Legate Tournon arrived in Guangzhou from Macau and the formal discussion of Bouvet's *Gujin* took place in July.[75] Advocates and critics of accommodation both presented arguments. Bishop (technically vicar apostolic) Álvaro de Benevente, OESA (Bai Wanle 白萬樂 (1646–1709) of Jiangxi province, a known defender of accommodation, travelled to Guangzhou with a group of Jesuits to participate in the discussion. Benevente had approved the printing of Bouvet's *Gujin* in 1702.[76] However, the Legate's rigid mind was already made up. One notes that the opponents of accommodation included Jesuit outliers like Claude de Visdelou (Liu Ying 劉應) (1656–1737), a scholar of Chinese literature, who had once been close with Bouvet, but who supported Tournon because he agreed that the Chinese were atheists.[77] Since the text of Bouvet's *Gujin* existed only in Chinese, Tournon had to rely upon others to read it for him. In choosing two critics of accommodation as revisers—Visdelou and an English Dominican Thomas Croquer (Croker) (1657–1729), OP—a negative judgment of the manuscript was assured.[78] Also contributing to the assessment was Tournon's translator, the Italian Lazarist Luigi Antonio Appiani (Bi Tianxiang 畢天祥) (1663–1732).

Tournon condemned Bouvet's *Gujin* in a way that foreshadowed some of the very worst features of European arrogance and superiority that would emerge in China a century later. First, he criticized Bouvet for having his book begin with a sympathetic forward by a "heathen Mandarin" instead of an approbation by a Christian bishop.[79] This was a reference to Han Tan's forward. Tournon's arrogance prevented him from learning about or respecting the formalities of Chinese culture. Conversely, of course, Bouvet was also using Han Tan's status to help counter opposition from critics of accommodationism. That might have had some effect if Tournon had been more sensitive to the Chinese environment, but Tournon acted as if he were still in Europe and as if European values were universal in application.

Tournon's condemnation also complained that the preface by this non-Christian Mandarin "gives the impression that we are coming from Europe in order to learn the teaching of the Chinese instead of propagating the Teaching of Jesus Christ." Actually Han Tan's preface refers to the missionaries with the honorific "*jun*" 君 which was used when addressing someone of equal or higher status. In his condemnation on July 17, 1705, Tournon demanded that all the printed copies of Bouvet's *Gujin* be recalled.[80] His ruling was precipitious and foolish because the book had not yet even been printed. Hand-copied Chinese texts sometimes gave the misleading appearance of being printed from wood-blocks and Tournon's advisors apparently failed to notice the difference.[81]

The Kangxi emperor had read Bouvet's *Gujin* in 1704. When he received word of Tournon's condemnation of the book in 1705, he had difficulty understanding Tournon's objections. Consequently, the ironic situation followed in which a Chinese monarch ordered the work to be translated into a European language so that Tournon could read it for himself.[82] The Jesuit Father Kilian Stumpf (Ji Li'an 紀理安) (1655–1720) feared that Tournon might see an attempt to translate the condemned work as a form of Jesuit obstinance in refusing to accept his condemnation and provoke Tournon's anger. Nevertheless Bouvet had been corresponding with Prémare, Hervieu,

Foucquet, Gollet, and other Jesuits about Figurism since 1703. He would now call upon Prémare and Hervieu to make a Latin translation. Meanwhile, the Kangxi emperor ordered Bouvet to go to Rome to deal with issues involving the Chinese rites. He and Fr. Sabino Mariani (Sha Guo'an 沙國安) were entrusted with imperial gifts for the Pope and departed from Beijing on January 2, 1706. However, because of the Kangxi emperor's anger with Tournon, the gifts were recalled and Bouvet returned to Beijing in September.

Two slightly different copies of a Latin translation of Bouvet's *Gujin* exist. Both appear to be in Prémare's handwriting. The undated, but apparently earlier translation is entitled "Caelestis doctrinae vera notitia" (The true conception of the Heavenly Teaching).[83] It includes Han Tan's preface (see figure 1.2). Consequently, Bouvet might have sent a copy of the *Gujin* to Prémare as early as 1703. The second translation is entitled *De cultu celesti Sinarum veterum et modernorum* (On the celestial cult of the ancient and modern Chinese) and dated 1706. The translators are identified as Prémare who was based in Jiangxi and Julien-Placide Hervieu, SJ (He Cangbi 赫蒼璧) (1671–1746) who had been based in Huangzhou-fu 黃州府 in eastern Hubei province. The apparently later 1706 translation adds a title page that identifies the author, translators, and date. It omits Han Tan's preface and makes notable changes in the text, such as removing the name of the Daoist philosopher Laozi from the opening paragraph of part two and replacing it with a reference to di 帝 (emperor).[84] Unlike the Figurists, Matteo Ricci and most other missionaries regarded Daoism as irredeemably atheistic. The removal of a reference to Laozi would probably have been a way of making Bouvet's *Gujin* less offensive to anti-Figurist missionaries.

The 1706 translation also replaced the "Conclusion" with an "Author's Epilogue." This is significant because while the "Conclusion" had focused on later Song dynasty Neo-Confucian terminology, such as *Taiji* 太極 (Supreme Ultimate) and *li* 理 (principle), the "Author's Epilogue" focused on ancient Chinese texts, referring to the legendary Fu Xi 伏羲, to the ancient Chinese term for God *Shangdi* 上帝, *Shang Tian* 上天 (Heaven Above, i.e., God), and *Tian Ye* 天爺 (Heavenly Father). Whereas ancient Confucian texts had been regarded since Ricci as a basis for accommodation between Chinese antiquity and Christianity on the level of natural morality, Neo-Confucianism had been viewed as atheistic. Consequently, removing the references to Neo-Confucian terminology would have made the essay less incendiary to anti-accommodationist clerics.

While the first translation of the *Gujin* gives the appearance of being more of a draft, the second translation is in a more presentable form. The Church historian Claudia von Collani believes that Prémare sent his translation "Caelestis doctrinae vera notitia" to the departing Bouvet in Guangzhou under urgent conditions because Bouvet wanted to take the manuscript to Rome with him to use in defending the Jesuit position on the Chinese Rites.[85] Prémare may indeed have done so, but it is the translation entitled "De cultu celesti Sinarum veterum et modernorum" that would seem to have been the more finished and appropriate version of the translation to take to Rome. It is unclear how Bouvet would have instructed Prémare to make the edits to the manuscripts described above unless the first translation had been sent to him between 1703 and 1706.

NOTES

1. *Yijing* 易經 (Classic of Changes), hexagram 13, translated in James Legge, *The I Ching* (Oxford: Clarendon Press, 1899), p. 86.

2. Philippe Pons, *Macao*. Sarah Adams, tr. (London: Reaktion Books 2002), p. 9.

3. C. R. Boxer, *Seventeenth Century Macau in Contemporary Documents and Illustrations*. C. R. Boxer, ed. & tr. (Hong Kong: Heinemann (Asia), 1984), p. 14.

4. Pons, p. 63–64.

5. Joseph de Prémare, SJ, *Selecta quaedam Vestigia praecipuorum Christianae relligionis dogmatum ex antiquis Sinarum libris eruta* (hereafter *Vestigia*), 1725, f. 305a; Joseph de Prémare, SJ. *Vestiges des principaux dogmes chrétiens tirés des anciens livres chinois* (hereafter *Vestiges*). Edited and translated by Augustin Bonnetty & Paul Perny (Paris: Bureau des Annales de Philosophie Chrétienne, 1878), p. 475.

6. Ma Ruose (Prémare), "Jing chuan yilun" 經傳議論 (A discussion of the Classics and their Commentaries). 1710. Bibliothèque nationale France, Chinois 7164. f. 1a.

7. Carlos Sommervogel, SJ, "Joseph de Prémare." In *Bibliothèque de la Compagnie de Jésus*. 12 vols. (Brussels: Schepens & Paris: Picard, 1890–1932) 9: 784, and 1196.

8. Claudia von Collani, *P. Joachim Bouvet. Sein Leben und sein Werk* (Nettetal: Steyler Verlag, 1985), p. 23.

9. Ma (Prémare), "Jing chuan yilun," p. 1a.

10. François Froger, *Relation du premier voyage des François à la Chine fait en 1688, 1689 et 1700 sur le vaisseau l'Amphitrite*. Ed. E. A. Voretzsch (Leipzig 1926) VIII f.

11. Dehergne, Joseph, SJ. *Répertoire des Jésuites de Chine de 1552 à 1800*. (Rome: Institutum Historicum S.I., 1973), p. 210.

12. Chen Xinyu 陳欣雨, Lizu yu Wenzixue de Ma Ruose de *Yijing* Yanjiu: *Zhouyi Lishu* yu *Taiji Lueshuo* 立足于文字學的馬若瑟的《易經》研究：以《周易理數》與《太極略說》為例 (Establishing a Foothold on the Philology of Joseph de Prémare's Research on the *Classic of Changes:* a Study of the *Yijing Numerology* and *The Abridged Discourse on the Great Ultimate*), *Aomen ligong xuebao* 1 (2017), p. 85.

13. Benjamin A. Elman, *From Philosophy to Philology: Intellectual and Social Aspects of Change in Late Imperial China* (Cambridge, MA: Harvard University Press, 1984), p. 3–6.

14. Ma Ruose [Prémare], *Jing zhuan yilun*. 1710. preface, p. 1b–2a.

15. Lackner, "A Figurist at Work," p. 35, considers it probable that Prémare was the only French Figurist who was deeply influenced by a Chinese scholar (Liu Ning).

16. The current list of Twenty-Six Dynastic Histories evolved gradually. Prémare's reference to reading Twenty-One Dynastic Histories is explained by the fact that it was not until 1739, three years after Prémare's death, that the *Ming Shi* 明史 (History of the Ming Dynasty) (compiled 1678–1739) was completed and an imperial decree was issued to print Twenty-Two Histories, thus increasing the number by one. Han Yu-shan 韓玉珊, *Elements of Chinese Historiography* (W. M. Hawley: Hollywood, CA, 1955), p. 193–95.

17. Ad Dudink, "The Rediscovery of a Seventeenth-Century Collection of Chinese Christian Texts: the Manuscript *Tianxue jijie*," *Sino-Western Cultural Relations Journal* 15 (1993): 19.

18. Knud Lundbæk, *Joseph de Prémare (1661599–1679 and 156–1736), SJ: Chinese Philology and Figurism*. Acta Jutlandica LXVI:2 (Aarhus: Aarhus University Press, 1991), p. 142–45.

19. Nicolas Standaert, ed., *Handbook of Christianity in China. Volume One: 635–1800* (Leiden: Brill, 2001), p. 401.

20. The late Italian scholar Giuliano Bertuccioli located a copy of Liu Ning's unpublished preface to Ricci's *Jiaoyou lun* in the National Library of Russia and reproduces the copy in facsimile. See his article "Two Previously Unknown Prefaces of Ricci's Jiaoyou Lun and Martini's Qiuyou Pian by Liu Ning and Shen Guangyu," in *Western Humanistic Culture Presented to China by Jesuit Missionaries (XVII–XVIII Centuries)*. Ed. Federico Masini (Rome: Institutum Historicum S.I., 1996), p. 101–18.

21. Dudink, "The Rediscovery," p. 19 and Standaert, ed., *Handbook*, p. 435

22. The 1710 estimate of Liu Ning's death is made by Xiao Qinghe 肖清和 "Qing chu Rujia Jidutu Liu清初儒家基督徒刘凝生平事跡" *Zhongguo Dianji Yu Wenhua* 《中国典籍与文化, No. 4, 2012 (总第83期), p. 45–46. A slightly later estimate of 1715 is made by Li Zhen 李真, "Shilun Ming-Qing zhi ji lai Hua Yesuhuishi yu Rujia Jidutu zhi xueshu jiaowang" 试沦明清之 际來华耶稣会士与儒家基督徒之学术交往：以马若瑟与刘凝为中心 *Beijing Xingzheng Xueyuan xuebao* 《北京行政学院学报》 2015年第2期123頁.

23. Ma Ruose (Prémare), "Jing chuan yilun" 經傳議論 (A discussion of the Classics and their Commentaries). Bibliotheque nationale France, Courant 7164. f. 1b.

24. Dudink, "The Rediscovery," p. 19.

25. Xiao Qinghe 肖请和, *Suoyin Tianxue: Ma Ruose de Suoyin Shenxue tixi yanjiu* "索隐天学：马若瑟的索隐神学体系研究" *Xueshu Yuekan* 《学术月刊 / Academic Monthly》 48 (01) (January 2016) p. 159.

26. Witek, p. 195.

27. Witek, p. 227, fn. 185.

28. Witek, p. 202.

29. Han, Qi 韓琦. "Kexue yu zongjian: Yesuhui shi Bai Jin de *Yijing* yanjiu" 科學與宗教之間：耶穌會士白晉的《易經》研究 (The space between natural science and religion: The Jesuit Joachim Bouvet's study of the *Yijing*). In 東亞基督教再詮釋 (A reinterpretation of East Asian Christianity). Edited by Tao Feiya 陶飛亞 and Liang Yuansheng 梁元生。 Hong Kong: 香港中文大學崇基學院宗教與中國社會研究中心, 2004. p. 420–22. See also Wu, Min 吳旻 & Han Qi 韓琦, "Liyi zhi zheng yu Zhongguo Tianzhujiao tu: yi Fujian jiaotu he Yan Dang de chongtu wei li," 禮儀之爭與中國天主教徒：以福建教徒和顏璫的冲突為例 (The Chinese Rites Controversy and Chinese Catholics: the case of the conflict between the Fujian Christians and Bishop Charles Maigrot). *Lishi yanjiu* 歷史研究 2004 (6): 85.

30. Witek, p. 227.

31. Letter of Joachim Bouvet, SJ to Leibniz, November 8, 1702. In Gottfried Wilhelm Leibniz, *Der Briefwechsel mit den Jesuiten in China (1689–1714)*. Ed. Rita Widmaier (Hamburg: Felix Meiner Verlag, 2006), p. 390–91.

32. D. E. Mungello, *Curious Land: Jesuit Accommodation and the Origins of Sinology*. (Stuttgart: Franz Steiner Verlag,1985), p. 32f.

33. Witek, *Controversial Ideas*, p. 168–70.

34. Witek, *Controversial Ideas*, p. 140 & Chen Xinyu, p. 85.

35. For details on Bouvet's attempt to attract other researchers to his Apostolic Academy, see Collani, *P. Joachim Bouvet SJ*, p. 54–59.

36. For an annotated form of this letter, see Claudia von Collani, *Eine Wissenschaftliche Akademie für China*. Studia Leibnitiani Sonderheft 18 (Stuttgart: Franz Steiner Verlag, 1989), p. 81.

37. Collani, *Eine Wissenschaftliche Akademie*, p. 33.

38. Collani, *Eine Wissenschaftliche Akademie*, p. 35.

39. Nicolas Fréret to Fr. de Prémare, December 1732 in *Documents inédits relatifs a la Connaissance de la Chine en France de 1685 a 1740*. Ed Virgile Pinot (Paris: Librairie Orientaliste Paul Geuthner, 1932), p. 45.

40. For a detailed explanation of the differences between the Jesuit "historians" and Jesuit "symbolist theologians" (Figurists), see Nicolas Standaert, *The Intercultural Weaving of Historical Texts: Chinese and European Stories about Emperor Ku and His Concubines*. (Leiden: Brill, 2016), p. 116–50.

41. For a brief summary of the differences in Figurism between Bouvet, Foucquet and Prémare, see Paul A. Rule, *K'ung-tzu or Confucius: The Jesuit Interpretation of Confucianism* (Sydney, Australia: Allen & Unwin, 1986) p. 154–56.

42. Less prominent Figurists included John-Alexis de Gollet, SJ (1664–1741), Jean-François Noëlas, SJ (1669–1740), and Jean-Baptiste-Joseph de Grammont, SJ (1736–1812?). See Claudia von Collani, "Daoismus, Figurismus, Historismus, Die Chinamissionare und die ersten Übersetzungen des *Daodejing*." In *Uroffenbarung und Daoismus. Jesuitische Missionshermeneutik des Daoismus* (Berlin: Europäischer Universitätsverlag GmbH, 2008), p. 31–38.

43. Letter of Prémare to Fr. LeGobien, November 1, 1700, *Lettres édifiantes et curieuses*, vol. 9 (Lyon, 1819), p. 242.

44. Prémare to LeGobien, p 243.

45. Prémare to LeGobien, p. 244.

46. Prémare to LeGobien, p. 246.
47. Prémare to LeGobien, p. 247.
48. Prémare to LeGobien, p. 248.
49. Joseph Sebes, SJ, *The Jesuits and the Sino-Russian Treaty of Nerchinsk (1689)*. (Rome: Institutum Historicum S.I. 1961).
50. Antonio Sisto Rosso, OFM., *Apostolic Legations to China of the Eighteenth Century* (South Pasadena: Perkins, 1948), p. 131.r
51. Propaganda limited Spanish and Portuguese influence by using "vicar-apostolics" to circumvent the Spanish and Portuguese territorial prerogatives of appointing bishops in their respective world spheres. It was based on legal and canonical grounds for Rome to appoint a vicar-apostolic who lacked any territorial basis for appointment.
52. Edward J. Malatesta, SJ, "A Fatal Clash of Wills: The Condemnation of the Chinese Rites by the Papal Legate Carlo Tommaso Maillard de Tournon," in *The Chinese Rites Controversy: Its History and Meaning.* Edited by D. E. Mungello. Monumenta Serica Monograph Series XXXIII (Nettetal, Germany: Steyler Verlag, 1994), p. 212–15.
53. Kilian Stumpf, SJ, *Acta Pekinensia*. Edited by Paul Rule & Claudia von Collani. Vol. I. (Rome: Institutum Historicum Societatis Iesu, 2015) p. 687–99.
54. P. Pelliot, "La *Brevis Relatio*," *T'oung Pao* 23 (1924): 367–68. The work was republished several times in Europe, the first of which was *Brevis Relatio eorum quae spectant ad declarationem Sinarum Imperatoris KamHi circa Caeli, Confucii et avorum cultum, datum anno 1700* . . . (Augsburg-Dillingen 1703).
55. Antonio Sisto Rosso, OFM, *Apostolic Legations to China of the Eighteenth Century* (South Pasadena: P. D. & Ione Perkins, 1948) p. 138–46.
56. Claudia von Collani, "Tianxue benyi—Joachim Bouvets Forschungen zum Monotheismus in China," *China Mission Studies (1550–1800) Bulletin* X (1988): 11–15.
57. Collani, "Tianxue benyi," p. 24 & Stumpf, *Acta Pekinensia*, p. 23–29.
58. D. E. Mungello, "Unearthing the Manuscripts of Bouvet's *Gujin* after Nearly Three Centuries," *China Mission Studies (1550–1800) Bulletin* X (1988): 36–39.
59. Ad Dudink, "The Chinese Christian Books of the Former Beitang Library," *Sino-Western Cultural Relations Journal* 26 (2004): 53.
60. P. Pelliot, "Melanges sur quelques manuscrits sinologiques conservés en Russie," *T'oung Pao* 29 (1932): 106–8.
61. Collani, "Tianxue benyi," p. 16.
62. Mungello, "Unearthing," p. 41–43.
63. Collani, "Tianxue benyi," p. 21.
64. Stumpf, *Acta Pekinensia*, p. LXXVIII.
65. Fang Chao-ying, "Han T'an." In *Eminent Chinese of the Ch'ing Period, 1644–1912*. Edited by Arthur Hummel (Washington, D.C.: Government Printing Office, 1943) p. 275 and D. E. Mungello, *The Forgotten Christians of Hangzhou* (Honolulu: University of Hawaii Press, 1994), p. 173–74.
66. D. E. Mungello, *Forgotten Christians*, p. 16. See also Nicolas Standaert, *Yang Tingyun, Confucian and Christian in late Ming China*. (Leiden: Brill, 1988).

67. Shang Huqing's major work was *Bu Ru wengao* 不儒文告 (The Touchstone of True Knowledge) (1664). See D. E. Mungello, *The Spirit and the Flesh in Shandong, 1650–1785* (Lanham, MD: Rowman & Littlefield, 2001), p. 38–62.

68. The *Tian Ru tongyi kao* sometimes bears the expanded title of *Tianzhujiao Rujiao tongyi kao* 天主教儒教同異考 which also means "An examination of the similarities and differences between the Heavenly Teaching and the Literati Teaching."

69. Mungello, *Forgotten Christians of Hangzhou*, p. 230 & Fang Chaoying, "Han T'an." In *Eminent Chinese of the Ch'ing Period* (Washington, D.C.: United State Government Printing Office, 1943) p. 275. [275–76]

70. Dudink, "The Chinese Christian Books of the Former Beitang Library," p. 56. For a brief history of the Beitang Library, see H. Verhaeren, CM, *Catalogue de la Bibliothèque du Pé-t'ang* (Beijing: Imprimerie des Lazaristes, 1949) p. v–xxxiii.

71. Fang Chao-yin, "Han T'an," in Hummel, p. 275–76 & Pelliot, "La Brevis Relatio," p. 365–66.

72. Han T'an preface, in Bouvet, "Gujin jing Tian jian Tianxue benyi," Xujiahui Library copy, p. 1a–b. See. Also Adrian Dudink, "The Chinese Christian Texts in the Zikawei 徐家匯 Collection in Shanghai: a Preliiminary and Partial List," *Sino-Western Cultural Relations Journal* 33 (2011): 5.

73. Claudia von Collani, "Charles Maigrot's Role in the Chinese Rites Controversy." In *The Chinese Rites Controversy*. Ed. D. E. Mungello (Nettetal, Germany: Steyler Verlag, 1994), p. 169.

74. For a detailed, annotated record of Tournon's visit to China, see Stumpf, *The Acta Pekinensia* I.

75. Collani, "Tianxue benyi," p. 23.

76. Collani, "Tianxue benyi," p. 20

77. Collani, "Tianxue benyi," p. 18–19 & Stumpf, *Acta Pekinensia*, I, p. 26, fn.64

78. Collani, "Tianxue benyi," p. 24.

79. For a German translation of Tournon's decree, see Collani, "Tianxue benyi," p. 25–26

80. Collani, *P. Joachim Bouvet*, p. 53.

81. Henri Cordier, *L'imprimerie sino-européenne en Chine* (Paris: Imprimerie Nationale, 1891) p. 6 made the same mistake in including both the *Tianxue benyi* and the *Gujin jing Tian jian* in his article of printed Sino-European works in China.

82. Collani, "Tianxue benyi," 28 & Stumpf, *Acta Pekinensia*, p. 47–48.

83. Bouvet, "Caelestis doctrinae vera notitia," Biblioteca Capitolare Fabroniana, Pistoia, Ms. 53.

84. Cf. Bouvet, "Caelestis doctrinae vera notitia," part 2, p 1 with Bouvet, "De cultu celesti Sinarum veterum et modernorum," p. 74b.

85. Collini, "Tinxue benyi," p. 29.

Chapter Two

Drama versus History

Fire is the second of the Five Elements

PRÉMARE'S STATURE AS A SINOLOGIST

If one were to ask who was the greatest European Sinologist of the eighteenth century, there is little dispute that it would be one of the China Jesuits, but which one? There is a tradition among twentieth-century French Sinologists dating from Virgil Pinot (1932), Henri Bernard-Maitre (1935), Paul Demiéville (1970), and Jacques Gernet (2009) to praise Antoine Gaubil, SJ as the greatest eighteenth-century Sinologist. But Gaubil's works, unlike Prémare's, were not suppressed. And so while Gaubil's research on Chinese astronomy, history and chronology was published and his reputation was well established during the eighteenth century, most of Prémare's works remained unpublished.

The Sinologist Abel Rémusat (1788–1832) claimed that only two men occupied the highest rank among China missionaries—Prémare as a grammarian and philologue and Gaubil as an astronomer and historian. Rémusat wrote: "It would be difficult to decide which one of the two was better at Chinese: perhaps Prémare had penetrated deeper into the genius of the language and knew certain refinements more completely; but Gaubil was drawn toward more serious objects and applied himself to more important points in the deep enlightenment that he had acquired."[1] By comparison, Rémusat added that other notable Jesuits, such as, Philippe Couplet, François Noël, Dominique Parrenin, Jean Amiot, and Pierre-Martial Cibot were not the equal of Prémare in his profound knowledge of the Chinese language. Similarly, the eminent Jesuits Adam Schall, Ferdinand Verbiest, and Claudio Grimaldi had not achieved what Gaubil had achieved in astronomy nor had Martino Martini, Claude de Visdelou, and Joseph de Mailla equaled Gaubil in their research on Chinese history and antiquities.

Rémusat's assessment of Jesuits with knowledge of Chinese history and antiquity is based on incomplete knowledge. He gives no indication of being familiar with Prémare's magnum opus—the *Vestigia*—which deals extensively with Chinese history and Chinese historians. Although Rémusat was familiar with Fourmont's correspondence with Prémare, this familiarity did not extend to the *Vestigia* which Prémare sent to Fourmont shortly before his death and which was preserved in the Royal Library.

Rémusat summarized Prémare's involvement with Figurism in the following way:

> It was in being occupied with deep research on Chinese antiquities, that Fr. Prémare was led to embrace a curious system, which had seduced several of the missionaries of China, and, what is very remarkable, precisely those who had a greater understanding of the ancient Chinese authors. This system, of which we have already spoken several times, consisted of research in the Jing and in the literary monuments of the centuries which had preceded the burning of the books [213 BC], of traces of traditions which are supposed to have been transmitted to the authors of these books by means of the founding patriarchs of the Chinese empire. The sometimes obscure meaning of these passages, the diverse interpretations that had been given to different epochs, the allegories contained in the *Book of Odes*, the enigmas of the *Book of Changes* (*Yijing*), the analysis of several symbols, also served for the missionaries partial to these ideas as an argument to fortify them in an opinion that they regarded as favorable to the propagation of Christianity. It was certainly in this view, and not in order to excite a vain curiosity, that they attached themselves to the propagation of these extraordinary notions.[2]

Rémusat quoted a revealing passage from a letter Prémare wrote to the French proto-Sinologist Etienne Fourmont (1683–1745):

> The final and ultimate aim to which I consecrate this *Notitia* [*Linguae Sinicae*], and all my other writings so that, if I am able, that all the earth may know that the Christian religion is as old as the world, and that the God-man is very certainly known to it or to those who have invented the hieroglyphs of China, and composed the Jing. That, my dear, is the sole motive that has sustained and animated me during more than thirty years in my studies.[3]

However, in Fourmont, Prémare was dealing with an unsympathetic correspondent. According to Rémusat, Fourmont believed Figurism was not credible and said "the ancient Chinese were not prophets."[4]

PRÉMARE'S TRANSLATION OF *THE ORPHAN OF ZHAO*

Only two of Prémare's substantive works were published in the century following his death. The first was a translation of a Chinese drama published to popular acclaim in Paris in 1735 and the second was a history published in 1770. The drama had less substance than the history, but nevertheless evolved into one of the most influential works of Chinoiserie in the eighteenth-century. The history was less subject to the distortions of Chinoiserie and was an important contribution to the European knowledge of ancient Chinese history. These two works—a drama and a history—reveal the breadth of Prémare's knowledge of China. Both were mere anticipations of Prémare's most imaginative work, the *Vestigia*, in which he transforms history into symbolical theology. And yet both works were subjected to the suppressive forces of the eighteenth-century intellectual gatekeepers of Europe who distorted and diminished the original contents of these works.

One work which circumvented the ban on Prémare's publications was the Preliminary Discourse published together with Gaubil's translation of the *Classic of History* (*Shujing*) in 1770 and edited by Joseph de Guignes. But in terms of establishing Prémare's reputation and in terms of his influence, a far more important work was his translation of the Chinese drama *Zhaoshi gu'er* 趙氏孤兒 (*Orphan of Zhao*) which had a significant impact on the popular sphere of European culture.

Prémare's status as a leading eighteenth-century Sinologist is based in large part on the great number of Chinese texts in which he was knowledgeable. These encompassed history, philosophy, religion, literature, and drama. Dramatic art had flourished in the Yuan dynasty (1270–1368) when the Mongols dominated China. We know the names of at least sixty-seven playwrights and the titles of 378 dramas from that brief period.[5] Ji Junxiang 紀君祥, one of the less prominent of these Yuan dynasty writers, wrote the drama *Zhaoshi gu'er* (*Orphan of Zhao*). The drama deals with the tragic story of the house of Zhao and is based on an event that occurred in the state of Jin 晉 in the middle of the sixth century and approximately a century before the birth of Confucius.[6] The play's subject matter is serious and its underlying morality theme has an affinity to Christianity. Moreover, its setting fell within the timeframe which Prémare's Figurist views accepted as historical—the Eastern Zhou, unlike the Western Zhou which he regarded as symbolical. In his "Ancient History," Prémare dated the beginning of Chinese history from 722 BC.

Chinese traditional drama was poetic and the songs were as essential to the drama as the script, much like the chorus was essential to the script of a Greek drama.[7] Yuan drama typically consisted of dialogue and songs in which the songs were chanted by the protagonist or chief actor. However, the protagonist could play more than one character in the play. In the original *Orphan of Zhao*, the protagonist played three characters. Prémare translated the drama from the only anthology of Yuan drama widely available at his time—the *Yuan qu xuan* 元曲選 (A Selection of Musical Dramas) of 1616–1617.[8] However, Prémare's translation of the *Orphan of Zhao* omitted the arias and contains only the stage directions, monologues, and dialogues. Ironically, the surviving Yuan dynasty block-print of the *Orphan of Zhao* reverses this emphasis by omitting the stage directions and the dialogues and providing only the text of the arias, which Prémare omitted.[9]

Ji Junxiang was indebted to Sima Qian's *Shiji* (Historical Records) for the story of the Orphan of Zhao.[10] Ji appears to have been the first to treat the theme as a form of vernacular literature. His play is divided into five acts (*jue*) and a wedge (*zhizi*) which serves as a prologue. Prémare never clearly stated why he chose to translate this particular play, but he may have been attracted to it as a characteristic Chinese morality drama of good versus evil. Specifically, the Orphan of Zhao expressed a favorite Chinese theme of filial piety and the responsibility to avenge wrongs done to one's family. The story is set in the sixth-century BC Warring States period when centralized authority had collapsed and feudal warlords engaged in perpetual warfare in which might dominated over right. *Orphan of Zhao* tells the tragic story of the near-extermination of the powerful Zhao clan and the orphan Zhao's culminating revenge.

An underlying current of the play involves the thirst for power that leads to murder. The general theme is a universal one, but the specific form of the theme is Chinese. In a monologue from the prologue, the military leader Tu Angu told how he destroyed his civilian rival Zhao Dun. He revealed his brutal nature by openly revealing how he trained a fierce dog to attack a strawman dressed in his rival's clothes. After telling the king that this dog could detect traitors, Tu released the dog who immediately attacked Zhao Dun. Tu then sent a forged command from the king to Zhao Dun's son to commit suicide, offering the choices of strangling, poisoning or stabbing. Tu followed up by eliminating the entire Zhao clan and its domestic servants, failing however to kill the male heir who became the orphan of Zhao.

The orphan escaped death by the benevolence of a physician who allowed his own son, in a mistaken case of identity, to be executed in the orphan's place. The orphan took the physician's name and was raised as Cheng Bo. As the intricate plot unwound, this Cheng Bo was ultimately adopted by the very same man who killed his father and grandfather—Tu Angu who, of course, was unaware of the orphan's descent from the house of Zhao! So the grandson of Zhao Dun—the Orphan of Zhao—not only survived, but after becoming aware of his descent, he avenged his clan by destroying Tu Angu.

The translation of the *Orphan of Zhao* may have been an attempt by Prémare to move away from controversial issues. After completing the *Vestigia* in May of 1725, the anti-Figurist pressures of the Rites Controversy and exile in Guangzhou seem to have diverted Prémare to non-Figurist projects. One of these projects was his translation of the *Orphan of Zhao*. In 1731 he sent it and several other manuscripts to Fourmont. However the carriers passed the *Orphan of Zhao* manuscript to the Jesuit Jean Baptiste Du Halde (1674–1743) who published it in 1735 (see figure 2.1).[11] Fourmont protested against this unauthorized publication in an angry exchange of letters with Du Halde.[12] However, given Fourmont's tendency to sit on the manuscripts Prémare sent him rather than comply with Prémare's request to disseminate them, it is difficult to give Fourmont's protests much credence.

In spite of the original *Orphan of Zhao* being of only average quality as a Chinese drama and in spite of imperfections in the translation, the work achieved enormous attention, in part, because it was the only Chinese drama to have been translated and, in part, because *Le petit orphelin de la maison de Tchao* appeared at the peak of the European enthusiasm for Chinoiserie. Chinoiserie was a product of global cultural exchange in which Chinese art works were carried to Europe where they were transformed into Sino-European images that had only a distant relationship to the Chinese originals. The *Orphan of Zhao* presents a clear case of this transformation. The significance of Prémare's translation errors was tempered by the fact that Chinoiserie itself was a process of distortion by which elements from a foreign culture were transformed into meaningful European images.[13] Viewed in the context of cultural exchange, Prémare's translation was a pioneering and influential work.

English translations of the *Orphan of Zhao* in Du Halde's *Description de la Chine* appeared in 1736 and 1741 and a separate edition of the play appeared in 1762. It was also translated into German and Dutch.[14] In addition to translations, there were five adaptations made in the eighteenth century. The Englishman William Hatchett adapted Prémare's work under the title *The Chinese Orphan: an Historical Tragedy*, but Hatchett's primary concern was not artistic. The theme of an orphan's revenge was used by Hatchett to create a political satire attacking the British political leader Robert Walpole for his power-hunger.[15] Essentially a political pamphlet, Hatchett's work was never staged.

In Vienna the Abbé Pietro Metastasio adapted the drama at the request of the Empress Maria Theresa who insisted on a time limit for the presentation and only five performers. Metastasio's operatic treatment entitled *L'Eroe cinese* (The Chinese Hero) was produced in 1752, although much of the original work was omitted.[16] The most famous adaptation was made by Voltaire whose *L'Orphelin de la Chine* (1753) completely distorted the original work to promote his Enlightenment cultural agenda.[17] Like Hatchett, Voltaire de-emphasized the role of the orphan and the theme of revenge. The timeframe was moved forward seventeen centuries from the sixth-century BC to AD 1200 and Genghis Khan was introduced as a main character! Little remained of the original Chinese play, except the story of the orphan, and even the orphan of Zhao was replaced by an orphan of the Chinese imperial house who did not grow to maturity and so the theme of filial revenge was eliminated.[18]

Voltaire added to the characters a learned scholar-official named Zamti who served as the voice of Voltaire's idealization of Chinese moral values and who convinced Genghis Khan to adopt the acclaimed tolerance of Chinese civilization. Voltaire removed the original theme of the revenge killings of the orphan of Zhao in order to exalt a conception of Chinese civilization as a model of Enlightenment values, all of which was a fictional projection of his imagination. This drama was first presented in the Comédie Française in 1755 with two outstanding French performers and it became one of the most popular French plays of the eighteenth-century.[19] In a first for French drama, the costumes and scenery of contemporary France were replaced by the imagined recreation of the costumes and scenery of China. With the staging of Voltaire's adaptation, the total transformation of the *Orphan of Zhao* from Prémare's Chinese translation into European Chinoiserie was complete. Voltaire's dramatic success inspired an English adaptation by Arthur Murphy whose *Orphan of Zhao* was a theatrical success staged in 1759 in London.[20]

The intellectual gatekeepers of eighteenth-century Europe applauded Voltaire's adaptation of Prémare's translation because it was a vehicle used to promote Enlightenment values then in vogue. Voltaire was praised, without regard to his distortion of Chinese culture, in the name of Enlightenment values that attacked traditional religion and exalted deism and rationality. On the other hand, Prémare elsewhere was criticized for distorting Chinese culture in the name of a radical theory of Christianity and an outmoded hieroglyphic analysis.

A final eighteenth-century instance of the influence of Prémare's *Orphan of Zhao* may have been in an unfinished tragedy called *Elpenor* by the great German author Johann Wolfgang von Goethe (1749–1832). Goethe sent Schiller a fragment of the work in 1798, but eventually abandoned it.[21] However, unlike other eighteenth-century contemporaries, his interest did not extend to the excesses of Sinomania.

PRÉMARE'S ANCIENT HISTORY OF CHINA

There is a certain irony in the publication of Prémare's manuscript "L'ancienne histoire du monde suivant les chinois" (The ancient history of the world according to the Chinese).[22] While the missionaries' exile in

Guangzhou and Macau continued with no end in sight, news of the Yong Zheng emperor's unrelenting enmity toward Christianity continued to be relayed from the few Jesuits left at the court in Beijing. Prémare realized that his prayers for the return of the expelled missionaries to their flocks in China might not be granted. In fact, the China mission was in a fight for its survival. In this kind of sensitized environment, Prémare sought to avoid any direct violation of his superiors' ban on the dissemination of his research. But since he believed that a Figurist interpretation of ancient Chinese texts provided hope for the eventual acceptance of Christianity among the literati, he tried to find ways of circumventing the ban on publishing his works.

The prominent Parisian scholar Etienne Fourmont was crucial to this hope by providing a channel through which Prémare's works might be disseminated to European intellectuals. With this aim in mind, Prémare sent Fourmont several Figurist manuscripts. One of these was the first sixteen chapters of his chronology of ancient China. The manuscript consisted of 142 sheets with the French text on the recto side and the notes, mostly quotations from Chinese texts which were written, on the verso side.[23] This is the same scholarly format that Prémare used in his *Vestigia*. Illness prevented him from sending the remaining chapters. Moreover, he had a presentiment that his life was entering its final phase and he knew he needed to act promptly, so he enclosed this manuscript with his letter of November 10, 1730, to Fourmont. Prémare gave Fourmont permission to edit the work. He hoped that Fourmont might present it to the *Académie des Inscriptions et Belles-Lettres*. He begged Fourmont not to mention his authorship as that could cause great difficulty with his superiors.

Fourmont never presented Prémare's manuscript to the *Académie des Inscriptions et Belles-Lettres*. The manuscript lay in obscurity for forty years until one of his students published it. Joseph de Guignes (1721–1800) became a student of Fourmont in 1736 and was awarded the post of Chinese interpreter of the French king in 1741. After Fourmont's death, Guignes succeeded him as secretary-interpreter for Oriental Languages in the Royal Library. Guignes' most famous book was a disseminationist attempt to prove that the Chinese were an Egyptian colony.[24] Guignes included Prémare's work as an eighty-page introduction to the 1770 publication of Fr. Antoine Gaubil's translation of the *Classic of History* (*Shujing*) (see figure 2.2). The French Sinologist Henri Cordier (1849–1925) said the book reflected Guignes' rich imagination and lack of critical facility.[25]

This was Gaubil's most famous publication and its inclusion of Prémare's essay on Chinese antiquity nicely juxtaposed the works of the two leading Sinologists among China Jesuits. Prémare and Gaubil represented intellectually opposing points of view about the decipherment of ancient Chinese texts with Prémare interpreting these texts as theological symbolism and Gaubil interpreting them as history. Guignes applied a heavy editor's hand to Prémare's text, even though he lacked the knowledge of Chinese antiquity needed to make these revisions and consequently he made mistakes. As an editorial gatekeeper he removed all explicit references to Figurism on the exaggerated ground that Figurism had been completely rejected by the China missionaries.[26] Nevertheless, certain elements of Figurism remained. While Figurism had been suppressed and driven underground, it had not been destroyed. The ideas embodied in it were too dynamic to eradicate.

Guignes also inaccurately changed the title from Prémare's "Ancient History of the World according to the Chinese" (L'ancienne histoire du monde suivant les chinois) to "Preliminary Discourse, or Research on the Times Prior to Those on Which the Classic of History speaks, and on Chinese Mythology (*Discours Preliminaire, Ou Recherches sur les temps antérieurs à ceux dont parle le Chou-king, et sur la Mythologie Chinoise*). In fact, in treating material that extended to the beginning of the Eastern Zhou (770 BC), Prémare was covering material contained in the *Shujing* (*Classic of History*). Ironically, the thesis of Prémare's "Ancient History" was so grounded in Figurism, that Guignes was unable to remove these defining characteristics. In fact, Figurism appears in the first sentence of Prémare's "Ancient History" which states:

> There has been published here in Europe a great many books which treat Chinese history, but you would fall into error if you believed that everything is as certain as they say ... No one has spoken in detail of who precedes [the ancient figure] Fu Xi. It is reasonably said that these are myths. It should be added that what follows Fu Xi is no less mythical.[27]

Traditional Chinese chronologies commonly claimed that the first three dynasties—the Xia, Shang, and Zhou—were historical and assigned them dubiously precise years with sight variations, such as, 2205–1784 BC, 1783–1135 BC and 1134–247 BC, respectively. Prémare noted that there was no consensus among Chinese authors on these early dates. However, he argued that, based on his examination of what he referred to as historical "monuments," the antiquity of Chinese history extended back only to 722 BC.[28] This was approximately the time when the Western Zhou ended and the Eastern Zhou was established. He does not challenge the historicity of the Eastern Zhou.

In his suppressed work, the *Vestigia*, Prémare explained the fundamental Figurist point about the non-historical nature of the first three dynasties in the following way:

> The reader would perhaps be led to suspect, by all that precedes and by what follows in this article, that I want to affirm that the three dynasties 三代 *Sandai*,

of which the *Classic of History* makes mention, are not [historically] real, but purely symbolic. This is why I am going to give all my thoughts here.

It is very true that several savants, very erudite, think that the *Classic of History* is not a profane and common history, but a very profound teaching hidden under the appearance of history. I do not wish to express any opinion below. I leave to the Chinese their histories, as one reads about them in Sima Qian and others. I go even farther. In supposing that it may be certain that these three dynasties have never existed, the opposing opinion [that these three dynasties existed] is profoundly rooted in the spirit of the Chinese of this time. And this error, if there is an error, has grown from roots so ancient that, in my view, the Chinese will never be able to be cured of this malady, if there is a malady. Far from being offended, they will applaud the praise that we will give to the *Jing* (Classics), in our refraining from asking the useless question above, and to the remarkable things that we have discovered, especially if we demonstrate that all things converge toward a single reality.

So I am going to continue to completely explain the wonderful teaching hidden in the *Classic of Changes*, *Classic of History*, and the *Classic of Odes*. Far from my thoughts of wishing to force anyone to adopt my position, I ask on the contrary that I be informed of my errors, if one thinks that I have committed them. My aim is to extract from these very ancient monuments the vestiges of the august mysteries of the true religion.[29]

Prémare drew from numerous standard Chinese histories in writing his "Ancient History." When the Jesuit missionaries arrived in China during the late Ming dynasty, there were two main genres of comprehensive histories. One was a composite style (*jichuan* 紀傳) going back to Sima Qian's *Shiji* 史記 (Records of the Grand Historian) (104–87 BC) and the other consisted of an annalistic style (*biannian* 編年). According to recent research by the Sinologist Nicolas Standaert, the missionaries arrived at the time of the emergence of a new historiographical genre which transformed the two genres of the composite and annalistic styles into a new genre—*gangjian* 剛鑑.[30]

The standard (normative) historiographical tradition had been established in the Song dynasty (960–1279) in the form of annalistic histories that blended narrative and morality in history. The most notable of these was *Zizhitongjian* 資治通鑑 (Comprehensive Mirror for Aid in Governance) (composed 1067–1084) by Sima Guang 司馬光. Whereas Ming annalistic (comprehensive mirror) texts were written as aids in governance, Ming *gangjian* (outline and mirror) texts were composite works which attempted to appeal to the broader Ming reading public by emphasizing clear language, easy readability and a wider span of Chinese history. These *gangjian* histories were used extensively by missionary authors in China, including Prémare.

Prémare drew extensively from the annalistic histories of the Song period, but he made most creative use of *gangjian* texts, particularly the *Lushi* 路史

(Grand History) (1170) of Luo Bi 羅泌 (d. after 1176). The *Lushi* covered a large span of time from the mythological era to the Eastern Han (25–220). The work has a strong moralistic tone that reflects Luo's views as a Daoist and anti-Buddhist.[31] Luo Bi has been criticized for his "strong moralistic and anti-Buddhist views." However, since Zhu Xi, who wrote his highly influential historical work *Zizhi tongjian gangmu* (Chronicle of the Comprehensive Mirror for the Aid of Government) (1172) at the same time as Luo Bi, imposed the moralistic judgment of Neo-Confucianism on China's history, one wonders to what extent such moralistic judgments of history were simply characteristic of Chinese historiography.

In his "Ancient History," Prémare cited the most famous composite history, Sima Qian's *Shiji* (Records of the Grand Historian) (compiled 104–87 BC).[32] He also cited the "great history . . . in 294 volumes" of Sima Guang 司馬光—the Comprehensive Mirror for Aid in Governance.[33] This annalistic history is said to have been the most important work of history since Sima Qian's *Shiji*.[34] Prémare was aware of the historical significance of these two works. He cited both Sima Guang's Comprehensive Mirror and Zhu Xi's influential *Zizhi tongjian gangmu* 資治通鑑綱目 (Outline and Detail of the Comprehensive Mirror for Aid in Governance) in claiming that a second epoch of history began in 425 BC.[35] However he noted that some push the beginning of this epoch back to 770 BC, the time of the European Romulus.

Prémare claimed that the first epoch of Chinese history was defined by one of Sima Guang's assistants, Liu Shu 劉恕 (styled Liu Daoyuan 劉道原) (1032–1078).[36] Liu wrote *Sizhi tongjian waiji* 資治通鑑外紀 (Additional Chronicle to the Comprehensive Mirror for Aid in Governance) (1078). While Sima Guang's work covered 403 BC–AD 959, Liu Shu's *Waiji* extended its coverage back to earliest times as well as forward into his own times.[37] Liu's work, which is incomplete and contains only one chapter on ancient times, begins its treatment with Pan Gu who was a creator of the world.[38] Prémare cited other historians who treated this earliest period. He praised Luo Bi's *Lushi* "in which one finds almost everything that can be desired on ancient times; he does not omit the Xia [dynasty], but he adds a great number of treatises of unusual erudition." He praised Yuan Liaofan 遠了凡 of the Yuan dynasty (1270–1368) for adapting everything that others preceding him had said of this earliest period and for inserting appropriate critical judgments of a large number of savants, which was of great assistance to Prémare.[39]

Prémare stated that the second epoch of history was defined by Sima Zheng 司馬貞 (fl. 720).[40] [Sima Zheng is commonly called Xiao Sima 小司馬 (Lesser Sima) to distinguish him from the famous Han historian Sima

Qian.] Sima Zheng wrote an introduction to Sima Qian's Shiji called *Sanhuang ji* 三皇紀, which dealt with the mythical period of Fu Xi.[41]

According to Prémare, the third epoch of Chinese history was defined by Sima Qian. The fourth epoch was defined by Jin Luxiang 金履祥 (1232–1303) who wrote *[Zizhi] Tongjian qianbian* [資治]通鑑前編 (Prologue to the Comprehensive Mirror for Aid in Governance).[42] Jin sought to cover the years before Sima Guang's great work and so added a prologue that covered 2357 BC to 403 BC.[43] Prémare said the fifth and last epoch was covered by Sima Guang's history and extended from the civil wars of King Wei Lie (威烈) 425 BC down to the conquest of China by Qin Shi Huangdi, the First Emperor, whose reign began in 246 BC.[44]

Prémare criticized later Chinese historians for blindly following Liu Shu's *Waiji* and for not carefully examining China's antiquity. He was dubious of the authoritative Zhu Xi's claim that:

> in tracing the symbols [Fu Xi] became the first father of letters. It follows however, from what I have reported down to here, that the letters existed a long time before Fu Xi, if one can use the terms before and after in a chronology as confused as this one.[45]

After presenting the various accounts of China's antiquity, Prémare wrote:

> If one were forced to choose between so many different opinions, I would be in an embarrassing situation, not having found any author who had been thought to prove that one opinion should be believed rather than the others.[46]

This ambiguity was one of the grounds that caused him to view the accounts of Chinese antiquity as allegorical rather than historical.

The nature of an allegorical story typically transcends its specific meaning to assume universal significance. Prémare reveals this interpretative inclination in the following:

> The *Shanhaijing* (*Classic of Mountains and Seas*) said that Huangdi gave an order to an obedient *long* 龍 (dragon) to slay Chiyou and to throw him into the dark valley of evil. As to what our poets express by different names, such as, Neptune, Glaucus, etc., the ancient Chinese call them all *long* (dragons) which usually designates good spirits. It is often said the Chi You is not dead. Huangdi paints his description in order to frighten the whole universe.[47]

In the *Vestigia*, Prémare explains that Chi You is a symbolic form of Satan.

FROM HISTORY TO SYMBOLISM

Catastrophic floods play an important role in Chinese mythology and are probably linked to the frequent overflow of rivers produced by the shallow riverbeds and flat terrain of northern China. There are four main flood myths.[48] However, these four myths all seem to be related in that they each emphasize different aspects of a similar destructive force. One flood myth involves the god of water Gonggong as narrated in the *Guanzi*, *Guoyu*, and *Huainanzi*. Another flood myth involves the creatrix Woman Wa. Yet another flood myth involves Gun who also appears in the fourth flood myth involving emperor Yu. The Yu myth became the dominant flood myth in China when it was absorbed into Confucian morality and the Mandate of Heaven (*tianming* 天命) by which rulers should be chosen on the basis of morality and ability rather than might and cleverness.

Prémare and Bouvet agreed that the meaning of the Yu flood lay not in actual flooding, but rather in its symbolic meaning. In this interpretation, the Flood represented

> the sins and crimes coming from the rebellion of Lucifer and of Adam which spread throughout the world as malevolent and injurious water. Christ alone has been able to remedy such a great evil, in attacking the evil at its source and draining by his death the fountain of these evils. This admirable teaching, lost through the lapse of time, is being revealed again; so we interpret these ancient monuments spiritually and divinely.[49]

Prémare drew from the opening chapter of the *Classic of History*, the "Record of Yao" (Yao dian 堯典), to explain the fundamental polarities in his interpretation. When the emperor Yao called for a man who would serve him in ruling, someone proposed Gun 鯀, but Yao rejected him, saying he "smoothly speaks, but his actions are perverse."[50] In seeking someone to help deal with the flooding, the emperor said:

> the great waters everywhere are injurious, extensively they embrace the mountains and rise above the hills, vastly they swell up to Heaven. The lower people groan. Is there anybody whom I could let regulate it? All said: Oh, Gun, indeed! The emperor said: Oh, he is offensive. He neglects (my) orders, he ruins his kin.

When his advisers nevertheless praised Gun, Yao appointed him to be the minister of works (sikong 司空) and to drain the waters from the flooded land.[51] But after nine years of unsuccessful labor, Yao removed him and banished him to Mount Yu (*Yushan* 羽山) and the task was given to his son, Yu 禹. Prémare interprets Gun and his nine years of unsuccessful labor as symbols of Adam:

It is in vain that Adam had wept 900 years for his sin; he had been unable to find any remedy for the evils that his defect has caused for his posterity.[52]

He added:

It is now easy to see how Adam is well symbolized in the type of the ancient Gun. When King Yao had spoken of the waters of the Flood the words that I have reported above, he asked who would be able to develop a remedy for such a great evil. Everyone replied that it is Gun. Yao refused him and said: "Enough! Be off!" He has violated the law and lost the human race. Can Adam be designated more clearly?[53]

Yao replaced Gun with his son Shun who was successful in controlling the flooding and was chosen by Yao to succeed him on the throne. Prémare quoted the *Classic of History* to say: "Shun being mounted on the throne, he 'banished Gun to Feather-Winged Mountain (Yushan 羽山) and hurled Gonggong into the abyss of darkness.'"[54] He quoted another *Classic of History* passage to say: "The world pacified and the Flood quelled, Yu attained the throne."[55]

REJECTION BY PARISIAN INTELLECTUALS

Unlike Bouvet, Prémare was an isolated Jesuit in China who had few contacts with prominent people—either Chinese or Europeans. When he encountered an article in the 1721 volume of the *Mémoires de Trevoux* about an Italian Jesuit astronomer and philosopher named Melchior della Briga (1686–1749), he attempted to contact him.[56] Fr. Briga was an astronomer and philosopher based in Rome who deciphered Egyptian hieroglyphs. Briga claimed that the hieroglyphs demonstrated that the ancient Egyptians had known about the Holy Trinity.[57] Struck by the parallels to his own Figurist interpretations of ancient Chinese texts, Prémare wrote to Briga, but there is no record of any reply. However, Prémare used Briga's thesis as a means to introduce himself and his Figurist theories to the Parisian academician Étienne Fourmont (1683–1745). He had learned about Fourmont in reading a 1722 volume of the *Mémoires de Trevoux*. That journal had published an extract of a paper on Chinese hieroglyphs that Fourmont had presented at a meeting of the Académie des Inscriptions et Belles-Lettres.[58]

Fourmont's study of the Chinese language began when Jean-Paul Bignon asked him to help reform the *Bibliothèque du Roi*. Bignon was a powerful figure and by 1721 had control of almost every official cultural institution in Paris.[59] The valuable Chinese collections in the royal library were uncatalogued and inaccessible to scholars because of language difficulties. Their classification had initially been undertaken by a Chinese named Arcadio Huang (1679–1716) who had been born in Fujian province and been brought to Europe by Bishop Artus de Lionne in 1702.⁶⁰ Bignon had invited Huang to begin an inventory of Chinese works in the royal library and, after Huang's death from tuberculosis in 1716, Fourmont completed it. This included the recently-acquired Chinese collection of 1,845 volumes which had been brought back from China by Fr. Jean-François Fouquet, SJ in 1722. With Bignon's support, Fourmont became responsible for ordering and cataloging Chinese (as well Indian and Tartar) books for the royal library. In China, Fr. Prémare purchased a great number of Chinese books that were regularly dispatched to France.⁶¹ Writing from Macau on November 3, 1733, Prémare despaired over the worms devouring the books he had collected with so much care over the years.⁶² He wrote of giving the best-preserved books to Bignon's nephew, a mate on one of the French ships in the harbor, to deliver to his uncle in Paris.

Over the years from 1716 until his death in 1745, Fourmont's works on Chinese became the object of great controversy in the French academic world. By 1729 he had produced a "Grammaire Chinoise," although it was not published until 1745. At that time in France the Jesuits monopolized publications on China through the writings of their fellow missionaries.⁶³ Fourmont's critics felt that he was claiming a degree of knowledge that he simply did not have. Prémare tried to disabuse Fourmont of his belief that the Chinese used grammars. Unlike European students who learned to compose using the rules of grammar, Chinese students learned by memorizing classical texts.⁶⁴ The Chinese followed models rather than abstract rules. Fourmont refused to believe this, not only because it was at odds with his training as a Classicist, but also because he had found in the Chinese collection of the royal library what he believed were Chinese grammars.⁶⁵

Two of these works that he had found were the well-known Kangxi dictionary, the *Kangxi zidian* 康熙字典 (1716), and an obscure dictionary which he calls the *Haipian* 海篇.⁶⁶ The characters in the *Kangxi* dictionary were arranged on the basis of 214 radicals (*bu* 部) (the fundamental component of each character) and the number of strokes in each character. These 214 radicals had been developed by the Ming dynasty lexicographer Mei Yingzuo 梅膺祚 (1570–1615) in his dictionary *Zihui* 字彙.⁶⁷ Mei modified the arrangement that had been used in the ancient Shuowen dictionary to develop a new basis for arranging characters which served as a lexical aid to make the definitions of characters more accessible to readers. However, Fourmont mistakenly thought that these 214 radicals (classifiers) were part of the grammatical structure of the Chinese language and functioned like a key to understand Chinese.

Fourmont was not the first European to believe that the 214 radicals were part of the grammatical structure of the Chinese language. Numerous scholars in seventeenth-century Europe had believed that it was possible to recover the Primitive Language given by God to Adam and Eve in the Garden of Eden (Genesis 2:19–20). Some scholars even believed that Chinese was the Primitive Language. While many scholars were dubious about the possibility of recovering the Primitive Language, some thought that it was possible to construct a universal language using the common structure and features that all languages were thought to share.[68]

The search for a universal language was based on the assumption that it was possible to discover Real Characters, that is, symbols and sounds whose representation of things and ideas was natural or "real" rather than conventional. Francis Bacon was the first to propose the development of a universal language. Some of the most eminent seventeenth-century savants were involved in this search for a universal language. This group included the polyhistor Leibniz and Athanasius Kircher, SJ. Information about Chinese from the missionaries played an important role in stimulating this search.

In 1674 in Berlin, the proto-Sinologist Andreas Müller proposed the possibility of developing a *Clavis Sinica* (Key to the Chinese language) which would apply certain universal principles of language to help one learn Chinese at an accelerated rate.[69] Müller failed to complete his proposal. However, his proto-Sinological successor at the Great Elector's court in Berlin, Christian Mentzel, also proposed a *Clavis Sinica*, although his proposal made less ambitious claims than Müller's. Mentzel also used the 214 radicals of the *Kangxi* dictionary, but his Key seems to have been more like a grammar than a key which would expedite the learning of Chinese. However, the 214 radicals of the *Kangxi* dictionary were, as Prémare realized, not a grammar, but a lexical arrangement for creating a more efficient way to access the definitions of Chinese characters.

Lacking Bouvet's acute diplomatic and political skills, Prémare was naïve in dealing with a Parisian intellectual like Fourmont whose worldly ambitions were entirely at odds with Prémare's self-effacing qualities. Fourmont's prominence was built on his claims to expertise in the Chinese language which were tenable in Europe only because of the unsophisticated nature of European Sinology. Actually, rather than being a Sinologist, Fourmont belonged to the preliminary group of proto-Sinologists.[70]

In his attempt to enlist Fourmont as an intermediary, Prémare trusted him and sent him his manuscripts in the naïve belief that Fourmont shared his motivation. He expressed this belief in his letter of November 28, 1730, to Fourmont: "Sometimes it occurs to me that perhaps these matters that I am writing so much to you about, may be of more interest to a missionary in

China than to an academician in Paris. However, I have always trusted you. I am sure that you put Christianity far above the Academy . . . Take whatever I send you and use it as your own property . . . I pray you again, you and M. Raguet, not to tell anybody that I am sending you some of my works."[71]

Sadly, Prémare's trust in Fourmont was misplaced. The prominent French Sinologist Henri Cordier drew a very unflattering portrait of Fourmont as a "vain pedant" and a "mediocre soul who failed to grasp great ideas."[72] Cordier called him "a sycophant" and described him as having an "envious nature, having recourse to any intrigue in order to reach the aim of his ambition." When Prémare sent Fourmont a copy of "Notitia Linguae Sinicae" with the request that he circulate it, Cordier claimed that Fourmont suppressed the manuscript because its quality was so superior to Fourmont's own work that its dissemination would have embarrassed him.

NOTES

1. Abel Rémusat, "Joseph Henry Prémare, Missionnaire a la Chine," *Nouveaux Mélanges Asiatiques*. Vol. 2. (Paris: Schubart & Heideloff, 1829), p. 262–63.

2. Rémusat, "Prémare," p. 265–66.

3. Rémusat, "Prémare," p. 266, does not give the date of Prémare's letter to Fourmont.

4. Rémusat, "Prémare," p. 267.

5. Liu Wu-chi, "The Original Orphan of China," *Comparative Literature* 5 (3) (Summer 1953): 193.

6. Ch'en Shou-yi, "The Chinese Orphan: a Yuan Play. Its Influence on European Drama of the Eighteenth Century," *Tien Hsia Monthly* III (2) (1936): 91.

7. Liu, p. 195–96.

8. W. L. Idema, "The Orphan of Zhao: Self-Sacrifice, Tragic Choice and Revenge and the Confucianization of Mongol Drama at the Miing Court," *Cina.* No. 21, XXXth *European Conference of Chinese Studies Proceedings* (1988), p. 160–62.

9. Idema, p. 162.

10. Liu, p. 200 & Idema, p. 170.

11. The manuscript of Prémare's translation is preserved in the Biobliothèque Nationale France, Paris, Manuscrit BNF, Fonds français 25510. It was published in Jean-Baptiste Du Halde, SJ, *Description géographique, historique, chronologique, politique, et physique de l'empire de la Chine et de la Tartarie chinoise*. 4 vols. (Paris: P. G. Lemercier, 1735) III, 339–78.

12. Henri Cordier, *Bibliotheca Sinica.* 5 vols. (Paris: Librairie Oriéntale & Americaine, 1906–1907) III, 1787–88.

13. A century after Du Halde's publication of Prémare's translation of the *Orphan of Zhao*, the Sinologist Stanislas Julien published a list of Prémare's translation errors in *Tchao-Chi-Kou-Eul, ou l'Orphelin de la Chine* (Paris: Moutardier, 1834).

14. Ch'en, p. 89 & Liu, p. 203–5.

15. William W. Appleton, *A Cycle of Cathay: the Chinese Vogue in England during the Seventeenth and Eighteenth Century* (New York: Columbia University Press, 1951), p. 82–86.
16. Liu, p. 205–6.
17. Liu, p. 206–9.
18. Min Tan, *The Poetics of Difference and Displacement* (Hong Kong: Hong Kong University Press, 2008) p. 20–21. See also Appleton, p. 84–85.
19. Min Tan, p. 21–22.
20. Ch'en, p. 101.
21. Adolf Reichwein, *China and Europe: Intellectual and Artistic Contacts in the Eighteenth Century*. J. C. Jowell, tr. (London: Kegan Paul, 1925), p. 133–36.
22. BNF, Bréquigny 18, I.
23. Knud Lundbæk, *Joseph de Prémare (1666–1736), S.J.: Chinese Philology and Figurism*. (Aarhus, Denmark: Aarhus University Press, 1991) p. 49 & 161.
24. Joseph de Guignes, *Mémoire dans lequel on prouve que les Chinois sont une colonie égyptienne* (Paris: Desaint & Saillant, 1759).
25. Henri Cordier, "Les études chinoises sous la Révolution et l'Empire," *T'oung Pao*. Second series. 19 (2) (May 1918–May 1919): 63–64.
26. Lundbæk, p. 165.
27. Joseph de Prémare, "Discours Preliminaire" In *Le Chou-king, un des livres sacrés des Chinois* (Paris: N. M. Tilliard, 1770) p. xliv.
28. Prémare, "Discours Preliminaire," p. lvi.
29. *Vestigia* f. 94a-95a; *Vestiges*, p. 173–74.
30. Nicolas Standaert, *The Intercultural Weaving of Historical Texts: Chinese and European Stories about Emperor Ku and His Concubines* (Leiden: Brill, 2016), p. 15–17.
31. While praising Luo Bi's *Lushi* as richly imaginative in the literary and philosophical sense, Chun-shu Chang criticizes Luo Bi's approach for being "completely uncritical and inconsistent" with "strong moralistic and anti-Buddhist views." See *A Sung Bibliography (Bibliographie des Sung)*. Ed. Yves Hervouet (Hong Kong: The Chinese University Press, 1978), p. 87–88.
32. Prémare, "Discours Preliminaire," p. lv & liv refers to Sima Qian as Se-ma-tsien.
33. Prémare, "Discours Preliminaire," p. liv–lv refers to Sima Guang as Se-me-kouang.
34. G. Lewin, *Sung Bibliography*, p. 71–72.
35. Prémare, "Discours Preliminaire," p. lv refers to Zhu Xi as Tchu-hi.
36. Prémare, "Discours Preliminaire," p. liv, cv & cviii refers to Liu Daoyuan as Lieou-tao-yuen.
37. R. de Crespigny, *Sung Bibliography*, p. 72.
38. Yuan Ke, *Dragons and Dynasties: An Introduction to Chinese Mythology*. Selected and translated by Kim Echlin & Nie Zhixiong (London: Penguin Books, 1993) p. 1–3 & Anne Birrell, *Chinese Mythology: An Introduction* (Baltimore: The Johns Hopkins University Press, 1993), p. 25.
39. Prémare, "Discours Preliminaire," p. liv, lxx, lxxiij & cxiij refers to Yuan Liaofan as Yuen-leao-fan.

40. Prémare, "Discours Preliminaire," p. liv refers to Sima Zheng as Si-ma-tching.
41. William Frederick Mayers, *Chinese Reader's Manual* (Shanghai: American Presbyterian Mission Press, 1874), p. 198–99.
42. Prémare, "Discours Preliminaire," p. liv refers to Jin Luxiang as Kin-gin-chan.
43. A. W. Sariti, *Sung Bibliography*, p. 77.
44. Prémare, "Discours Preliminaire," p. liv–lv.
45. Prémare, "Discours Preliminaire," p. cij.
46. Prémare, "Discours Preliminaire," p.lxj.
47. Prémare, "Discours Preliminaire," p. cxxviij.
48. Birrell, *Chinese* Myths, p. 33–35 & Chinese *Mythology*, p. 146
49. Vestigia, f. 90a; *Vestiges*, p. 167.
50. Bernhard Karlgren, *The Book of Documents*. In *Museum of Far Eastern Antiquities* (Stockholm) Bulletin number 22 (1950), p. 3. Yao tien, 10–11. Cf. James Legge translated Yao's words in the same passage as follows: "Is there a capable man, to whom I can assign the correction *of this calamity?* All *in the court* said, 'Oh! There is K'wan.' The emperor said, 'Alas! no, by no means! He is disobedient to orders, and tries to injure his peers." *The Chinese Classics*. James Legge, tr. 5 vols. (Oxford: Oxford University Press, 1893) III, 24–25.
51. Mayers, *Chinese Readers Manual*, p. 95.
52. *Vestigia*, f. 90a; *Vestiges*, p. 169.
53. *Vestigia*, f. 90a-91a ; *Vestiges*, p. 168–69. The passage is from *Shangshu Zhengyi* 尚書爭議. Yao 堯. 122上。In *Shisan jing zhu shu* 十三經柱疏。Ruan Yuan 阮元, ed. 2 vols. (Beijing: Zhonghua Shuju Chuban,1806; reprinted 1980).
54. *Vestigia* f. 91r-v; *Vestiges,*p. 169, Shangshu *Zhengyi* 尚書爭議, 舜典。128下。Cf. Legge, III, 40
55. *Vestigia*, f. 91r–92r; *Vestiges*, p. 169. Shangshu *Zhengyi* 尚書爭議, 舜典。136上。Cf. Legge, III, 60–61.
56. Antoine Gaubil, SJ, *Correspondence de Pékin 1722–1759*. Ed Renée Simon (Geneva: Librairie Droz, 1970), p. 616.
57. Lundbæk, p. 22.
58. Lundbæk, p. 22–26.
59. Cécile Leung, *Etienne Fourmont (1683–1745) Oriental and Chinese Languages in Eighteenth-Century France* (Leuven, Belgium: Leuven University Press, 2002), p. 129–32.
60. Danielle Elisseeff, *Moi Arcade interprete chinois du Roi-Soleil* (Paris: Les Éditions Arthaud, 1985) & Jonathan D. Spence, "The Paris Years of Arcadio Huang," in *Chinese Roundabout: Essays in History and Culture* (New York: W. W. Norton, 1992), p. 11–24.
61. Rémusat, "Prémare," p. 274 & Leung, p. 136–37.
62. Lundbæk, p. 193, fn 26.
63. A. Brou, SJ, "Les Jésuites sinologues de Pékin et leurs éditeurs de Paris," *Revue d'histoire des Missions* 11 (1934): 551–66.
64. Leung, p. 189
65. Etienne Fourmont, *Meditationes sinicae*. 4 parts. (Paris: Bullot, 1737) II, 60, and 124–26.

66. A copy of this *Haipian* dictionary is found in the Vatican Library (Borgia Cinese 262–63). See Mungello, *Curious Land*, p. 217–18.

67. Roy Andrew Miller, "Mei Ying-tso," in *Dictionary of Ming Biography 1368–1644*. Eds. L. Carrington Goodrich & Chaoying Fang. 2 vols. (New York: Columbia University Press, 1976) II, 1061–62.

68. Mungello, *Curious Land*, p. 174–97.

69. Mungello, *Curious Land*, p. 198–203.

70. Mungello, *Curious Land*, p. 13–14.

71. Translated by Knud Lundbæk, *Joseph de Prémare*, p. 51.

72. Henri Cordier, "Les études chinoises sous la Révolution et l'Empire," *T'oung Pao,* second series, 19 (2) (May 1918–May 1919): 60.

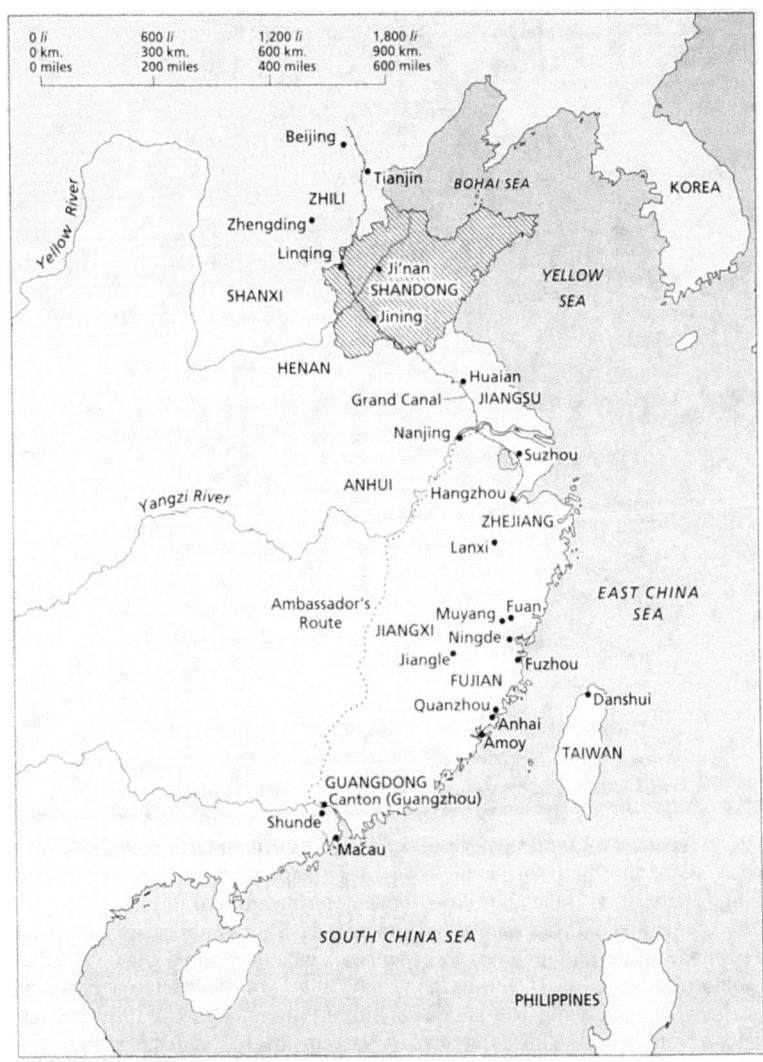

Map 1. *Eastern China ca. 1700.* The Ambassador's Route, from Guangzhou (Canton) in the south to the capital Beijing in the north, was the route travelled by Jesuit missionaries into China. The southern part involved an overland route (indicated by dotted lines) and the northern part was the Grand Canal. Apart from two years in Beijing, Prémare spent 1698–1724 in Jiangxi province, through which the Ambassador's Route passed. He and most other missionaries were expelled to Guangzhou in 1724 and then further expelled to Macau in 1733 where he died in 1736. *Source*: D. E. Mungello. *The Spirit and the Flesh in Shandong, 1650–1785* (Rowman & Littlefield, 2001).

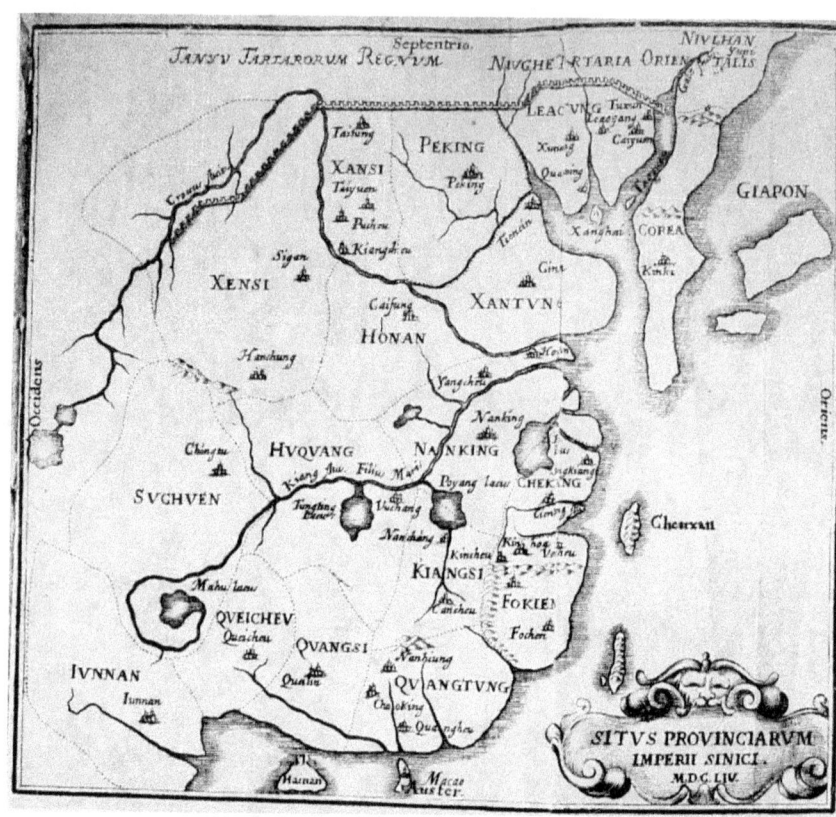

Map 2. *Seventeenth-Century Provinces of China.* Martino Martini, *De bello tartarico historia* (Milan: Gio. Battista Bidelli, 1654). This map clearly delineates the province of Kiangsi (Jiangxi) with the Gan River flowing northward into Poyang Lake and then into the Yangzi River. These waterways formed part of the Ambassador's Route. There were several mission stations along this waterway, including Nanchang (labelled on the map south of Poyang Lake). During the years 1700–1714, Prémare was based mainly at Jianchang, located about 130 km due south of Poyang Lake. The Christian scholar-official Liu Ning retired to his hometown of Nanfeng in 1702, remaining there until his death in 1710. Nanfeng is not labelled on Martini's map, but it was only 30 km south of Jianchang and it was apparently during these years that Prémare and Liu had their most substantive intellectual contact. *Source*: Martino Martini's *De bello tartarico historia* (1654).

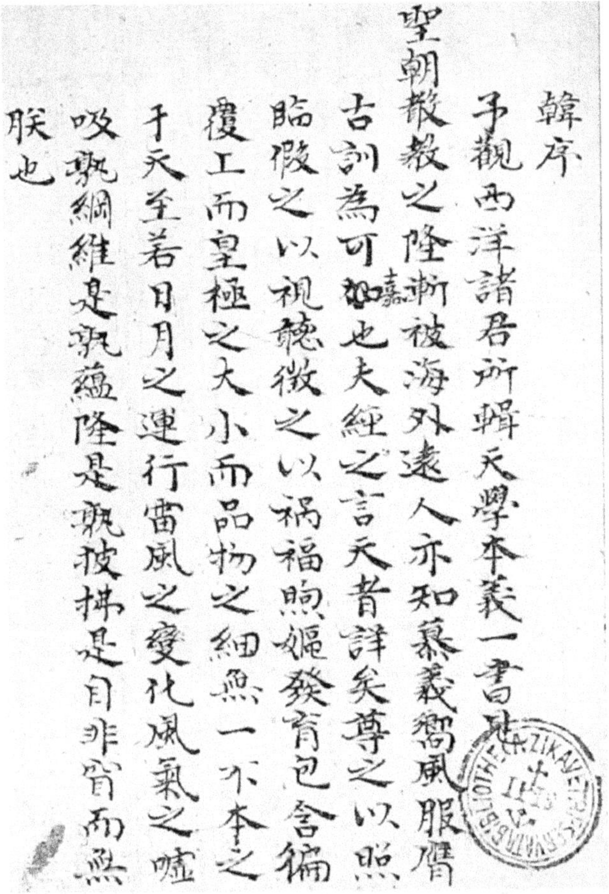

韓序

予觀西洋諸君所輯天學本義一書也
斷被海外遠人亦知慕義馭風服膺
古訓為可如也夫經之言天者詳矣尊之以照
臨微之以視聽微之以禍福煦嫗發育包含徧
覆工而皇極之大小而品物之細無一不本之
于天至若日月之運行當風之變化風氣之噓
吸呃綱維是冀蘊隆是覲被拂是自非宵而熙
朕也

聖朝散教之隆

嘉

Figure 1.1. The eminent scholar-official Han Tan's preface (1703) to Joachim Bouvet's *Gujin jing Tian jian Tianxue benyi* 古今敬天鑑 天學本義 (An Examination of the original meaning of the Heavenly Teaching in the ancient and modern expression 'revere Heaven'). Zikawei (Xujiahui 徐家匯) Library, Shanghai. Although Han Tan was not a Christian, he admired the Jesuits at the court in Beijing. The Jesuits realized that Han's preface bestowed status on Christianity in China, but the Papal Legate Tournon criticized the inclusion of a preface by a Chinese non-believer in a Christian work. Image courtesy of the Zikawei (Xujiahui) Library, Shanghai.

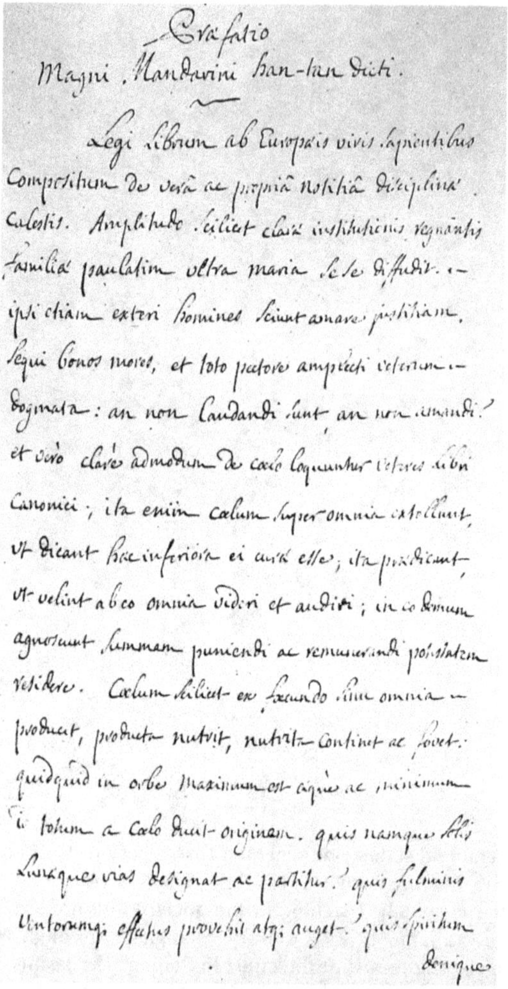
Praefatio
Magni Mandarini han-tan dicti.
Legi librum ab Europaeis viris sapientibus
compositum de verâ ac propriâ notitiâ disciplinae
caelestis. Amplitudo scilicet clarae institutionis regnantis
familiae paulatim ultra maria sese diffudit. –
ipsi etiam exteri homines sciunt amare justitiam,
sequi bonos mores, et toto pectore amplecti veterum –
dogmata: an non laudandi sunt, an non amandi?
et vero clare admodum de caelo loquuntur veteres libri
canonici; ita enim caelum super omnia extollunt,
ut dicant haec inferiora ei curae esse; ita praedicant,
ut velint ab eo omnia videri et audiri; in eo dominum
agnoscunt summam puniendi ac remunerandi potestatem
residere. Caelum scilicet ex faecundo sinu omnia –
producit, producta nutrit, nutrita continet ac fovet:
quidquid in orbe maximum est aeque ac minimum
id totum a caelo ducit originem. quis namque solis
lunaeque vias designat ac partitur? quis fulminis
ventorumque effectus provehit atque auget? quis spiritum
denique

Figure 1.2. The first page of Prémare's Latin translation of Han Tan's preface to Bouvet's *Gujin jing Tian jian Tianxue benyi* translated as *Caelestis disciplina vera notitia* (A Report on the true teaching of Heaven), Biblioteca Fabroniana, Pistoia, MS. 53. 1703 (?). Han Tan's preface was later removed in a revised translation made in 1706 by Prémare and another Jesuit, Julien-Placide Hervieu, entitled "De cultu Caelesti Sinarum veterum & modernorum." This was one of several editorial changes made because of Rites Controversy criticism of the Jesuits by the Papal Legate Tournon and his supporters. Reproduced with the permission of the Biblioteca Fabroniana.

TCHAO CHI COU ELL,
OU
LE PETIT ORPHELIN
DE LA MAISON DE TCHAO.
TRAGEDIE CHINOISE.

SIÉ TSEE,
OU PROLOGUE.

SCENE PREMIERE.

TOU NGAN COU, *seul.*

'HOMME ne songe point à faire du mal au Tigre, mais le Tigre ne pense qu'à faire du mal à l'Homme. Si on ne se contente à tems, on s'en repent. Je suis *Tou ngan cou*, premier Ministre de la *Guerre* dans le Royaume de *Tsin*. Le Roy *Ling cong* mon Maître avoit deux hommes, auxquels il se fioit sans réserve, l'un pour gouverner le Peuple, c'est *Tchao tun*; l'autre pour gouverner l'Armée, c'est moi; nos Charges nous ont rendus ennemis: j'ai toujours eu envie de perdre *Tchao*, mais je ne pouvois en venir à bout. *Tchao so* fils de *Tun* avoit épousé la fille du Roy, j'avois donné ordre à un assassin de prendre un poignard, d'escalader la muraille du Palais de *Tchao tun*, & de le tuer. Ce malheureux en voulant exécuter mes ordres, se brisa la tête contre un arbre, & se tua. Un jour *Tchao tun* sortit pour aller animer les Laboureurs au travail, il trouva sous un

Tome III. sff

Figure 2.1. Prologue to Prémare's *Tchao Chi Con Ell* [*Zhao Shi Gu Er*] *ou Le Petit Orphelin de la Maison de Tchao. Tragedie Chinoise* (Paris, 1735). This first translation of a Chinese drama by Prémare was received with great enthusiasm in Europe and transformed by the eighteenth-century form of European assimilation of Chinese culture called Chinoiserie. Several dramatists adapted this drama, the most famous case of distortion being that of Voltaire who rewrote and slanted the drama to exemplify the values of the Enlightenment. *Source: Tragedie Chinoise.* Paris, 1735.

DISCOURS PRELIMINAIRE,

Ou recherches sur les tems antérieurs à ceux dont parle le Chou-king, & sur la Mythologie Chinoise, par le P. de Premare.

ON a publié jusqu'ici en Europe beaucoup de livres qui traitent de l'Histoire Chinoise ; mais on tomberoit dans l'erreur, si on se persuadoit que tout cela est aussi certain qu'on le dit. Ces Ecrivains ne conviennent point du tems où l'on doit fixer le commencement de la Chine. Les uns disent que Fo-hi a été son premier Roi ; & pour le sauver du déluge, ils ont recours à la chronologie des Septante, encore ont-ils bien de la peine d'en venir à bout. Les autres commencent par Hoang-ti, s'appuyant sur l'autorité de Se-ma-tsien, Auteur ingénieux & poli, mais qui n'est pas si sûr qu'ils le pensent. D'autres enfin, suivant, à ce qu'ils croient, Confucius, débutent par l'Empereur Yao. Aucun n'a parlé en détail de ce qui précede Fo-hi ; on dit pour raison que ce sont des fables ; on devroit ajoûter que ce qui suit Fo-hi n'est pas moins fabuleux. Pour moi j'en ai toujours jugé autrement, & je crois que ces sortes de fables doivent être recueillies avec soin. George le Syncelle ne nous a conservé que de simples tables chronologiques des anciens Rois d'Egypte ; & les Savants sont bien aises de trouver dans ces premiers âges de quoi exercer leur critique. La Chronique des Chinois, ouvrant un champ encore plus vaste, donne aux Curieux un plus beau jour pour faire paroître leur érudition & leur esprit. C'est pourquoi j'ai dessein de ramasser ici tout ce que j'ai trouvé dans un assez grand nombre d'Auteurs Chinois, qui ont rassemblé tout ce qu'ils ont appris des anciens tems, & je commence avec eux par la naissance du monde.

Figure 2.2. The first page of Prémare's ancient history of the world according to the Chinese, published as *Discourse Preliminaire* (composed 1730), together with Antoine Gaubil's *Le Chou-king* (Paris 1770). Prémare applied Figurist theory to material in the *Shujing* (*Classic of History*) down to the beginning of the Eastern Zhou (770 BC) and interpreted it figuratively rather than historically. Source: *Discours Preliminaire* (composed 1730), published together with Antoine Gaubil's *Le Chou-king*. Paris, 1770.

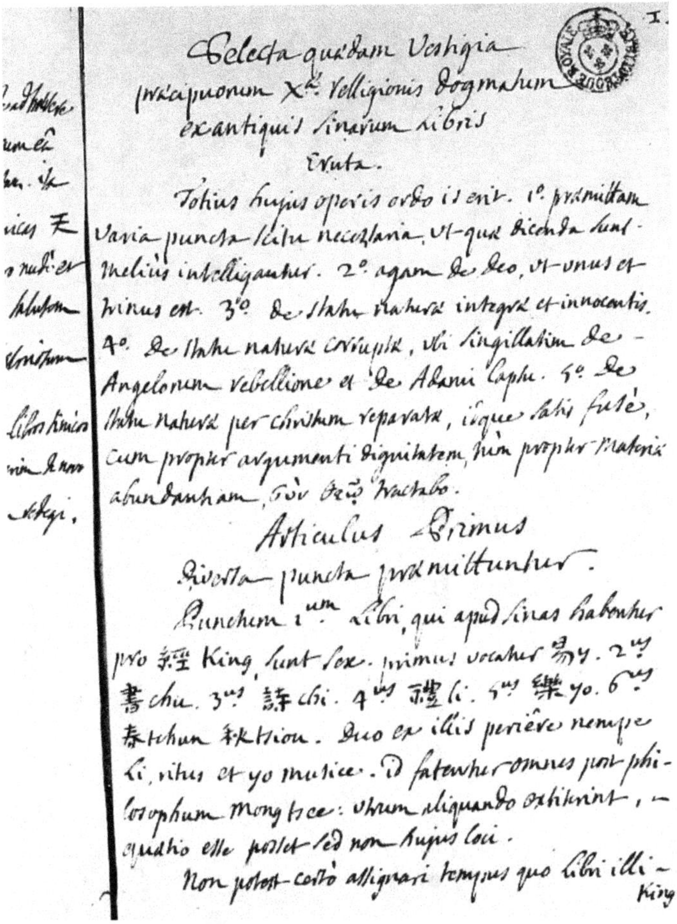
Selecta quaedam Vestigia
praecipuorum X^ae. Relligionis dogmatum
ex antiquis Sinarum Libris
Eruta.

Totius hujus operis ordo is erit. 1°. praemittam varia puncta scitu necessaria, ut quae dicenda sunt melius intelligantur. 2°. agam de Deo, ut unus et trinus est. 3°. de statu naturae integrae et innocentis. 4°. de statu naturae corruptae, ubi singillatim de Angelorum rebellione et de Adami lapsu. 5°. de statu naturae per christum reparatae, idque satis fuse, cum propter argumenti dignitatem, tum propter materiae abundantiam, τοῦ θεοῦ tractabo.

Articulus Primus
Diversa puncta praemittuntur.

Punctum 1um. Libri, qui apud Sinas habentur pro 經 King, sunt sex. primus vocatur 易 y. 2us 書 chu. 3us 詩 chi. 4us 禮 li. 5us 樂 yo. 6us 春秋 tchun tsiou. Duo ex illis periere nempe Li, ritus et yo musicae. id fatentur omnes post philosophum Mong tsee: utrum aliquando extiterint, quaestio esse posset sed non hujus loci.

Non potest certo assignari tempus quo libri illi King

Figure 3.1. The first page of Prémare's *Selecta quaedam Vestigia praecipuorum Christianiae relligionis dogmatum ex antiquis Sinarum Libris Eruta* (Certain selected vestiges of principal Christian religious teachings extracted from the ancient Chinese books). Canton, 1725. Bibliothèque Natonale France, Chinois 9248. Prémare began composing the work in 1713, just prior to his two-year stay in Beijing where he worked with Joachim Bouvet, SJ on Figurist texts. After having disagreements about Figurism with Bouvet, he returned to Jiangxi province and continued to work on the *Vestigia*. He was forced to go to Canton in 1724 where he completed the manuscript in 1725. Reproduced with the permission of the Bibliothèque National France.

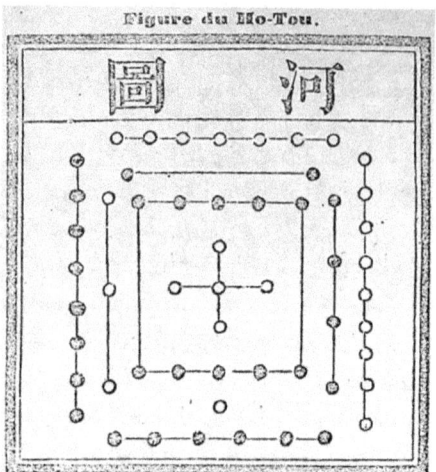
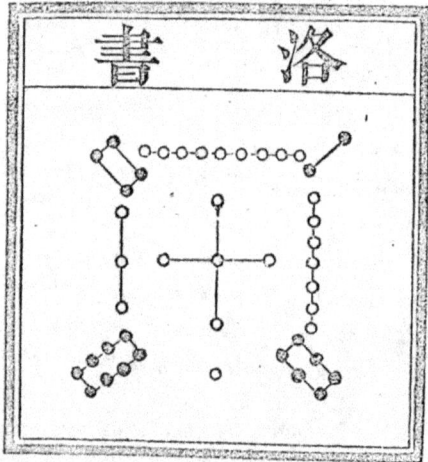

Figure 3.2. The Yellow River Chart (Hetu 河圖) (top) and the Luo River Book (*Luoshu* 洛書) (bottom) (Bonnetty & Perny, *Vestiges*, p. 376). The Luo River Book and its complement the Yellow River Chart were regarded by many Chinese commentators as the ultimate source of Chinese nonary (9) cosmography. Bouvet's Figurism emphasized mathematics more than Prémare whose Figurism was based more on texts. *Source*: Bonnetty & Perny, *Vestiges des principaux dogmes chrétiens tirés des anciens livres chinois*. (Paris, 1878).

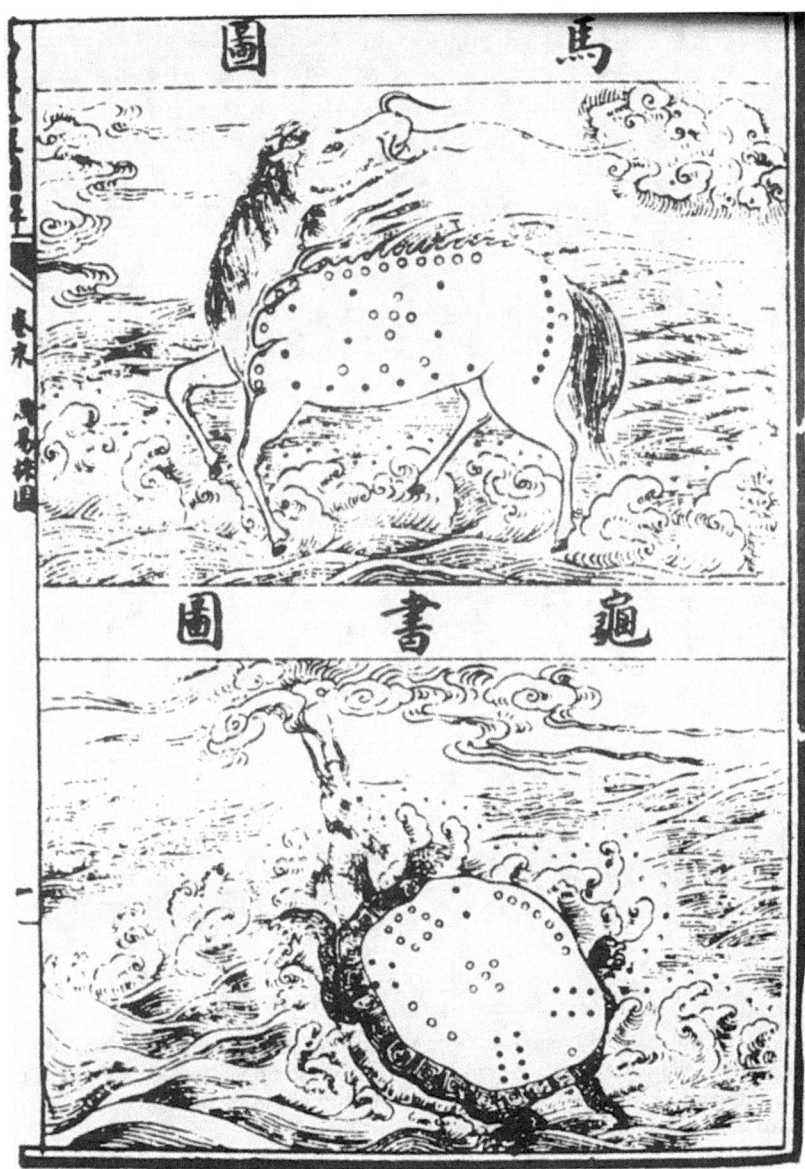

Figure 3.3. The ancient nonary diagrams on the side of a horse emerging from the Yellow River (*Hetu*) and on a tortoise shell emerging from the Luo River (*Luoshu*). Reproduced in Lai Qutang 來瞿唐, *Zhouyu caitu* 周易彩圖, p. 1a. In Lai Qutang, *Yijing tujie* 易經圖解 (Taipei: Guangtian reprint, 1975). The dots in both figures are grouped into segments of 1 to 9. The nonary diagram was regarded by Chinese commentators as having cosmological significance. *Source*: Lai Qutang, *Yijing tujie* 易經圖解 (Taipei: Guangtian reprint, 1975).

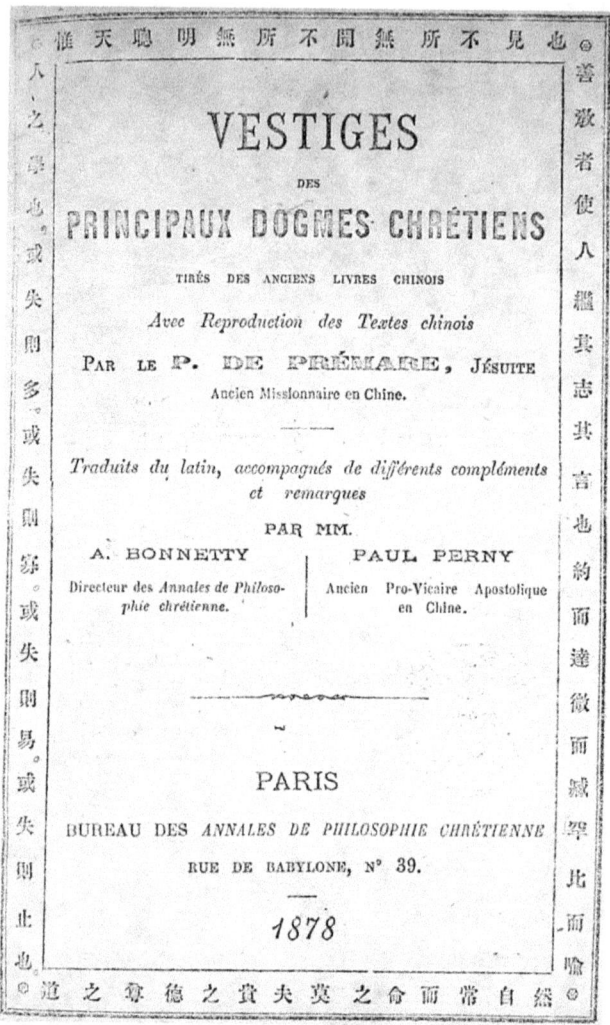

Figure 3.4. Title page of Prémare's *Vestiges des princiipaux dogmes chrétiens tirés des anciens livres chinois*. Edited and translated by Augustin Bonnetty & Paul Perny. Paris, 1878. This work by Bonnetty and Perny was a mixture of translation and commentary, some of which disagreed with Prémare's Figurist theories.

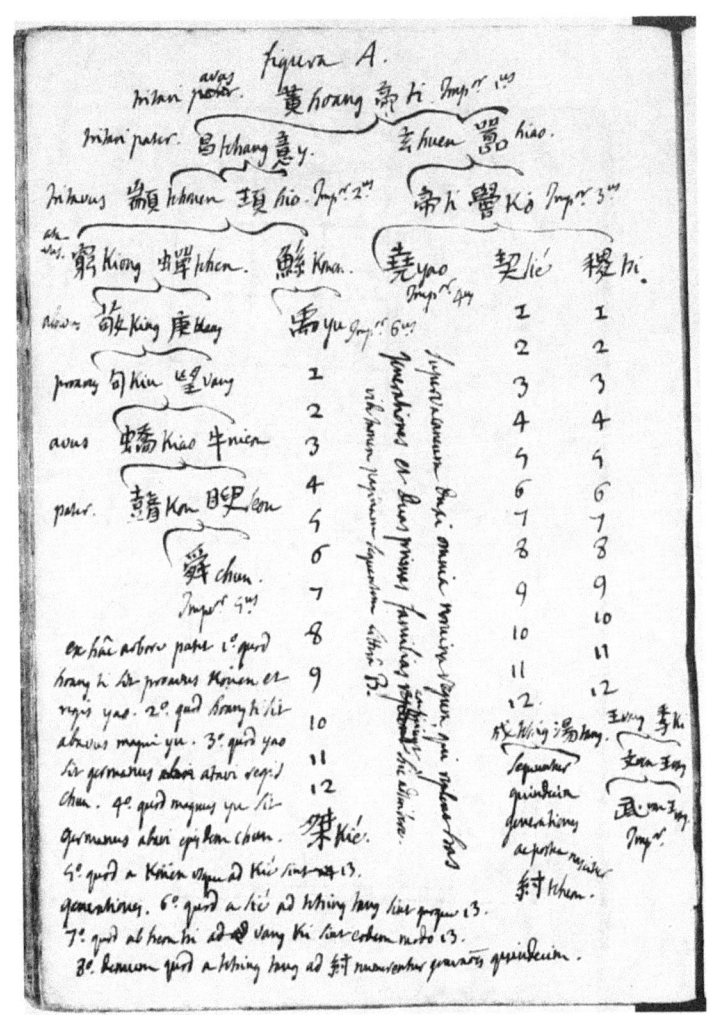

Figure 3.5. Genealogical Table of Chinese Antiquity (*Vestigia*, f. 306v). Bibliothèque Nationale France, Chinois 9248. Prémare constructed this table of generations dating from the first emperor, the Yellow Emperor Huangdi 黃帝, down to the founder of the Zhou dynasty King Wu (traditionally 1122 BC). His aim was not to delineate history, but rather to point out the discrepancies in Chinese texts and to argue that the discrepancies could be resolved by interpreting the texts as metaphorical rather than historical in nature. Reproduced with the permission of the Bibliothèque National France.

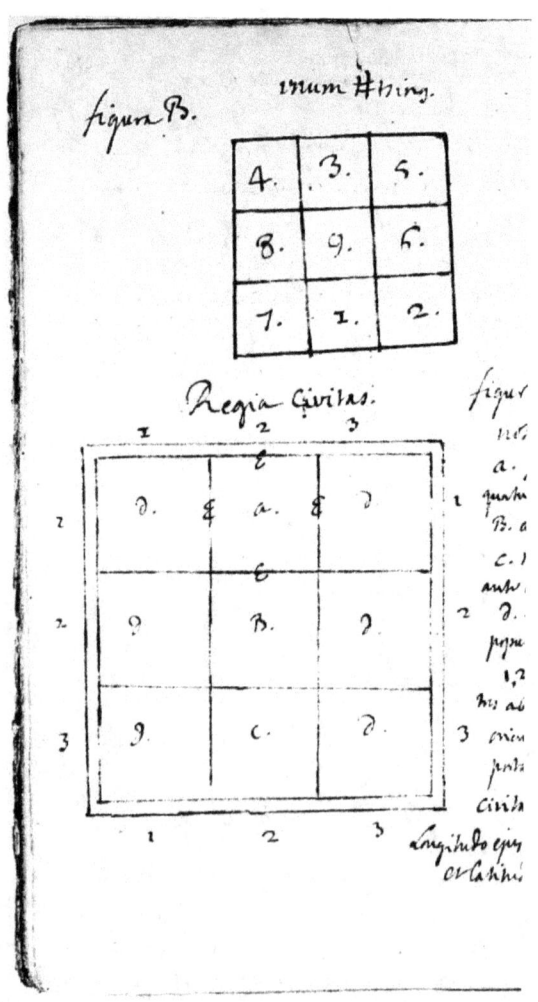

Figure 3.6. The traditional Chinese *Jing* 井 (well-field) Diagram and the Royal City Diagram (*Vestigia*, f. 97v). Bibliothèque Nationale France, Chinois 9248. The divisions in both of the diagrams reflect a nonary cosmology. Reproduced with the permission of the Bibliothèque National France.

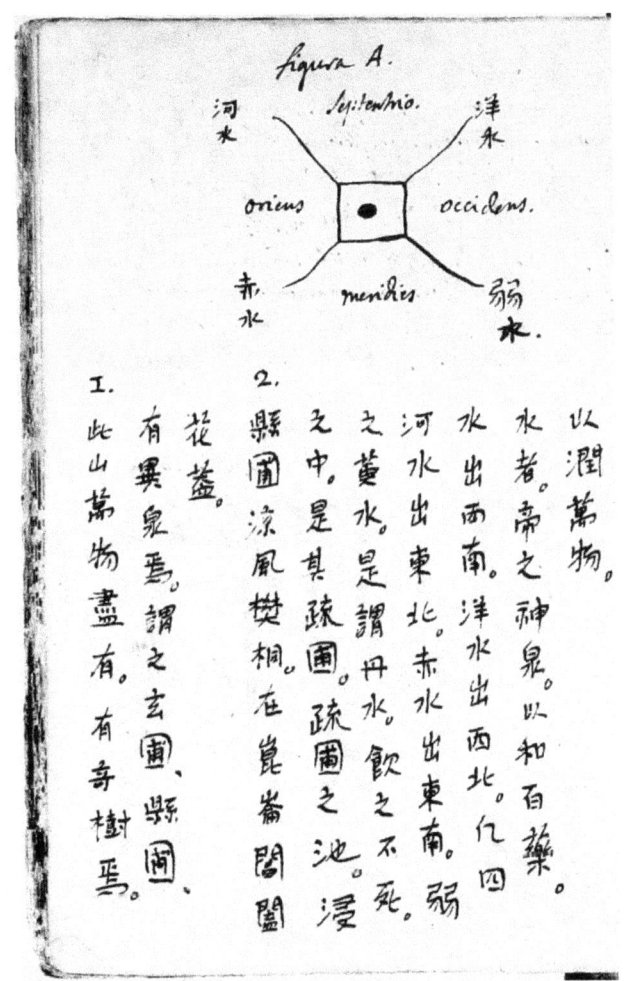

Figure 4.1. The Kunlun Mountain Earthly Paradise, based on the *Shanhaijing* (*Classic of Mountains and Seas*) (*Vestigia*, f. 65v). Bibliothèque Nationale France, Chinois 9248. The four directions north, south, east, and west (the latter two are reversed from their usual positions) surround the fountain of immorality at the center of the world. From this fountain, four rivers flowed out into the world. Prèmare regarded this drawing as a Chinese depiction of the Garden of Eden in Genesis. Reproduced with the permission of the Bibliothèque National France.

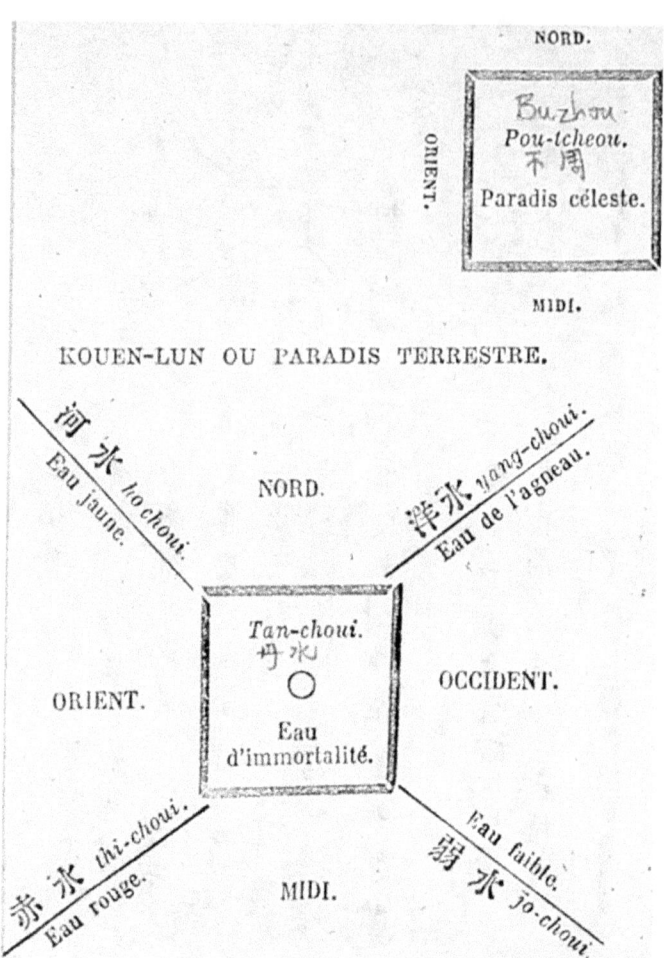

Figure 4.2. The Kunlun Mountain Earthly Paradise and the Buzhou Mountain Celestial Palace, based on the *Shanhaijing* (*Classic of Mountains and Seas*). Adapted by Bonnetty and Perny in *Vestiges*, p. 132. The Kunlun Mountain was part of an ancient East Asia tradition of religious cosmography. Located in central Asia or northern Tibet, it was regarded as the center of the world and depicted as such in numerous Buddhist wheel-maps. Adapted by Bonnetty and Perny in *Vestiges* (Paris, 1878).

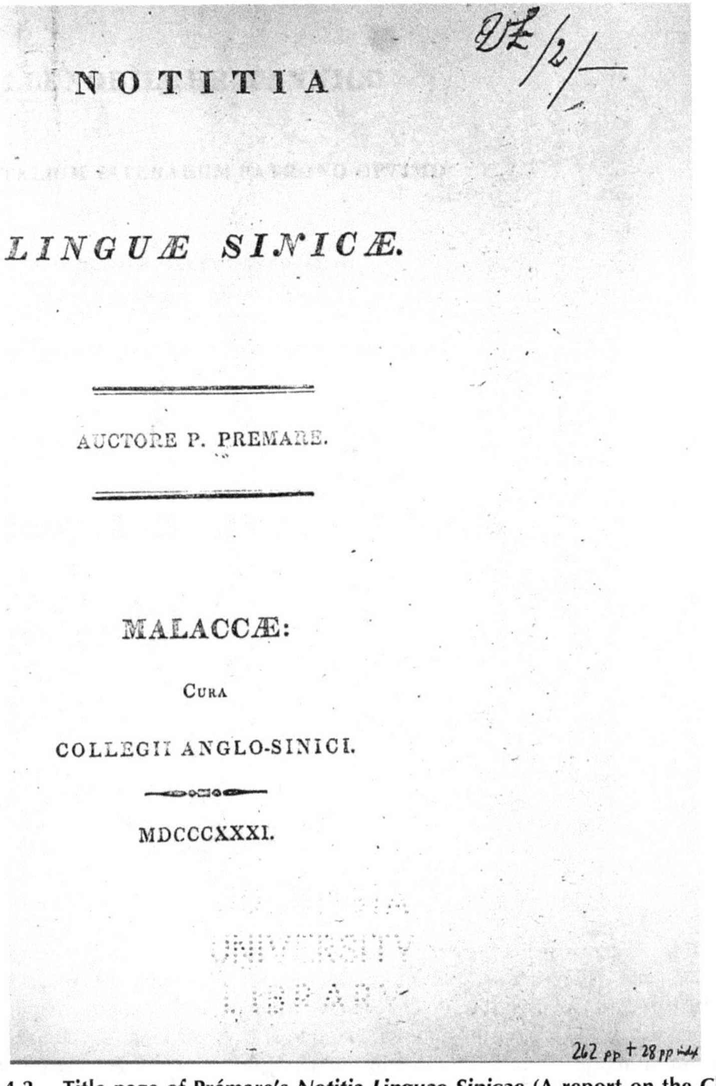
NOTITIA

LINGUÆ SINICÆ.

AUCTORE P. PREMARE.

MALACCÆ:

CURA

COLLEGII ANGLO-SINICI.

MDCCCXXXI.

262 pp + 28 pp

Figure 4.3. Title page of Prémare's *Notitia Linguae Sinicae* (A report on the Chinese language). Malacca, 1832. This work was a Latin adaptation of Prémare's Chinese philological work *Liushu shiyi* (The true meaning of the six kinds of characters), which was influenced by Liu Ning's *Liushu guai* (Explanation of the six kinds of characters). Source: Prémare. *Notitia Linguae Sinicae* (A report on the Chinese language). Malacca, 1832.

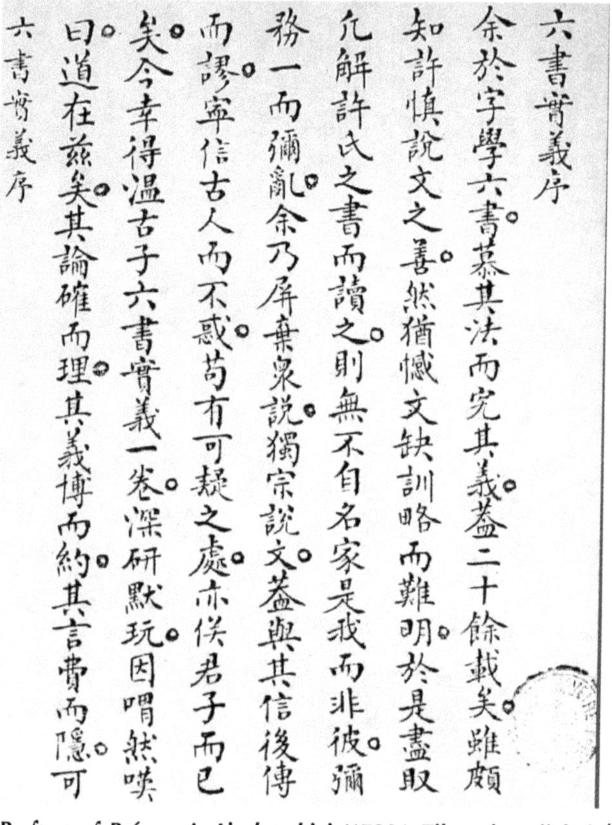

六書實義序

余於字學六書慕其法而究其義蓋二十餘載矣雖頗
知許慎說文之善然猶憾文缺訓略而難明於是盡取
凡解許氏之書而讀之則無不自名家是我而非彼彌
務一而彌亂余乃屏棄衆說獨宗說文蓋與其信後傳
而謬寧信古人而不惑苟有可疑之處亦俟君子而已
矣今幸得溫古子六書實義一卷深研默玩因喟然嘆
曰道在兹矣其論確而理其義博而約其言費而隱可

六書實義序

Figure 4.4. Preface of Prémare's *Liushu shiyi* (1720.) Zikawei (Xujiahui 徐家匯) Library, Shanghai. This work shows the deep influence of the Chinese literatus Liu Ning upon Prémare. Liu had used the ancient Chinese *Shuowen* dictionary to compile a work that explained the six classes of Chinese characters. Liu's philological scholarship also influenced Prémare's Figurist theories in the *Vestigia*. Source: Prémare. *Liushu shiyi* (1720). Zikawei Library, Shanghai.

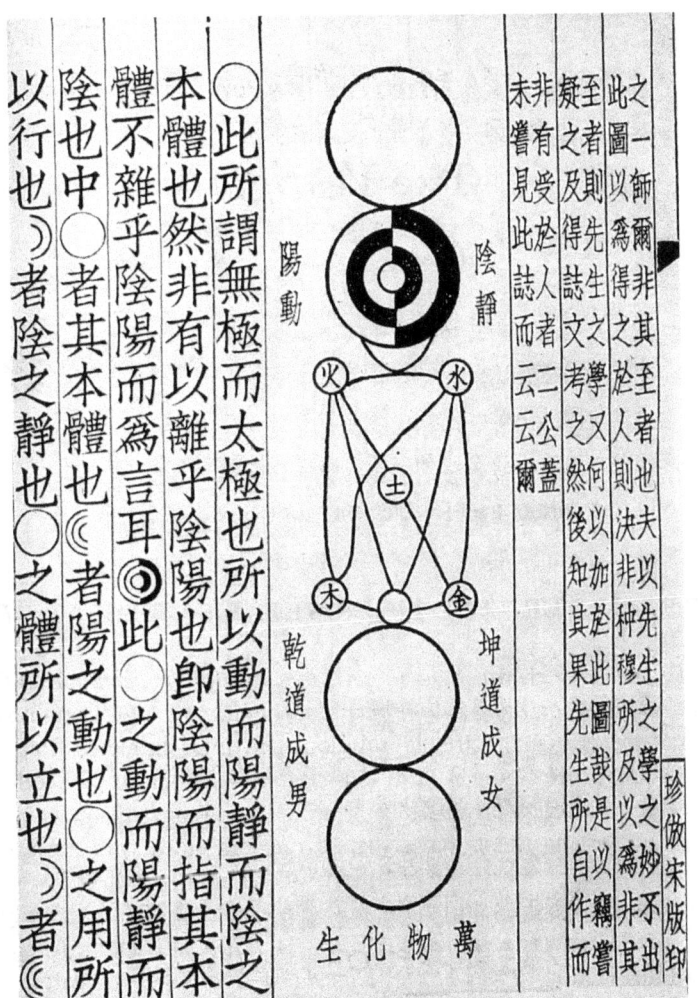

Figure 5.1. The Diagram of the Supreme Ultimate (*Taiji tushuo* 太極圖說) by Zhou Dunyi (1017–1073). Li Guangdi edited *Xingli jingyi* 性理精義 (The essential meaning of Neo-Confucianism), at the order of the Kangxi emperor, 1715–1717. This famous diagram depicted the Neo-Confucian view of creation as a cyclical process of generation and corruption. The first line of Zhou Dunyi's description said: "*Wuji er Taiji*" 無極而太極 (Ultimate Nothingness and yet the Great Ultimate). Although many missionaries regarded the cyclical Neo-Confucian view of creation as in conflict with the Judeo-Christian notion of Creation *ex nihilo* (out of nothing) described in Genesis, Prémare's Figurism was more accommodating of Neo-Confucianism and he translated this phrase as "without limit and yet at the same time, the great limit" (*sine termino et inde magnus terminus*). Source: Zhou Dunyi (1017–1073). Li Guangdi edited *Xingli jingyi* 性理精義 (The essential meaning of Neo-Confucianism), at the order of the Kangxi emperor, 1715–1717.

Chapter Three

The *Vestigia*

Wood is the third of the Five Elements

THE STRUCTURE AND FIGURIST BASIS OF THE *VESTIGIA*

Prémare's major work was *Selecta quaedam Vestigia praecipuorum Christianae relligionis dogmatum ex antiquis Sinarum libris eruta* (Certain selected vestiges of the principal Christian religious teachings extracted from ancient Chinese books) (see figure 3.1). It is a large manuscript of 329 folio sheets whose argument relies on citations from a wide range of ancient Chinese works. Many of the sheets have writing on both sides with the Latin text on the recto side of the sheet and the Chinese citations on the verso side, although sometimes the Latin and Chinese are mixed. The main body of the work (f. 1a–314b) was completed on May 21, 1725, at Canton. An appendix with an introduction to the *Yijing* (*Classic of Changes*) was dated on May 18, 1725.

Bouvet provided the stimulus for Prémare's *Vestigia*. Bouvet had first voiced Figurist ideas in 1697.[1] In his role as recruiter, leader, and first Chinese teacher of Prémare, he might have introduced Figurist ideas to Prémare as early as 1698 on the long journey from France to China. In the following years, they remained in contact, with Prémare sending thirty-six letters to Bouvet in the years 1703–1708. A starting date for the *Vestigia* could be deduced from Prémare's comment in the text that it had been "over twelve years [*duodecim et amplius annis*] since scrutinizing with care the Chinese antiquities."[2] The last page of the manuscript is dated May 21, 1725.[3] Projecting back twelve years in time from the date on the manuscript would indicate that his research began around 1713. Significantly, this would be about the time when he was called to Beijing to work on Figurist texts (1714–1716) in Bouvet's *petit Academie Apostolique*.

The *Vestigia* consists of five parts divided into sections. The first part presents fifteen key points from the ancient *Jing* 經 (classics), with the emphasis on the *Classic of Changes* (*Yijing*), in arguing that the main teachings of Christianity could be recovered from the ancient Chinese books. The second part of the *Vestigia* quotes passages from ancient texts that reveal a knowledge of God as both one and the Trinity. The third part presents selected cultural remains indicating that the Chinese believed in a terrestrial and a celestial paradise. The fourth part presents vestiges in China of humanity's fall from grace in the forms of Lucifer and Adam. The fifth and final part recounts Chinese legends which reflect the teaching that the state of fallen humanity is repaired by Christ.

THE CHINA JESUITS' TRANSITION FROM THE FOUR BOOKS TO THE FIVE CLASSICS

Prémare's bold hypothesis was based on a remarkable breadth of knowledge of ancient Chinese texts.[4] His knowledge went far beyond the Confucian Four Books (*Sishu* 四書) studied by earlier Jesuits. Around 1200 Zhu Xi's spirit of skepticism toward the Five Classics (*Wujing* 五經) had caused a shift in literati emphasis toward the Four Books.[5] Ricci affirmed this emphasis, in part, because the Four Books were more comprehensible than the Five Classics with their obscure literary allusions and, in part, because the Four Books suited the needs of Ricci's accommodation method. Consequently, the early China Jesuits focused on the Four Books rather than the Five Classics in an attempt to blend Christianity with the currently dominant philosophy of the Chinese literati. Their Riccian accommodative emphasis generated a long-term collaborative translation project that published five European-language editions of the Four Books between 1662 and 1711.[6] The most famous product of these editions was the fourth edition, *Confucius Sinarum Philosophus* (Paris, 1687), which translated three of the Four Books, omitting only the *Mencius*.

However, there were a number of elements of Neo-Confucianism, preeminently manifested in the work of Zhu Xi, that conflicted with Christianity. In order to explain these conflicts, Ricci argued that the ancient Chinese texts revealed the presence of natural religion, that is, the moral and spiritual truths discernible through human reason, as opposed to divine Revelation. Whereas the "ancient literati" (*gu ru* 古儒) or "early literati" (*xian ru* 先儒) had adhered to this natural religion, "later literati" (*hou ru* 後儒), including Zhu Xi, had diverged from it, in part, because of the entry of Buddhism into China and its distorting influence.⁷ In the Jesuit translation *Confucius Sinarum philosophus,* these "later literati" were referred to as *Neoterici Interpretes* (Modern Interpreters).⁸

Whereas the seventeenth-century China Jesuits struggled with translating the Four Books, the Christian literati were more inclined, with their more advanced level of literacy, to focus on the Five Classics. There was a loose tradition of literati converts who developed and refined a Confucian-Christian synthesis, following Xu Guangqi's defining phrase *bu Ru yi Fo* 補儒易佛 (Repair the Literati Teaching and displace Buddhism). Zhang Xingyao defined three stages of this process in his work *Tianjujiao Rujiao tongyi kao* 天儒同異考 (An Examination of the Similarities and Differences between the Heavenly Teaching and the Literati Teaching) (1672–1725).⁹ In the first stage, he defined how the Literati Teaching (Confucianism) and Christianity agreed (*he* 合). In the second stage he defined how Christianity could "repair" (*bu* 補) Confucianism, and in the third stage he defined how Christianity "transcended" (*chao* 超) Confucianism.¹⁰

The Christian literatus Shang Hujing 尚祜卿 (b.1619) of Jinan in Shandong province produced a long work of approximately 166,500 characters entitled *Bu Ru wengao* 補儒文告 (A Warning to Repair the Deficiencies of the Literati), dated 1664.¹¹ Shang described the role that the Heavenly Teaching (Christianity) could play in "repairing the Literati Teaching" (*bu Ru* 補儒).¹² Copies of these works by Zhang and Shang circulated among the China Jesuits.

Prémare focused on a far broader range of texts than the earlier Jesuits. He gave particular attention to the Five Classics as well as Daoist texts and other ancient works from which he made extensive citations. His theories were shared by a small group of China Jesuits, some more timid than others, who were condemned by an outpouring of harsh criticism from both fellow China missionaries and from most eighteenth-century European savants. Not only was Figurism condemned as intellectually unsound, but it was also regarded as a threat to the Christian mission in China.

In 1733 a leading China missionary Antoine Gaubil, SJ (1689–1759) responded to a letter from the prominent European scholar Nicolas Fréret, expressing his delight in Fréret's wit in coining the name "figuriste" to refer to missionaries like Bouvet, Foucquet, and Prémare whose system was "untenable."¹³ Gaubil believed that the Figurists' system ran the risk of destroying the mission and he praised his Jesuit superiors for preventing the dissemination of their ideas. The Figurists would, he wrote, have better served the mission if they had composed works of which they were capable, such as, a Chinese dictionary or by translating several books and analyzing ancient Chinese prophecies without having recourse to false or unintelligible vestiges. In comparison with the Figurists, Gaubil's scholarship was more anchored in conventional reality and less inclined than Prémare toward leaps of the imagination.

Gaubil wrote that much of what the Figurists argued could have been proven without claiming that the mysteries of the Trinity, of the Holy Eucharist, etc. were clearly delineated in these Chinese books and without transforming the ancient Chinese kings into saints of the Old Testament or persons of the Holy Trinity. Moreover, Gaubil argued, it could have been proven without placing the terrestrial paradise in China, Mesopotamia, and the Indies and without declaring that the three ancient dynasties of the Xia, Shang, and Zhou were unreal. Gaubil noted that anyone in China accused of declaring these three ancient dynasties to be unreal was committing a crime punishable by death.

Gaubil's criticism was shared by other China Jesuits, including Kilian Stumpf, SJ (Ji Lian 紀理安, 1655–1720), an important administrator in the Beijing mission. He was director of the Bureau of Astronomy in 1711–1719, apostolic notary during the papal legation of Tournon, and occupied the highest China mission office of Jesuit Visitor in 1714–1718. However, he (unlike Bouvet) fell out of favor with the Kangxi emperor who denied him the usual burial honors at his death in 1720.[14] Concerned with practical issues, Stumpf was an administrator who could not appreciate the imaginative impulses of Bouvet. He criticized Bouvet's obsessive interest in the *Classic of Changes*, an interest that he had been "rolling in front of him like the rock of Sisyphus for more than 20 years."[15] He rejected Bouvet's request for three or four co-workers to assist in his Figurist research.[16] Stumpf claimed that most of the China Jesuits believed Bouvet had become deranged in his obsessive pursuit of research on the *Classic of Changes*. However, Stumpf exaggerated the reasons why Bouvet's previous collaborators Prémare, Gollet, and Foucquet had distanced themselves from Bouvet. Their differences with Bouvet dealt with aspects of Bouvet's research and did not represent a rejection of Figurism as a whole.

Because of the negative reactions among both the China Jesuits and clerics and intellectuals in Europe, the Figurists were silenced and any publication of their works was banned. The manuscript of Prémare's *Vestigia* remained on a library shelf in Paris for a century until taken up in the nineteenth century and published in a French adaptation.

THE TEXTUAL SOURCES OF FIGURISM

The fundamental premise of Prémare's thesis was that the understanding of the ancient writings of China had been entirely lost to the Chinese.[17] These writings included three of the ancient *Jing* 經 (Classics) as well as non-Confucian texts of ancient philosophers. Prémare quoted several prominent literati to support his premise, although they differed about exactly when the teachings of the ancients had been lost. Some dated the loss to the Qin burning of the books in 213 BC. Others dated the loss to the death of Mencius in the third-century BC; still others to the death of Confucius in the fifth-century BC, and some traced the loss to even earlier.[18] Prémare quoted Confucius himself (*Lunyu* 3.24) to confirm that these teachings were lost. But he also quoted Su Shi 蘇軾 (Dongpo 東坡) (1036–1101) who said the teachings were lost after the death of Confucius. In addition, he quoted the leading Neo-Confucian philosopher Zhu Xi who said that the teachings were lost after the death of Mencius when the Literati became tainted with the errors of Daoism and Buddhism.[19]

Prémare divided the body of ancient writings into four categories that he used to reconstruct the lost teachings of the ancients. The first category consisted of the Six *Jing*, of which he regarded only four as extant in a reliable form: the *Yijing* 易經 (Classic of Changes), *Shujing* 書經 (Classic of History), *Shijing* (Classsic of Odes), and *Chunqiu* 春秋 (Spring and Autumn Annals). He claimed that the *Liji* 禮記 (Record of Rites) as well as the *Yuejing* 樂經 (Classic of Music) were lost.[20] Prémare noted there was no agreement among scholars about when the *Jing* were composed. He also noted that four different major commenters on the *Jing* had emerged: Sima Qian 司馬遷 (ca.145–90 BC), Zuoshi 左氏 (Zuo Qiuming 左丘明) who is said to have been a contemporary of Confucius, Kong Anguo 孔安國 (second-century BC, a descendant of Confucius), and Mao Chang 毛萇 (second-century BC, associated with the Maoshi 毛詩 text of the *Shijing*).[21] The Four Books (*Sishu* 四書) were not included in Prémare's list of sources for reconstructing the ancient teaching of China.

The second category of Prémare's sources included Daoist works: Laozi's *Daodejing* 老子道德經 (the Way and the Power) (third-century BC), the *Zhuangzi* 莊子 (forth-century BC), *Guanyinzi* 關尹子 (an admirer of Laozi, dated 604 BC), *Liezi* 列子 (semi-legendary sage dated ca. 400 BC), *Huainanzi* 淮南子 (pseudonym of Liu An 劉安, d. 122 BC, grandson of the Han founder), and *Sunzi* (unidentified) as well as several savants who lived shortly after the Jin 晉 dynasty was established in AD 265.[22]

A third category of Prémare's sources were works in harmony with the *Jing*, but of uncertain origins. These included the *Zhouli* 周禮 (Rites of Zhou), the *Yili* 儀禮 (Rites of Yi), several chapters from the *Liji* 禮記 (Record of Rites), the *Shanhaijing* 山海經 (*Classic of Mountains and Seas*), and the *Erya* 爾雅 thesaurus.

The fourth and final category of Prémare's sources included works which he described as inferior to the others, but nevertheless usable. These included the *Shuowen jiezi* 說文解字 dictionary by Xu Shen 許慎 (ca. 55–149?), *Lüshi chunqiu* 呂氏春秋 (The Spring and Autumn of Master Lü) by Lü Buwei 呂不

韋, *Lushi* 路史 (A Grand History) by Luo Bi 羅泌 (fl. ca. 1170), and *Tongzhi* 通志 (Comprehensive History) by Luo Bi's son Zheng Qiao 鄭樵 (1104–1162).[23]

Prémare claimed that the ancient Chinese books had been damaged by two main causes. First, they had been destroyed because of political instability. He mentioned five destructive events in Chinese history dating from 221 BC to AD 951.[24] Secondly, the *Jing* had been corrupted by commenters, such as, the three differing commentaries on the *Spring and Autumn Annals* (*Gongyang* 公羊, *Guliang* 穀梁, and *Zuozhuan* 左傳).[25] Prémare quoted Ouyang Xiu 歐陽修 (1007–1072) as saying: "I hate all the commentaries because they have disfigured the Spring and Autumn Annals" (*Yu yan zhong shuo zhi luan Chunqiu* 予厭衆說之亂春秋).[26] Prémare claimed that the *Classic of History* had become confused when later prefaces were mixed in with the text.

THE FIGURIST REINTERPRETATION OF THE *JING* (CLASSICS)

Prémare quoted the Tang Emperor Xuanzong 玄宗 (r. 713–755) on the loss of the true meaning of the *Jing* after the death of Confucius: "The more one is removed from the source by years, the greater has been the disparity between the source and the streams. There is nevertheless a true meaning and this meaning is not at all arbitrary. It should be restored to give the [text] unity because the natural and sublime meaning of the ancient *Jing* cannot have a double meaning and be true."[27] In giving this and other quotations, Prémare usually quoted the Chinese text without giving a detailed citation. He may have been following a Chinese literary practice which often assumed that the reader had knowledge of the canonical texts being quoted. He followed up this quote from the Emperor Xuanzong by citing the adage: "Believe the *Jing*, but do not believe the commentaries." (*Xin jing bu xin chuan*. 信經不信傳.)

As a foreigner, Prémare's attempt to assist the Chinese in clarifying the original meaning of their *Jing* seems audacious. But it becomes far less audacious in light of his belief that truth and the fundamentals of true religion were universal. This belief opened his mind to a willingness to accept that fundamental truths were found in ancient Chinese texts from which European Christians could learn. He placed the ancient Chinese *Jing* on a level of sanctity comparable to Christian Scripture in the sense that the *Jing* anticipated the Revelation of Scripture. His willingness to do so was rare among Europeans of that time. This was unlike Riccian accommodationists who were willing to accept only that ancient Chinese texts contained natural morality. It was also unlike the European philosophes who were willing to accept Chinese culture only in their distortions of Chinoiserie. Prémare believed that the controversial nature of his theories fell within the parameters of the traditional literati debates over the meaning of the *Jing*. Prémare adhered to the traditional Chinese literati path of studying the ancient Chinese texts. For Prémare, the truths that the Figurists were unearthing in the *Jing* were neither distinctly Chinese nor European—they were universal. Europeans overwhelmingly rejected Prémare's reinterpretation as heterodox and false. By contrast, the Kangxi emperor, a Manchu who ruled over different ethnic groups, gave support to the Figurists' reinterpretation of the *Jing*.

The teaching of the orthodox transmission of Confucian doctrine was first formulated by the philosopher Mencius (fourth century BC) at the end of his book—*Mengzi* 7B:38.[28] Mencius claimed a transmission in the teaching from Yao and Shun down to Confucius and, by implication, to himself. This transmission became for the Confucians, the criteria of truth. After the fall of the Han dynasty and the intervening centuries of Daoist and Buddhist dominance, the Tang philosopher Han Yu 韓愈 (768–824) led the revival of Confucianism with the same claim of the orthodox transmission of Confucian doctrine.[29]

Zhu Xi 朱熹, like Mencius and Han Yu before him, claimed to be the direct heir of this orthodox transmission and he was the first to use the term *daotong* 道統 (Transmission of the Dao) to describe this transmission. He first used the term *daotong* in his 1194 preface to the *Zhongyong* (Doctrine of the Mean).[30] For Zhu, the line of transmission was passed from the Emperors Yao, Shun, and Yu down through the Shang dynasty founder Tang 湯, to the Zhou dynasty founders Wen 文 and Wu 武, to Confucius, to Zeng Zi 曾子 and Zisi 子思 to Mencius. He eliminated the Han and Tang Confucians from the line of transmission and chose Zhou Dunyi 周敦頤 (1017–1073) and the Cheng brothers—Cheng Hao 程顥 (1032–1085) and Cheng Yi 程頤 (1033–1107)—as his Confucian link to antiquity.[31] He purged the tradition of Buddhist elements, but accepted the Daoist elements in Zhou Dunyi's diagram of the *Taiji* (see figure 5.1).

Although Prémare did not agree with Zhu's line of transmission, he followed Zhu's model in attempting to redefine the line of transmission. Prémare claimed that he wished to continue the teaching interrupted since Mencius and criticized the Song philosophers Zhou Dunyi, the two Cheng brothers, Zhang Zai 張載, and Zhu Xi. In doing so, he was adhering to a very traditional way of rejecting past interpreters as diverging from the true Transmission of the Dao and seeking to replace the Song Neo-Confucian philosophers' interpretation with a new interpretation—Figurism.

Prémare compared the literati, especially in the Song dynasty, to the Jews. In their attempt to subjugate the *Jing* to the political regime of the empire, they paralleled the Jews who saw the Messiah only in terms of temporal glory for Judea. Prémare referred to their philosophy as "the system of those Chinese rabbis" (*systema istorem rabinorum Sinensium*).[32]

In shifting the focus from the Four Books to the Five Classics, Prémare and other Figurists diverged from the earlier China Jesuits, dating from Matteo Ricci, who sought accord with the Chinese through emphasizing the Four Books (*Sishu* 四書). The greater literary fluency of the Figurists enabled them to go beyond the Four Books to incorporate books outside of the Confucian tradition, particularly the Daoist literature referred to as the Huang-Lao teaching. The Confucian tradition had avoided Daoist literature because its metaphorical and intuitive nature conflicted with the Confucian discursive and deductive emphasis. Daoist texts were inappropriate for constructing an examination system which would create a socio-economic system based on formal education and on examinations which would generate a class of scholar-officials.

Prémare quoted several literati who cited the *Classic of Changes* as the primary *Jing*—the origin and source of all the other *Jing*. Although sometimes a critic of Zhu Xi, at other times Prémare relied on his great authority. He quoted Zhu Xi as saying: "The *Classsic of Changes* . . . is like the source which has given birth to letters; it is like the father of the true teaching."[33] Prémare regarded the *Changes* as providing the means of restoring all the *Jing* to a coherent system of teachings.

Prémare described a traditional view which claimed that Paoxi shi 庖犧氏 (i.e., Fu Xi 伏羲) wrote the *Classic of Changes* by observing the images in the sky and the uniform laws on earth, examining different species of birds and animals, and conceiving of tracing eight three-lined figures.[34] The historian Luo Bi 羅泌 (fl. ca. 1170) in his Lushi 路史 attributed the same acts to Shi Huang 史皇 who is said to have lived a long time before Fu Xi and who had invented writing. Prémare contradicted a traditional account by denying that King Wen (Wen Wang 文王), the Duke of Zhou (Zhou Gong 周公), and Confucius offered explanations of the lines of the *Changes* and he noted that the Song Literatus Ouyang Xiu 歐陽修 said Confucius did not write the Ten Wings (*Shi Yi* 十翼) which interpret the lines of the hexagrams.[35] At this point Prémare introduced the Figurist claim of Joachim Bouvet that Fu Xi was not Chinese, but rather a universal figure of humankind designated in Biblical tradition as Henoch (Enoch). Henoch is said by Bouvet to have written the *Changes*, however the written language had been invented long before by Seth, the son of Adam.

Prémare's methodology throughout the *Vestigia* involved quoting ancient texts and writings of literati to support each point in his arguments. He quoted several literati to support his claim that the *Changes* was the primary or foundational *Jing*, such as, Zhu Xi's claim that the *Changes* had given birth to letters and was like the father of true teaching.[36] Prémare regarded the *Changes* as providing the means for restoring all the *Jing* to a coherent system of teachings. His approach to the work was expressed in this quotation from Lieou-ell-tchi (?): "Supreme truth (*li Dao* 理道) has no physical shape, but it has an image that can be seen. The Way (*Dao* 道) cannot be expressed by words, but if there are images, then they can be expressed with words. The *Classic of Changes* is a book that makes exhaustive use of images."[37]

Prémare believed that the *Jing* contained a mathematical and figurative form of reasoning. Chinese characters were hieroglyphic and enigmatic, but they were images borrowed from believable things in order to graphically represent the power and kindness of the Creator. It began with their science of numbers which led to the eight trigrams (*gua* 卦) which led to images (*xiang* 象). Words were uttered in conformity with thought. Fu Xi generated these figures and the two diagrams—the Luo River Diagram (*Luoshu* 洛書) and the Yellow River Chart (*Hetu* 河圖)—from which he generated the eight trigrams (see figures 3.2 and 3.3). Prémare quoted Zhu Xi as saying: "The entire *Classic of Changes* contains exclusively metaphorical words, symbols, and parables."[38] Luo Bi's *Lushi* added that the language of the ancient sages was largely hidden in metaphors and parables.

Daoism distrusted words. Although the discursive nature of the Confucian tradition tended to regard the anti-discursive and intuitive nature of the Daoist tradition as alien, the Figurist emphasis on figurative and metaphorical language made Prémare more open to accepting the reasoning of Daoist works like the *Zhuangzi* and *Liezi*. Prémare claimed that Confucians, such as, the historian Liu Shu 劉恕 (T. Daoyuan 道原) (1032–1078) who wrote the *Sizhi tongjian waiji* 資治通鑑外紀 (Additional Chronicle to the Comprehensive Mirror for Aid in Government) (1078), misinterpreted these Daoist works as flawed and enigmatic accounts.[39] He quoted Liu Shu as saying: "The works Zhuangzi and Liezi contain only enigmas and fables."[40]

Although Prémare criticized past literati for their distortions of the *Jing*, he believed that contemporary literati were amenable to adopting the Figurist interpretation of the *Jing*. As an example, he cited Bouvet's persuasion of Li Guangdi 李光地 (1642–1718), who was highly trusted by the Kangxi emperor and appointed to serve as Grand Secretary from 1705 until his death in 1718. Li was an orthodox Confucian scholar and led several commissions for the official compilation of a number of works dealing with Zhu Xi, including *Zhuzi Quanshu* 朱子全書 (Complete Works of Zhu Xi) (1713), which was honored with the emperor's preface. Li also led the compilation of a Song Neo-Confucan collection *Xingli jingyi* 性理精義 (The Essentials of Neo-Confucianism) (1717) with the emperor's preface (1717).[41]

Li Guangdi was considered a master of the *Classic of Changes* and was often consulted by the emperor on its contents, as in predicting the outcome of a battle. Li was also responsible for compiling *Zhouyi zhezhong* 州易折中 (Annotations on the Book of Changes) (1715). Li had praised the emperor's idea of correlating the *Sanhuang* 三皇 (Legendary Three Emperors)—Fu Xi, Shen Nong and Huangdi—with the numerology of the Luo River Diagram (*Luoshu* 洛書) and the Yellow River Chart (*Hetu* 河圖). Bouvet's Figurist attempt to decipher these ancient materials using numerology was certainly known to Li.⁴² Prémare was working with Bouvet in Beijing during these years (1714–1717) and he would have been aware of Bouvet's contacts with the Kangxi emperor and Li Guangdi. Moreover, he agreed with Bouvet that the Chinese Literati were amenable to accepting Figurist interpretations of the *Jing*.

Prémare believed that the *Jing* referred to a holy and divine personage. If the *Jing* were explained in a "spiritual and divine manner" (*shen er ming zhi* 神而明之), following the same law proposed in the *Changes*, then the Chinese would again see the light of the holy law after so many centuries of darkness.⁴³ In order to bring this lost meaning to light, Prémare reinterpreted the meaning of *sheng ren* 聖人, which the literati traditionally translated as "sage," to *sanctus* or *sanctus vir* (saint, holy man). Prémare clarified in a note: "When modern literati speak of Confucius, they always call him by the name of 聖 *sheng* 人 *ren*, 'holy.' But in the *Jing* books, *sheng ren* is understood as 'holy of holies' [*sanctus sanctorum*], and the latter refers not to Confucius, nor is Confucius this Holy Man who is referred to in the *Jing*."⁴⁴ The last China Figurist, Pierre Martial Cibot, SJ (1727–1780), explained what Prémare meant by naming the *sheng ren* the saint.

> "The Heaven is the Saint invisible, the Saint is the Heaven who became visible and instructed men." How to understand the notes on the Saint in the *Yijing*? "That man is heaven and heaven is that man." How can we understand the words "the divine man," the "celestial man," and "unique man," the "most beautiful of men," the "highest of men," the "marvellous man," the "first born"? How can we understand what is said in so many ways by so many authors that he should die in pains and abjection, that will open the Heaven? I could write a whole book on that manner.⁴⁵

The scholar Pan Feng-chuan argues that Prémare interpreted *sheng ren* to be a reference to the second member of the Holy Trinity, that is, the Son in the "Father, Son and Holy Spirit," that is, Christ.⁴⁶

The shifting of sage to saint was a radical reinterpretation of the Chinese classics, shifting the emphasis from a humanistic, rationalized, deistic treatment of cosmic forces to a spiritualized and mystical focus. This interpretation released the classical literature from the restraints of the highly intellectualized Confucian tradition, manifested in literacy and the examination system. Simultaneously, this interpretation opened the classical literature to seeing the influence of the Chinese intuitive and anti-intellectual tradition found in the Daoist classics.

TRANSLATING THE *VESTIGIA*

Augustin Bonnetty (1798–1879) was born on March 11, 1798, at Entrevaux (Basses-Alpes). After four years in the seminary, he relinquished the priesthood and dedicated his life to philosophy and to the defense of the Catholic faith.[47] He went to Paris and in 1830 founded the *Annales de Philosophie Chrétienne* which he edited until his death. His main goal was to show how religion and science were in agreement. The *Annales* sought to show the universality of primitive revelation found in the myths and fables of all nations.[48] His emphasis on primitive revelation at the expense of reason caused the Archbishop Sibour of Paris to report him to the Congregation of the Index which in 1855 asked him to sign a statement affirming four orthodox propositions on the relationship between faith and reason. Bonnetty was very cooperative and signed the statement without any hesitation. However he had been warned that he was skirting a dangerous line. His situation had striking similarities to Prémare almost a century and a half before whose religious zeal and creative mind also carried him to the margins of unorthodoxy.

Bonnetty was one of the first scholars to take an interest in Prémare's *Vestigia*. However, he was cautious in dealing with this controversial work. His first publication on Prémare's *Vestigia* appeared as part of three articles in 1837 in the *Annales de Philosophie Chrétienne*. Two of the articles were signed by l'abbé A. Sionnet. The third was signed by Bonnetty.[49] Both authors were affiliated with the *Société Asiatique de Paris*. Antoine Matthieu Sionnet (1808–1856) was a theologian who studied Chinese under the French Sinologist Stanislas Julien.[50] He collaborated with Bonnetty during the early years of their research on Prémare's *Vestigia*. However, while Sionnet wanted to choose certain passages to make an analysis of the *Vestigia*, Bonnetty wanted to make a translation.[51] In 1839 a booklet was published that contained the contents of their three articles published in 1837 plus additional material, all of which was attributed to Sionnet rather than to Bonnetty.[52] Sionnet's interest was then distracted by other projects and that appears to have been the end of his work on the *Vestigia*. Segments of this 1837 essay were later included in the *Vestiges* (1878) of Bonnetty and Paul Perny (see figure 3.4). Bonnetty explains that the delay in bringing the project to completion was caused by the French Imperial Library mislaying the *Vestigia* manuscript.[53] When the *Vestiges* was eventually published, it made only passing reference to Bonnetty's collaboration with l'abbé Sionnet and simply listed the articles in the *Annales de Philosophie Chretienne* in which they collaborated.[54]

Sionnet recognized that Prémare's *Vestigia* contained extracts on the *Classic of Changes* that had never before appeared in Europe.[55] The principle vestiges of Christian teachings that were preserved were said to be almost entirely related to Daoism. Sionnet called Daoism "a sect that has always been considered foreign to China" and which came to China from the West. It appears that Sionnet confused Daoism with Buddhism because while Daoist texts date from ca. 300 BC, Buddhism did not enter China from India until the first century AD. Furthermore, it was Buddhism, not Daoism, that was often criticized by the Chinese as being a foreign teaching.

Sionnet believed that these vestiges of Christian teachings were developed by the Jews who emigrated with the dispersion of the Ten Lost Tribes of Israel eastward to China and developed Christianity in "the first centuries of our era." He added that there are similarites between the "cabala of the Jews and that of the Chinese."[56] This indicates that Sionnet was a disseminationist, in contrast to Prémare's *Vestigia* which implied that the vestiges of Christianity in the ancient Chinese texts were given directly by God to the Chinese. Unlike Sionnet who claimed that Biblical teachings were carried to China by foreign people from the west, Prémare argued that the Biblical teachings were indigenous to Chinese culture, although lost through the passage of time and through the Chinese misinterpretation of ancient texts.

Sionnet concluded his essay with four points, the first of which was: "The most ancient fragments of Chinese books contain nothing that comes close to the teaching of the holy [i.e., Biblical] saints." This is a fundamental contradiction of Prémare's Figurism which claimed that the *Classic of Changes* and other most ancient Chinese texts anticipated Biblical teachings. Sionnet's second point claimed that traits of resemblance between the ancient Chinese texts and Biblical teachings began to appear at least one-hundred years after the dispersion of the Ten Lost Tribes of Israel. The dispersion is traditionally dated to the conquest of Israel by the Neo-Assyrian Empire circa 722 BC. The third point claims that all of these authors belonged to the Daoist sect. Sionnet's fourth and final point claimed that the Daoist sect had been inspired by Judaism to purify China of materialistic doctrines.

Bonnetty eventually collaborated with Paul Perny, a missionary of the *Congrègation des Missions-Étrangères*, to translate and publish an adaptation of Prémare's manuscript. Fr. Perny had served for twenty-five years in China and had returned to Europe, tasked with supplying China missionaries the books needed to complete their apostolate.[57] He brought with him metal fonts of Chinese characters which were used to print the characters in their French adaptation of Prémare's *Vestigia* which was entitled *Vestiges des principaux dogmes chrétiens tirés des anciens livres chinois*. One can imagine what a challenge Prémare's manuscript was to them. It was a massive undertaking of decipherment which took over forty years to bring to publication in 1878 (see figure 3.4). One testament to the enormity of their task lay in the fact that since 1878 there has been very little scholarly research done on Prémare's

Vestigia. This is, in part, because Prémare's work uses a form of etymological analysis that is no longer fashionable or credible and, in part, because the mass and breadth of the Chinese works Prémare cited transcend the narrowly specialized fields in which most China scholars are trained.

The *Vestiges* was an ambitious work of over 500 pages, filled with extensive footnotes and certainly the most important work published by either Bonnetty or Perny. One wonders how the cost of publishing such a bilingual (French-Chinese) work was financed. In the preface, Bonnetty notes the skepticism of Jules Mohl, the director of oriental publications at the government printing-office, who said: "I would never have proposed the publication of this work, but I am very glad that you have undertaken it because it has a great deal to teach."[58]

Although presented as a translation, the *Vestiges* of Bonnetty and Perny is actually a book within a book. It is a translation interspersed by a commentary that is not always clearly distinguished from Prémare's original text. Moreover, the commentary frequently diverges in interpretation from Prémare's text. In fact, Bonnetty and Perny were not mere translators, but were attempting to create a work of independent scholarship by, on one hand, translating Prémare's *Vestigia* and supplementing it with annotations, and on the other hand, adding commentary that often disagreed with Prémare's interpretation and offered an alternate interpretation. They often rejected Prémare's Figuristic interpretation of ancient Chinese texts as metaphorical and treated them rather as historical, for example, they disagreed with Prémare's contention that the Xia, Shang, and Western Zhou dynasties were not historical.

Prémare constructed a genealogical table of the earliest rulers of China—from the Yellow Emperor Huangdi 黃帝 down to the founder of the Zhou dynasty King Wu (traditionally dated 1122 BC)—for the purpose of illustrating his theory that the ancient Chinese texts were metaphorical rather than historical (see figure 3.5).[59] Consistent with his usual pattern, he drew from authoritative Chinese sources to make his argument, in this case the great Han historian Sima Qian (145?–86? BC), whom he calls the "Chinese Herodotus," and the Song literatus Ouyang Xiu (1007–1072).[60] In order to resolve this important question of when Chinese history began, Sima Qian had woven together several genealogies. However, Prémare noted that Ouyang Xiu questioned Sima Qian's genealogy because of its discrepancies in terms of the ages of family relationships of the figures in the genealogy. For Prémare, this table was not a reflection of historical reality, but rather a heuristic device to show that these discrepancies provided further evidence for the Figurist claim that the ancient records of Chinese antiquity are, in essence, metaphorical. Prémare's tendency to present figures in this genealogical chart, such as Henoch (Enoch), under alternate names, shows that his figurative approach was at odds with the historical approach of Bonnetty and Perny.[61]

Bonnetty and Perny translated and reproduced Prémare's genealogical table.[62] However, they also generated an entirely new table in support of their disseminationist theory. This table is entitled "Table of Generations from Adam down to the age of Noah and his descendants, as the books carried to China present them, and rectified according to the Bible."[63] The Figurists did not claim that Biblical texts and teachings had been carried or disseminated from the Middle East to China. They believed that the Chinese had received a primitive revelation of true religion (Christianity) not through the established framework of the Old and New Testaments, but rather directly from God and that this revelation had been recorded in their ancient texts and later lost.

In one notable example of their differences with Prémare, Bonnetty and Perny said they attempted to offer a "more solid, more historical and more scientific" explanation by drawing from the work of the nineteenth-century scholar Le Chevalier de Paravey (1787–1871). Bonnetty published several of Paravey's articles in the periodical *Annales de Philosophie Chrétienne*. Paravey was a prolific, convinced "fundamentalist" and an arcane partisan of Biblical tradition whose style of scholarship fell out of fashion after 1871.[64] Paravey adhered to the Diluvian tradition as a form of apologetics in which he was making a reasoned defense of Christianity against intellectual objections. He identified the flood of Yao with that of the Noachic flood.[65] He regarded Yao as the son of Diku 帝嚳 (Noah).[66] Paravey dated the flood to 2357 BC and argued that this date corresponded to the period of the Five Emperors (Wu Di 五帝) of China.[67]

Paravey accepted the 1759 claim of Joseph de Guignes that the Chinese were an Egyptian colony.[68] He was also influenced by Guignes' edition of Gaubil's translation of the *Classic of History*—the *Chou-king*, published in 1770—to claim that the *Classic of History* began with the flood of Yao. Paravey was a prominent spokesman for the disseminationist belief that writing had originated in ancient Assyria, Egypt and Babylonia in a hieroglyphic form. The books and beliefs of these Middle Eastern cultures were said to have been carried to China. Disseminationist ideas in regard to China were not new for they had been expressed in the seventeenth-century search for a universal language by the polyhistor Athansius Kircher and others.[69] However, this was a new formulation of disseminationism.

The individual contributions of Bonnetty and Perny to the Vestiges are not clearly distinguished, but given Bonnetty's interest in the universality of primitive revelation and his lack of knowledge of Chinese, it is probable that Bonnetty was the primary author who depended upon Perny in dealing with Prémare's numerous Chinese citations. Bonnetty and Perny also cited Paravey's work to disagree with Prémare's claim that the ancient Three Dynasties (*Sandai* 三代)—the Xia, Shang, and Western Zhou mentioned in the

Classic of History—were unhistoric and purely symbolic.[70] Prémare and the other Figurists believed in the direct revelation of the "true religion" (*sanctae legis*) to the ancient Chinese rather than dissemination. Although largely lost, they believed vestiges of these august mysteries remained in the ancient texts and could be revealed if they were examined figuratively. They were to be found most prominently in the *Classic of Changes*, *Classic of History*, and *Classic of Odes*.

NONARY MATHEMATICS IN ANCIENT TEXTS

Bouvet was a mathematician and his knowledge of mathematics played a crucial role in elevating his status at the imperial court and in giving him access to the Chinese emperor. His application of Leibniz's binary system of numbers to the hexagrams of the *Book of Changes* formed the basis of his correspondence with the prominent European philosopher Leibniz in 1697–1707.[71] The scholar Han Qi has argued that Bouvet's research on the *Yijing* and the generation of Figurism should be viewed not as an isolated curiosity in Sino-Western cultural exchange, but rather as part of a broader intellectual exchange fostered by the Kangxi emperor.[72] This interchange involved the mathematics of calendrical science taught by the Jesuit missionaries in China. Based on Bouvet's research, the Kangxi emperor developed the view that the mathematics and calendrical science of Western learning had originated in China and he summarized this view in the phrase *Xixue Zhong yuan* 西學中源 (the Chinese origin of Western learning). The emperor supported Bouvet's research and this theory of the Chinese origin of Western learning became influential in China during the reign of the Kangxi emperor. Numerology was an important part of Bouvet's Figurist theories. Prémare, by contrast, gave greater emphasis to philology and to analyzing a comprehensive range of ancient Chinese texts. However, their differences were a matter of emphasis rather than kind. Prémare also linked his Figurist theories to the nonary system (a numerical system with a base of 9) which was very prominent in Chinese cosmology.

Prémare linked the nonary cosmography to his Figurist theories through the character *jing* 井, as in *jingtian* 井田 (well field system) which is commonly traced to the third chapter of *Mencius*.[73] The well-field system was a Chinese system of feudal land division in which square segments of land were divided into nine equal parts with eight family units and a ninth, central unit cultivated in common to provide rental payment to the feudal lords. Most scholars doubt that the *jingtian* system was ever really implemented, but it remained an important ideal in China of cooperative and fair taxation. It was incorporated into cosmological theories in the Han dynasty and the radical reformer Wang Mang attempted to implement it in AD 9, although his plan was revoked after three years.

Prémare drew two diagrams to illustrate the jing.[74] One diagram was a square divided into nine equal parts, labelled left-to-right and top-to-bottom 4, 3, 5, 8, 9, 6, 7, 1, 2. The 3×3 grid in this *jingtian* represented an ideal agrarian order (see figure 3.6). Prémare does not refer to the ideal city plan represented by the Ming Tang Jiu Shi Tu 明堂九室圖 (Diagram of the Nine Rooms of the Luminous Hall).[75] It is unclear whether the *Ming Tang* was a ruler's ancestral temple or an imperial audience hall. One of the versions depicts a nonary arrangement in which the numbers, whether read vertically, horizontally or diagonally, add up to fifteen. The numbering in Prémare's diagram does not exhibit this uniformity and any discernible pattern of numerical generation eludes this writer.

Prémare included a diagram of a second square figure divided into nine parts and labelled "Regia Civitas" (Royal City), implying a political and cosmological correspondence. Ancient Chinese cities were typically constructed as microcosmic reflections of the heavens with the capital city's north-south axis paralleling the celestial meridian[76] Prémare also referred to administrative divisions of China. He conceded he was unable to say if this nonary division of land existed in China before the flood, but he did affirm with more confidence that it had not existed since the flood. The sources of Prémare's numerological descriptions of China are unclear since he mentions only three indirectly-related sources—the *Huainanzi*, *Classic of Changes*, and *Xiaojing* 孝經 (Classic of Filial Piety).[77]

CHINESE MYTHICAL HEROES AS UNIVERSAL TYPES

In the fifth and last segment of the *Vestigia*, Prémare interpreted the figures from Chinese mythical history as universal types. In his view, these gods, heros and kings who formed a heroic age in China all converged in Christ.[78] They were typically born in an extraordinary way—from a virgin mother and with divine assistance. They typically invented divine music that united the disjointed elements of the world and especially heaven and earth. They received from on high the Yellow River Chart (Hetu) and the Luo River Diagram (Luoshu) which conveyed a nonary system of numbers that explained the mysteries of the world. Prémare quoted Luo Bi to describe these diagrams as "secret words of the celestial spirit announced to the holy king."[79] Prémare said that all of these figures have conquered Gonggong, Chiyou, and other monsters who represented different forms of the Demon.

Prémare claimed that the Chinese had no fixed agreement on who the Three Emperors (*Sanhuang* 三皇) and the Five Emperors (*Wudi* 五帝) were because they were not individuals, but rather types of representation. He claimed that for some, the Three Emperors were Fu Xi, Woman Wa, and Shen Nong while for others they were Suiren 燧人, Fu Xi, and Shen Nong, and for still others, they were Fu Xi, Shen Nong, and Huangdi (the Yellow Emperor). As for the Five Emperors, some believed they were Fu Xi, Shen Nong, Huangdi, Yao, and Shun; others believed they are Huangdi, Zhuan Xu 顓頊, Diku 帝嚳, Yao and Shun; and yet others believed they were Huangdi, Xiaohao 少暭, Diku, Yao and Shun.

Prémare drew from a wide range of Chinese sources in supporting his unorthodox argument. These sources included the famous Han philosopher and scholar-official Dong Zhongshu 董仲舒 (ca. 179–ca. 104 BC) who Prémare quoted as saying: "The three *huang* (emperors) are the three forces; the five *di* (emperors) are the five virtues. The three kings (*san wang* 三王) or founders of the [Xia, Shang, and Zhou] dynasties are the three luminaries. The five sires are the five mountains."[80] Prémare also cited the Song historian Liu Daoyuan 劉道原 (Liu Shu 劉恕)'s *Zizhi tongjian waiji* 資治通鑑外紀 (Additional Chronicle to the Comprehensive Mirror for Aid in Governance) (1078) in claiming that Liu proved that the ancient Chinese kings never existed. Occasionally, Prémare erred by citing a commentary instead of the original text, which seems to have been the case with his citation of a passage from the *Jifa* 祭法 chapter of the *Classic of Rites* (*Liji*).[81]

For Prémare, these character types as a whole were analogous to the person of Christ, but each one of them had a specific figurative meaning. Sui Huang 燧皇 discovered fire; Woman Wa conquered fire; Shen Nong was the good physician who did not hesitate personally to test the medicines he was prescribing; Hou Ji fed humans a specially nutritious grain; Xie 契 (minister of Shun) taught the law of life; Shun taught obedience; Yu accomplished great works; Cheng Tang (founder of the Shang dynasty) atoned for our sins; King Wen personally exemplified all virtues; and King Wu triumphed over tyranny.

In reading the numerous hand-written sheets of the *Vestigia*, one is struck by the impression of Prémare's isolation. As an active missionary, he must have had contacts with numerous Chinese and he indicated in correspondence his pastoral concern and sympathy for the struggles of the poor in China. He would have needed contacts with Chinese literati and book vendors in order to have assembled his extensive personal library and in purchasing Chinese books requested by European figures like Bignon. However, while he frequently mentioned books, he rarely mentioned any personal contacts with Chinese in the *Vestigia*. After the Jesuits were exiled to Guangzhou in 1724, his contacts with Chinese parishioners were much reduced. He had been working on the *Vestigia* since 1712 and he finished it in May 1725, approximately one year after he was exiled to Guangzhou. So he appears to have largely completed the research for the *Vestigia* while he was still at the missions in Jiangxi and working in relative isolation. The only other missionary he mentions in the *Vestigia* was his fellow Figurist Bouvet, but even then, he was referring impersonally to Bouvet's ideas.

The deeper one goes into the *Vestigia*, the greater the impression that Prémare's thought processes during the years when he was writing the *Vestigia* became increasingly detached from the outside world. Even though he performed his responsibilities as a missioner, he appears to have devoted himself to a separate life with his Chinese books. One gets the sense that in this separate life, he was working in a personal and spiritual dimension populated not by other people, but by what he felt was a personal and intense relationship with the Divine. This lack of contact with the outside world and with the give-and-take of debate seems to have fostered a distinctive style of argumentation that relied more on citations from Chinese texts than upon rhetorical development. This style impeded the reception of his ideas by other missioners and by European savants who did not share his vast knowledge of Chinese texts.

Prémare's physical and theological isolation in Jiangxi seems to have accentuated his conviction that the logic of his reasoning with its many citations of Chinese texts was so compelling that it needed no further refinement. By the time he was in closer contact with other missioners in Guangzhou and Macau, the situation there prevented him from receiving needed criticism and collaboration. The 1724 expulsion of missionaries to Guangzhou was very different from the 1665 expulsion during which they had openly debated issues surrounding the Chinese rites. By 1724, the China mission was traumatized and in danger of being destroyed. Prémare's works on Figurism were condemned by his superiors. He was silenced and he feared being recalled from China to face his accusers in Rome. This isolation denied him the interaction with peers as well as their criticism that he needed to make his reasoning and writing more complete. Consequently, his *Vestigia* remained an unfinished spiritual classic, still in the process of formation.

NOTES

1. John W. Witek, SJ, "Jean-François Foucquet: un Controversiste Jésuite en Chine et en Europe," in *Actes de Colloque de Sinologie: La Mission Française de Pékin aux XVIIe et XVIII Siècles* (Paris: Les Belles Lettres, 1976), p. 119.

2. *Vestigia*, f. 96r; *Vestiges*, p. 174.

3. *Vestigia*, f, 329r. In addition to the date of May 21, 1725, Prémare made minor additions to the text with the inscribed dates of May 2, 1725 (*Vestigia*, f. 86v) and May 18, 1725, (*Vestigia*, f. 327r).

4. Michael Lackner characterizes the extent of Prémare's knowledge of Chinese texts as "quite enormous," although he questions some of Prémare's interpretations of these texts. See his "A Figurist at Work—The Vestigia of Joseph de Prémare SJ," in *l'Europe en Chine*, p. 23, and 39

5. Wing-tsit Chan, "Chu Hsi's Completion of Neo-Confucianism." In *Etudes Song—Sung Studies. In Memoriam Etienne Balazs.* Edited by Francoise Aubin. Ser. II, #1, 1973, p. 83–85.

6. D. E. Mungello, "The Seventeenth-Century Jesuit Translation Project of the Confucian Four Books. In *East meets West: the Jesuits in China, 1582–1773*. Edited by Charles E. Ronan, SJ and Bonnie B. C. Oh. (Chicago: Loyola University Press, 1988), p. 252–72.

7. D. E. Mungello, *The Forgotten Christians of Hangzhou* (Honolulu: University of Hawaii Press, 1994), p. 78–80.

8. Philip Couplet, SJ et al, *Confucius Sinarum Philosophus*. (Paris, 1687, p. xxxv–xxxix.

9. Zhang Xingyao, *Tianjujiao Rujiao tongyi kao*. 3 juan. 1672–1715. Bibliothèque Nationale France, ms. Chinois 7171. Variant copies in the Xujiahui Library, Shangai and the Beitang Collection, Beijing.

10. Mungello, *Forgotten Christians of Hangzhou*, p. 100–7.

11. Shang Hujing, *Bu Ru wengao*. 1664. Unpublished manuscript in the Xujiahui Library (Shanghai Library).

12. D. E. Mungello, *The Spirit and the Flesh in Shandong, 1650–1785* (Lanham, MD: Rowman & Littlefield, 2001), p. 38–42.

13. Letter of A. Gaubil, SJ to N. Fréret, October 28, 1733. In Antoine Gaubil, SJ, *Correspondence de Pékin 1722–1759* (Geneva: Librairie Droz, 1970), p. 362–65.

14. Kilian Stumpf SJ, *The Acta Pekinensia or Historical Records of the Maillard de Tournon Legation*. Volume I December 1705–August 1706. Edited by Paul Rule and Claudia von Collani. (Rome: Institutum Historicum Societatis Iesu, 2015), p. l–li.

15. Reil, p. 160.

16. Reil, p. 164.

17. *Vestigia*, f. 6r-v; *Vestiges*, p. 31.

18. *Vestigia*, f. 9r; *Vestiges*, p. 34–35.

19. *Vestigia*, f. 7r-v; *Vestiges*, p. 32.

20. The extant *Liji* (Record of Rites) has no overall structure, but consists of forty-nine sections which originated at different times and in different contexts. The dates and origins of the different parts of the *Liji* have been subject to controversial debate throughout Chinese history. See Jeffrey K. Riegel, "Li chi." In *Early Chinese Texts: a Bibliographical Guide*. Ed. Michael Loewe (Berkeley: Institute of East Asian Studies, University of California, 1993), p. 293–97.

21. On Zuoshi, see Lowe, p. 69.

22. *Vestigia*, f. 22r–23r; *Vestiges*, p. 49–50.

23. Cf. Yves Hervouet, ed., *A Sung Bibliography (Bibliographie des Sung)* (Hong Kong: Chinese University of Hong Kong, 1978) p. dating from 221 BC to 87–88, and 173–74 and Nicolas Standaert, *The Intercultural Weaving of Historical Texts:*

Chinese *and European Stories about Emperor Ku and His Concubines.* (Leiden: Brill, 2016), p. 30–31, and 263–64.

24. *Vestigia,* f. 9r–10r; *Vestiges,* p. 35–36.

25. Anne Cheng, "*Ch'un ch'iu, Kung yang, Ku liang and Tso chuan.*" In *Early Chinese Texts: a Bibliographical Guide.* Ed. Michael Loewe (Berkeley: Institute of East Asian Studies, University of California, 1993), p. 67–76.

26. *Vestigia,* f. 11r-v; *Vestiges,* p. 38.

27. *Vestigia,* f. 14r-v; *Vestiges,* p. 41.

28. See Zhu Xi, *Mengzi jizhu* 孟子集注 (1177). In *Sishu jizhu* 四書集註 (1177) (Taipei: Yiwen Yinshu, 1969) . Cf. Legge, *Chinese Classics,* vol. 2, p. 501–2.

29. Wing-tsit Chan, "Chu His's Completion of Neo-Confucianism," p. 74.

30. Zhu Xi, "Zhongyong zhangju xu" 中庸章句序 (Commentary on the Doctrine of the Mean) preface (1194). In *Zhuzi daquan* 朱子大全 (Great Collection of Master Zhu) 76/21.

31. Wing-tsit Chan, "Chu Hsi's Completion of Neo-Confucianism," p. 75–81 and Wing-tsit Chan, "The Study of Chu His in the West," *Journal of Asian Studies* 35 (1976): 567.

32. *Vestigia,* f. 20r; *Vestiges,* p. 47.

33. *Vestigia,* f. 5r-v; *Vestiges,* p. 28. Zhu Xi wrote three commentaries on the *Book of Changes:* (1) *Zhouyi benyi* 周易本義 (Original meanings of the *Book of Changes*) in 12 *juan;* (2) *Yixue qimeng* 易學啟蒙 (Introduction to the Study of the *Book of Changes*) in 4 *juan*; and (3) *Yichuan*易傳 (Commentary on the *Book of Changes*) in 12 *juan.*

34. *Vestigia,* f. 3r–5v; *Vestiges,* p. 26–28.

35. *Vestigia,* f. 4r–5r; *Vestiges,* p. 26–27.

36. *Vestigia,* f. 5r; *Vestiges,* p. 28.

37. *Vestigia,* f. 17r-v; Vestiges, p. 44.

38. *Vestigia,* f. 16r-v; Vestiges, p. 43.

39. See R. de Crespigny article in *A Sung Bibliogrraphy (Bibliographie des Sung)* Ed. Yves Hervouet (Hong Kong: Chinese University Press, 1978) p. 72. Cf. Nicolas Standaert, *Intercultural Weaving,* p. 25–26.

40. Vestigia, f. 18r-v; Vestiges, p. 45.

41. Fang Chao-ying, "Li Kuang-ti" in *Eminent Chinese of the Ch'ing Period.* Ed. Arthur Hummel (Washington, D.C.: Government Printing Office, 1943), p. 473–75.

42. John W. Witek, SJ, *Controversial Ideas in China and in Europe: a biography of Jean-François Foucquet, SJ (1665–1741)* (Rome: Institutum Historicum S. I.), p. 204–6.

43. *Vestigia,* p. 19r & v & 20; *Vestiges,* p. 47.

44. *Vestigia,* f. 7v; *Vestiges,* p. 32, fn. 31.

45. Pierre Martial Cibot, "Essai sur la langue et les caractères des Chinois," in *Mémoires concernant l'histoire, les sciences, les arts, les moeurs, les usages, etc. des Chinois, par les Missionnaries de Pékin.* 17 vols. (Paris: Chez Nyon, Libraire, 1776–1814) vol. VIII, p. 133–266, and vol. IX, p. 282–430, translated in Knud Lundbæk, "Pierre Martial Cibot (1727–1780)—The Last China Figurst," *Sino-Western Cultural Relations Journal* XV (1993): 57.

46. Pan Feng-chuan 潘凤娟《翻译"圣人"：马若瑟与十字的索隐回转》(Translating the Saint: Joseph de Prémare's Figurist Torque of Chinese from Decem to Crucem), 国际比较文学 *International Comparative Literature* I (2018): 93.

47. M. Prevost, "Bonnetty." In *Dictionnaire de biographie française* (Paris: Librairie Letouzey et Ané, 1954) XVI, 1029–1030.

48. C. A. Dubray, "Bonnetty." In *The Catholic Encyclopedia* (New York, 1913) II, 43.

49. L'abbé A. Sionnet, "Analyse d'un Ouvrage Inédit du P. Prémare, sur les Vestiges des Principaux Dogmes chrétiens que l'on retrove dans les livres chinois," first article, *Annales de Philosophie Chrétienne*. Vol. XV (Nr. 85) (July 31, 1837), p. 7–24; A. Bonnetty, "Analyse d'un Ouvrage Inédit du P. Prémare," second article, p. 134–54; and l'abbé A. Sionnet, "Analyse d'un Ouvrage Inédit du P. Prémare," third article, p. 325–36.

50. A. Bonnetty, "Notice sur la vie et les ouvrages de M. l'abbé Sionnet," *Annales de philosophie chrétienne*, vol. 13 (1856), p. 441–42.

51. Bonnetty, "Notice," p. 444–45.

52. L'abbé Sionnet, *Vestiges de Dogmes chrétiens retrouvés dans les anciens livres chinois ou Analyse d'un ouvrage inèdit du P. Prémare.* (Paris: Gaume Frères, Libraries, 1839), p. 54.

53. Bonnetty, "Notice," p. 445.

54. Bonnetty & Perny, Vestiges, p. 1 lists *Annales de Philosophie chretienne*, vols. XIV, XV, XVI, XVIII, and XIX (2nd series).

55. Sionnet, *Vestiges*, p. 53.

56. Sionnet, *Vestiges*, p. 54.

57. *Vestiges*, p. Iv–v.

58. *Vestiges*, p. v.

59. *Vestigia*, f. 306v.

60. *Vestigia*, f. 306r.

61. *Vestigia*, f. 263r.

62. *Vestiges*, p. 478.

63. *Vestiges*, between p. 402 and 403.

64. Jean-Claude Drouin, "Un Esprit original du XIX° siècle: Le Chevalier de Paravey (1787–1871)," *Revue historique de Bordeaux et du département de la Gironde* (1970) p. 66.

65. *Vestiges*, p. 168, fn. B. See M. le chev. De Paravey, "Identité du déluge d'Yao et de celui de la Bible, ou le patriarche Noé retrouvé dans l'empereur chinois *Ti-ho*," *Annales de Philosophie Chrétienne*. Vol. XV (July 31, 1837), p. 380–95.

66. *Vestiges*, p. 402.

67. Drouin, p. 72.

68. Joseph de Guignes, *Mémoire dans lequel on prove que les chinois sont une colonie égyptienne* (Paris: Chez Desaint & Saillant, 1759).

69. D. E. Mungello, *Curious Land* (Stuttgart: Steiner Verlag, 1985) p. 185–88.

70. *Vestigia*, p. 94–95; *Vestiges*, p. 173, fn. C.

71. Mungello, *Curious Land*, p. 318–28. For a transcription (in the original French with a parallel German translation) of Bouvet's correspondence with Leibniz, see

Gottfried Wilhelm Leibniz, *Der Briefwechsel mit den Jesuiten in China (1689–1714)*. Rita Widmaier, ed. & Malte-Ludolf Babin, trans. (Hamburg: Felix Meiner Verlag, 2006)

72. Han, Qi 韓琦. "Bai Jin de 'Yijing' yanjiu he Kangxi shidai de 'Xixue zhong yuan' shuo" 白晉的《易經》研究和康熙時代的'西學中源'說。(Joachim Bouvet's Study of the *Yijing* and the theory of the 'Chinese Origin of Western Learning' during the Kangxi period), *Hanxue Yanjiu* 漢學研究 16:1:185–201.

73. *Mencius*. D. C. Lau, tr. (Middlesex, England: Penguin, 1970) IIIA.3 (p. 99–100) & III.i.3.13, 18 & 19 in James Legge, tr., *The Works of Mencius*. In *The Chinese Classics* (Oxford: Oxford University Press, 1893) II, 243–45.

74. *Vestigia*, p. 97b; *Vestiges*, p. 176–77.

75. John B. Henderson, *The Development and Decline of Chinese Cosmology* (New York: Columbia University Press, 1984) p. 72.

76. *Vestigia*, f. 97r–v; *Vestiges*, p. 176–77.

77. *Vestigia*, f. 99r–v; *Vestiges*, p. 179–80.

78. *Vestigia*, f. 258–59; *Vestiges*, p. 414–15.

79. *Vestigia*, f. 259r–v; Bonnetty and Perny in *Vestiges*, p. 414, fn. 1, give the citation of this quote as Luo Bi, *Lu shi*, Collection of Things Left by the Roadside, 1st part, l.v.

80. *Vestigia*, f. 260a–b; *Vestiges*, p. 416.

81. *Vestigia*, f. 261a–b; Vestiges, p. 416–17. The phrase Prémare cites does not appear in the *Liji* concordance.

Chapter Four

Daoism and Hieroglyphics in the *Vestigia*

Metal is the fourth of the Five Elements

THE TRIGRAMMATON FROM THE *DAODEJING*

Unlike most China Jesuits, Prémare found Daoist texts to be very complementary to Christianity, and he made frequent reference to the *Zhuangzi*, *Laozi*, and *Huainanzi* in his *Vestigia*. One of Prémare's more striking interpretations of a Daoist text was made of chapter 14 of Laozi's *Daodejing* (The Classic of the Way and its Power). He believed that the grouping of the characters *yi* 夷, *xi* 希, and *wei* 微 constituted a reference to the Christian God.[1] Prémare translated and commented on this passage as follows:

> We look for [spirits] but do not see them. This is called yi 夷. We listen for them, but do not hear them. This is called xi 希.... What is in some degree palpable, but which cannot however be touched is wei 微. On the subject of these three, it is in vain to pose questions in search of the meaning. They cannot respond to you at all. Seek it solely with the mind and you will understand that these three points are joined together and are only one.[2]

The implications of this passage would be drawn out by another Figurist, the China Jesuit Jean-François Noëlas (Nie Ruohan 聶若翰) (1669–1740), who along with Prémare was exiled to Guangzhou in 1724, then in 1732 to Macau where he died in 1740. Perhaps Noëlas and Prémare shared ideas on Figurism during the long hours of their exile, but if so, they would probably have spoken very quietly about this condemned theory. Noëlas is thought to have been the author of the first (albeit partial) translation of the *Daodejing* into a European language—*Liber Sinicus. Tao Te Kim inscriptus, in Latinum idoma Versus* (*Daodejing*—a Chinese text translated into the Latin language) (1721?).[3] The Figurist thesis of the work was conveyed in the subtitle: "Eleven chapters of the book *Daodejing* by which it is shown that the secrets of the most holy Trinity and the human incarnation of [the son of] God was once known by the Chinese people."[4] The unpublished manuscript was brought to Europe and eventually housed in the Royal Society Library in London.[5]

In 1820 the French Sinologist Jean Pierre Abel Rémusat (1788–1832) used Noëlas' work to compose a partial translation of the *Daodejing* into French.[6] The Hebrews had believed that the Tetragrammaton YHWH (in Latin letters) was the four-letter name of God (Yaweh). Rémusat carried the Figurists' interpretation of Laozi farther in claiming the Trigrammaton Yi-Hi-Wei (yi 夷, xi 希, and wei 微 or IHV) found in chapter 14 of the *Daodejing* was a Chinese transcription of the Hebrew Tetragrammaton YHWH.[7]

THE *SHANHAIJING* (*CLASSIC OF MOUNTAINS AND SEAS*)

Prémare also drew extensively from the *Shanhaijing* 山海經 (*Classic of Mountains and Seas*), which is an ancient Chinese description of the world (*descriptio mundi*) of about 31,000 characters in length. It consists of several layers of text compiled by different authors over a 600–800 year period from ca. 300 BC to AD 300, although some parts of it have been traced to the Shang dynasty (1500–1050 BC).[8] Its exact classification has been greatly disputed and it cannot be reduced to a single category of writing. The world picture of the *Classic of Mountains and Seas* consisted of an ethereal sky and a heavy earth separated by world mountains which supported the sky. An earthly rectangle of land was surrounded by water in all directions. These four seas were surrounded by four wildernesses. The earth's surface was divided into three concentric rectangles of land, sea and wilderness, with the central rectangle being 28,000 *li* (literally 14,000 km or 7,000 miles, but the number is meant figuratively) in length and 26,000 *li* in height, surrounded by the Four Seas, and then extending outward from the seashore to an undefined limit. The *Classic of Mountains and Seas* is divided into eighteen books (*juan* 卷). The first five books, entitled "The Five Treasuries of the Classic of Mountains" (*Wucang shanjing* 五臓山經) are regarded as the oldest part of the classic and it is from this part that Prémare drew.[9]

Prémare interpreted book 2 of the *Classic of Mountains and Seas* as describing a map of the Biblical Garden of Eden on Kunlun Mountain Kunlun Shan 崑崙山.[10] He presented the Kunlun Mountain as the cosmic axis (*axis mundi*) or center of the world where the sky connects with the earth. The Kunlun Mountain Range has both geographical and mythical significance. Geographically it is focused in central Asia or north of Tibet and runs eastward to divide the Yellow River and Yangzi River basins.[11] It was regarded by some as the source of the Yellow River. Unknown regions lie to the west of Kunlun while China and Korea lie to the east. Near the Kunlun Mountain Prémare placed the terrrestrial paradise, which is a closed and hidden garden (see figure 4.1). The garden is suspended on the middle of Kunlun Mountain, near a gate closed from heaven. Kunlun Mountain belonged to a tradition of religious cosmography in East Asia.[12] This type of map was centered on the Kunlun Mountain in central Asia. Numerous Buddhist wheel-maps used the Kunlun Mountain as their center.

In the middle of the terrestrial garden is the fountain of immortality from which the water of immortality (*dan shui* 丹水) originates.[13] Those who drink of this water do not die. The use of the character *dan* 丹 reflects Prémare's recasting of a Daoist term with Christian meaning. *Dan* meant cinnabar that was part of the Daoist quest for physical immortality, but it was reinterpreted by Prémare as spiritual immortality. Prémare regarded the *Classic of Mountains and Seas*' presentation of the fountain of immorality as a vestige of the Garden of Eden from Genesis. Four rivers flowed out from this fountain of immortality. Yellow Water (*he shui* 河水) flowed to the northeast.[14] Red Water (*chi shui* 赤水) flowed to the southeast.[15] Weak Water (*ruo shui* 弱水) flowed to the southwest.[16] Finally, the Water of the Lamb (*yang shui* 羊水) flowed to the northwest.[17]

To the north of the terrestrial paradise on Kunlun Mountain was the celestial paradise on Mt. Buzhou 不周 (see figure 4.2).[18] Prémare quoted the *Huainanzi* (Book [of the prince] of Huainan) to say "that the door of the north is opened in order to receive the wind which blows from the mountain Buzhou" (*Bei men kai yi na Buzhou zhi feng* 北門開以納不周之風).[19] Prémare interpreted the palace of the Lord below the Kunlun peak as being the terrestrial paradise (i.e. Garden of Eden): *Kunlun zhi qiu shi shi wei di zhi xia dou.* 崑崙之丘是實惟帝之下都.[20] Prémare continued to quote: "by the gate [to this terrestrial paradise] is an animal named *kaiming* 開明 who guards the entrance."[21] The gloss calls it a celestial animal. The Daoist Baopuzi 抱扑子 (Ge Hong 葛洪) (253–333?) called it a "spiritual animal" (*shenshou* 神獸). Prémare interpreted the name *kaiming* to be an allusion to the cherub with a flaming sword placed to the east of the Garden of Eden to guard the path that leads to the tree of life (Genesis 3:24). The *Classic of Mountains and Seas* compared the *kaiming* to an animal with a large body like a tiger and with nine heads and human faces turned toward the east.[22]

THE FALL OF THE ANGELS CHIYOU AND GONGGONG

Prémare continued his description of the terrestrial paradise by drawing from the *Classic of History* (*Shujing*). Contemporary Sinologists believe parts of the *History* contain the earliest writings that may date from the Zhou conquest ca. 1050 BC, although most parts were added later.[23] Prémare cited the *History* passage to claim that the ancient Xia dynasty (trad. 2000–1500 BC) king presided over a terrestrial paradise.[24] Prémare believed the Xia king may represent Adam, not in the historical sense, but rather as a figurative reference to Adam in the Garden of Eden. He cited *Zhuangzi*, *Huainanzi*, Sima Qian's *Shiji* (Historical Records), and Luo Bi's *Lushi* to describe a terrestrial paradise of innocence, simplicity, abundance, and happiness.[25] Luo Bi spoke of Hundun 渾沌, the legendary king whom the *Zhuangzi* refers to as chaos, as an innocent Adam.[26] The use of a legendary king from the imaginative work *Zhuangzi* rather than a historical work reflects Prémare's view that ancient Chinese texts should be interpreted figuratively rather than literally.

After discussing the vestiges of a state of human innocence found in ancient Chinese works, Prémare turned to the Fall. Of the two fallen natures—angelic and human—he dealt first with angels. His methodical argument, shaped by his Jesuit training, involved hieroglyphic analysis of passages from the *Classic of Changes* and of the mythical figures Chiyou 蚩尤 and Gonggong 共工.

He began with hexagram #1 *Qian* 乾 and focused on the sixth line (topmost of six undivided lines in the hexagram). The four-character *Yijing* text for this line is typically translated as "the dragon exceeding the proper limits" *kang long you hui* 亢龍有悔.[27] Prémare translated this line as "the rebellious and perverse dragon is punished for his arrogance."[28] He interpreted this rebel angel to be Lucifer and found a further reference to Lucifer in hexagram #36 *Ming Yi* 明夷 in which the sixth line (undivided topmost line of the hexagram) is typically translated as "shows the case where there is no light, but (only) obscurity. (Its subject) had at first ascended to (the top of) the sky; his future shall be to go into the earth."[29] Prémare translated this line as "Pride has blinded him: he has wished to rise to heaven and he has been thrown to the earth."[30]

Prémare next dealt with the Chinese fable of Yi 羿 the Archer and the ten suns, which he drew from the *Huainanzi* and the *Classic of Mountains and Seas*.[31] This fable is often treated as a catastrophic myth of world conflagration.[32] It is set during the time of the legendary King Yao when ten suns appeared in the sky at the same time. Yao ordered Yi the Archer to destroy them with arrows and Yi succeeded in hitting and destroying nine of ten suns, leaving one remaining sun. Nine crows who lived in these suns perished and their wings were broken. Prémare claimed that the Chinese, having lost the true teaching, were unable to explain the myth, but he argued that Christian law could explain it.³³ The nine crows represent the rebellious angels led by Lucifer who disputed with the living force of the Son of God, who in this myth is represented by King Yao. The one remaining sun represents the sun of justice and splendor of the eternal light. The archangel Michael is represented by Yi. Prémare drew from the *Shuowen* dictionary to make a hieroglyphic analysis of the character for Yi, which he divided into the upper part *yu* 羽 representing the wings of birds and the bottom part *shi* which he interprets as 干干 or *ping* 平 "to pacify, to still troubled movements." Michael chased the impure suns from the heaven. The black crows had their wings broken and were transformed into a serpent.

For Prémare, the two principal ancient Chinese symbols of Lucifer were the gods Chiyou and Gonggong. The fact that the Chinese placed Gonggong under six or seven monarchs who had different names and lived at different times reflected that Gonggong, as well as Chiyou, was symbolic and figurative rather than historical in nature.³⁴ Their figurative nature consisted of a unique type of being, which explained that the archetypal nature of their rebellion was based, not on historical circumstances, but rather on an inherent sense of pride and refusal to submit to the incarnate Son of God.

Prémare elaborated on Gonggong in his "History of the Ancient Chinese" ("*Histoire des vieux temps*"), the manuscript he sent to Etienne Fourmont with a letter dated November 10, 1730. This is an essay filled with a great deal of historical detail, which Prémare analyzed figuratively. He wrote that Gonggong reigned as a tyrant for 25 years and that his son was equally lacking in merit.³⁵ He died on the winter solstice and became a malign spirit.

According to the myth, the god of water, Gonggong, famous for his cruelty and anger, waged war against the god of fire, Zhu Rong 祝融. Gonggong rammed his head against Mount Buzhou and the mountain is said to have crumbled and the sky, deprived of its main support, collapsed.³⁶ Woman Wa is said to have repaired the damaged pillars with stones of five colors. However, Prémare doubted that Gonggong, given his humanlike size, was able by a blow of his head to have shaken Mount Buzhou (see figure 4.2). He is even more skeptical of the legend of the "queen of earth," Woman Wa, who although only a woman, flew to heaven in order to repair the pillars holding up the sky. As history, Prémare called these accounts described in the *Huainanzi* "pure fantasy."³⁷

Prémare conflated four different legends of catastrophic floods into one figurative meaning. Gonggong caused the flood by his malice and fighting with Zhurong. But Prémare denied that this flood had worldwide dimensions. Moreover, the *History* describes how a flood occurred during the reign of the legendary rulers Yao, Shun, and Yu and how it was finally subdued by Yu.³⁸ Prémare believed that those having experience with symbolic books, would be able to interpret Yao as the model/symbol of God, Shun as the figure/symbol of Christ as the Son of God, and Yu as the figure/symbol of the Son of Man.

THE SHADOW OF BOUVET

Bouvet hovered over Prémare in the manner of an older brother generating both benign influence and hostile tensions. He had recruited Prémare for the China mission, introduced him to the Chinese language, and, prior to 1717, served as a mentor. Bouvet's status in the Chinese imperial court and the Emperor's favor gave Bouvet power and influence that few other Jesuits enjoyed. In 1697, he had been the first to express the idea of Figurism by writing: "I hope to demonstrate the truth (of this proposition) in making an analysis of enigmatic figures of this book the *Yijing* [*figures éigmatiques de ce livre Yi king*] under which Fu Xi, the founder of the monarchy and the first philosophy of China, has concealed his principles."[39] Prémare was the first of Bouvet's "Figurist students" (Prémare, Foucquet and Gollet) to made an enthusiastic reference to Figurist ideas and to his discovery of Chinese hieroglyphics in his letter of 1704 to Bouvet.[40] During the five years 1703–1708, Prémare and Bouvet had an extensive correspondence.

Bouvet was not a confrontational personality. Fr. Benigne Vachet of the Missions Étrangères, who accompanied Bouvet and the Jesuits sent by Louis XIV on their voyage east from France to Siam in 1685, described Bouvet as a tranquil person, someone more fit to be a retiring Carthusian than a vocal Jesuit.[41] Vachet said few people got to know Bouvet on the trip to Siam. If someone spoke offensively to him, he would either remain silent or withdraw to his room. Foucquet said that in his later years Bouvet was normally "most firm and moderate."[42] Prémare agreed with Bouvet on the basic principles of Figurism, but their differences in style, substance and personality limited their collaboration. Bouvet inclined toward mathematics while Prémare inclined toward philology. Also, Bouvet was comfortable at the center of power in Beijing, but Prémare had reclusive tendencies. After two years of residing at the French residence there, he chose to return to the obscurity of Jiangxi province in 1717.

And yet Prémare showed no signs of hostility towards Bouvet in his *Vestigia*. While their collaboration was limited, signs of fundamental agreement were evident. One of these points of agreement was the Figurist interpretation of the flooding of Chinese antiquity. Four different forms of a flood myth have been delineated by scholars—the flood of the rebellious Gonggong, the flood in which Woman Wa saved the world, the flood associated with the large fish Gun, and the Yao-Shun-Yu flood told from a Confucian perspective in *Mencius* III.B.9.[43] Prémare voiced his agreement with Bouvet on the Figurist interpretation of the flood of Chinese antiquity.[44]

THE FLOOD

For the Figurists, the vast distribution of the malevolent and injurious water of the Flood symbolized that the sins and crimes involved in the rebellion of Lucifer and Adam were spread throughout the world. They believed that if the ancient Chinese texts were interpreted spiritually and divinely, it would be possible to see that Christ alone could remedy such evil by attacking it at its source and through his death draining the fountains of these evils. In this way, the teaching of the hieroglyphic characters contained in the ancient Chinese texts, although lost over time, would be recovered. Prémare claimed that it would be seen how the great Yu, who tamed the Flood, was a type of Christ. He climbed the mountain, sat on the chair of sorrow, shut off the impure water of the lower lake, and opened the fountains of justice.

Chiyou was a mythical Chinese god of war and a famous rebel. Prémare interpreted him to be a symbol of Lucifer who wanted to become equal to the Most High. But he fell from Heaven and became a mortal serpent.[45] This is signified hieroglyphically in the character for his name *chi* 蚩 by the bottom element *chong* 虫 (蟲) which means insect. Prémare noted that the character *chi* also signifies ignorance and blind covetousness. He cited Luo Bi as saying "that his covetousness was insatiable." Chiyou is also called *fan quan* 阪泉. The ancient *Shuowen* dictionary was cited to clarify that *fan* meant *po* 陂 in the sense of obstruction and that *quan* meant fountain. By extension, Lucifer was the first one who by his sin, obstructed the fountain of grace and divine munificence.[46]

Prémare cited the *Classic of History* which states that according to ancient teachings, Chiyou was the first to lead a rebellion and that this rebellion spread among the common people, engendering all sorts of crimes.[47] Prémare also cited the numerological Yellow River Chart and Luo River Diagram (*Hetu luoshu* 河圖落書) literature (see figures 3.2 and 3.3). According to legend, a dragon-horse waded in the Yellow River and a tortoise emerged from the Luo River, each with numerical markings of 1–9 dots on their backs and from which the hexagrams of the Book of Changes were generated. The Yellow River Chart and Luo River Diagram became the source of a nonary (based on number 9) cosmology that became prominent among Han Dynasty (206 BC–AD 220) and Song Dynasty (960–1279) metaphysicians.[48] Prémare briefly cited this nonary cosmology in referring to Chiyou having 81 brothers and there being 9 choirs of angels, in which 9 multiplied by itself yields 81.[49]

The Yellow Emperor [Huangdi 黃帝 as distinct from the more generic term for emperor with the same spelling, but different characters—Huangdi 皇帝 (emperor)] made a chariot that turned to the south and which was used to enchain Chiyou. However, Prémare noted that Chiyou was not dead because he embodied the figurative meaning of Satan rather than a historical meaning of someone from the past. Prémare cited the *Classic of Mountains and Seas* in which the Yellow Emperor ordered the winged dragon-spirit (*ying long* 應龍) to throw Chiyou into a black valley of misfortunes.[50] Prémare interpreted this winged dragon spirit to be the Archangel Michael and the black valley of misfortunes to be hell.[51]

At this point Prémare introduced the image of the Militant Holy Virgin of the Catholic Reformation whom he compared to the Chinese creatrix Woman Wa in power. He quoted from the Yellow River Diagram literature to say that "a divine Virgin was sent from heaven and gave to Huangdi weapons with which he vanquished Chiyou."[52] But just as the Archangel Michael has a counterpart in the rebel Chiyou, so too does the Militant Holy Virgin have a counterpart in the figurative representation of Eve in the *Classic of Odes* (*Shijing*). Prémare interpreted Mao ode 48 to deal with the temptation of Eve. The Chinese themselves have debated the meaning of this ode extensively.[53]

Prémare saw a second manifestation of Satan in the mythological god of water Gonggong 共工. Gonggong appeared in various forms—sometimes as a man and at other times as a snake with a human head and bright red hair.[54] He was ill-tempered and cruel. The first catastrophic destruction of the world is said to have occurred when Gonggong waged war against the god of fire Zhu Rong. Prémare quoted the *Waiji* (Additional Chronicle) by Liu Shu 劉恕 (Daoyuan 道原) (1032–1078) to say: "Gonggong fought with Zhu Rong. Conquered and trembling with anger, he struck his head against mount Buzhou" and caused the sky to fall.[55] Eventually Woman Wa is said to have defeated Gonggong, but elsewhere the legendary Yu is also said to have routed him. The attribution of Gonggong's defeat to several kings under much the same circumstances is interpreted by Prémare to indicate yet another case of the narrative representing not history, but rather symbolic stories of Satan and different manifestations of a figure who conquered demons.

Prémare cited the passage in the *Classic of Mountains and Seas* to say that "Gonggong had an assistant named Willow who had nine heads, ate the fruits of nine mountains, and lived on the north side of Mount Kunlun."[56] Prémare interpreted this allegory to correspond to the nine orders of rebellious angels who submitted to Lucifer. He located them on the north side of Moung Kunlun where they had fallen from Mount Buzhou, that is, from Heaven.

THE FALL OF HUMANITY

After the section devoted to the fall of the rebellious angels (symbolized by Chiyou and Gonggong), Prémare turned to the fall of humans, citing passages from the *Classic of Odes* and referring to figures representing the sinful Adam. He began with quoting from the Daoist texts *Zhuangzi* and *Huainanzi*. The *Huainanzi* consists of essays collected from scholarly debates at the court of Liu An 劉安 (179?–122 BC).[57] They reflect eclectic Huang-Lao 黃老 Daoism and other schools of that time. Prémare claimed that the *Zhuangzi* and *Huainanzi* both argued that the truth and virtue of early humans had been lost, thus corrupting humanity.[58] Prémare quoted Zhuangzi as saying, in an attack on the literati: "If truth and virtue had not been lost, what need would there have been for [Confucian] benevolence and righteousness?" Zhuangzi's claim that the excessive desire for knowledge was the cause of all wrongs was interpreted by Prémare to be a reference to Adam and Eve eating the fruit of the tree of knowledge.[59]

Prémare claimed that another figurative form of Adam was Hundun 渾沌 (Chaos). The Daoist Zhuangzi portrayed Hundun as the emperor of a central region of the world. Unlike the other emperors, he lacked the seven apertures in the head (eyes, ears, nostrils and mouth).[60] Since Hundun had no apertures, the other emperors tried to give him sight, hearing, smell and taste by boring one hole in his head each day, but on the seventh day, Hundun died. Figuratively, Hundan was a man of such innocence that he ignored evil. Prémare interpreted this story to mean that when Hundun's eyes were opened, he—like Adam—lost his blissful innocence.[61]

WOMAN AS EMBODYING TEMPTATION

Prémare next turned to the figurative forms of Eve as embodiments of temptation. When he cited the Chinese proverb: "Do not listen to the words of a woman" (*furen zhi yan bu ke ting* 婦人之言不可聽), he was not saying that a woman's words are not worth hearing, but rather that their words are dangerous.[62] He cited the Chinese commenter Tchu fong tching (?) to elucidate how this danger has played out in traditional accounts of the fall of the first three dynasties in Chinese history—the Xia, Shang, and Western Zhou. For Figurists, the fall of the Western Zhou signified the beginning of Chinese history.

Although the Xia dynasty is said to have ended when its last monarch Jie 桀 was destroyed by the Shang dynasty founder Tang 湯, the real cause of his fall was his favorite concubine Mei Xi 妹喜 on whom he wasted large amounts of wealth for her amusement.

Similarly, Prémare claims that the last ruler of the Shang dynasty, Zhou 紂, is often said to have been destroyed by the Zhou dynasty founder King Wu 武王. However, according to the commenter, the real cause of his defeat was the extravagance and degeneracy Zhou indulged in to please his notorious concubine Dayi 妲已. This included the construction of a vast pleasure palace where costly delicacies were hung from trees and wild orgies took place. The origins of cruel punishments were attributed to her, including the "roasting punishment" in which a criminal was tied to a hollow pillar with a fire inside.[63] The enchanting power of Dayi's beauty was so great that when King Wu captured her, it was difficult to find anyone willing to execute her.

Finally, Prémare claims that the real cause of the end of the last Western Zhou monarch, King You 幽, was not, as is often claimed, a rebellion led by [his son?] Marquis Shen 申, but rather the king's enchantment with his favorite concubine Bao Si 褒姒. She is said to have suffered such depression that King You spent vast sums of money in trying to entertain her, even issuing a false alarm calling for the forces of the feudal princes to assemble. Although these forces came and she laughed, when a real crisis later occurred, the feudal princes did not respond and the Western Zhou fell.

Prémare chose five passages from the *Classic of Odes* to allude to the happiness enjoyed in the state of human innocence and the miserable conditions of subsequent ages.[64] His arguments are somewhat belabored, which may partly stem from the literary and imaginative nature of these texts.[65] He also quoted the historian Luo Bi as saying in the *Lushi*: "after nature had been corrupted . . . all the birds of heaven and all the beasts of the earth, the reptiles and the snakes began to be hostile to man."

HIEROGLYPHICS AND ETYMOLOGY

During his exile in Guangzhou, Prémare made final changes to his *Vestigia* manuscript. It was essentially finished by May of 1725. He added one last notation to the manuscript on May 2, 1725, when he expressed his failure to include two relevant hexagrams from the *Changes* in his discussion of the fall of humans from their original state of innocence.[66] However he had included these hexagrams in his discussion of the personages who figuratively represent the types of Adam's sins. The first was King Miao or San Miao 三苗 from the *Classic of History*.[67] The legendary emperor Yu led an army to subdue the king of Miao and referred to him as ignorant, disrespectful and in rebellion against truth and virtue.[68]

Prémare's argument involved the hieroglyphic analysis of names and words. By hieroglyphic characters, the Figurists meant Chinese characters that were not merely ancient, but also spiritualized in content. The character *miao* contained a plane above and earth below. It was said to symbolize the human heart which had suffered dessication through its sins to become the arid earth of a desert. The character *san* (three) indicated the triple greed that was the source of all evil. Prémare believed this interpretation was reinforced by hexagram no. 18 of the *Changes*. The character for this hexagram *Gu* 蠱 (Prémare spelled it *tchong*) 011001 symbolized destruction. He analyzed the character into a top part consisting of three worms *chong* 蟲 and a bottom part consisting of *min* 皿 which he interpreted to stand for *xue* 血 (blood), that is, remorse by means of worms.[69]

Some of the clearest evidence of the influence of contemporary Chinese literati on Prémare is found in his most-recognized work of scholarship—*Notitia Linguae Sinicae* (An examination of the Chinese Language) (see figure 4.3). The *Notitia* is a Latin text derived from his Chinese work *Liushu shiyi* 六書實義 (The True Meaning of the Six Classes of Characters) in 1721 (see figure 4.4).[70] The *Liushu shiyi* was, in turn, based on Liu Ning's *Liu shu guai* 六書夬 (The Six Kinds of Characters).[71] Liu's use of the *Shuowen* dictionary in explaining the six classes of Chinese characters had a great influence on Prémare. The *Shuowen* compiler Xu Shen 許慎 had arranged the small seal script characters under 540 semantic classifiers using a system of etymological analysis that Prémare made extensive use of in composing the *Vestigia*. The *Liushu shiyi* is a brief 10,000 character work that follows traditional Chinese form with both a preface and a postscript, although the names are clearly literary names and probably pseudonyms. The preface is signed "A Venerable Scholar of the Golden Mean" (Zhezhong Wang 折中翁) and the postscript is signed "A Venerable Gentleman Who Has Learned Something New" (Zhixin Wang 知新翁).[72]

While much of Prémare's argument in support of Figurism was historical, another part was philological. This philological basis involved an analysis of the Chinese script which was influenced by Liu Ning. In his *Liushu shiyi*, Prémare used a question-and-answer form of dialogue which explored the *Classic of Changes*. The opening question in the essay asks what is the meaning of the "Great Appendix" of the *Changes* (*Yi dachuan* 易大傳).[73] The scholar answers that in earliest antiquity the knotting of ropes was used to keep records in governing. In later ages, sages changed from knots to using lines cut into bamboo or wood (*shu qi* 書契). The meaning contained in these lines was not a function of human invention, but rather was said to be inherent in the lines themselves. Prémare began by referring to the *Guai* 夬 hexagram (hexagram number 43 out of 64). In this hexagram, the inner (lower) part consists of the trigram *Qian* 乾 (three unbroken lines) which means Heaven while the outer (upper) part consisted of the trigram *Dui* 兌 (two unbroken lines topped by a broken line) which means speech. These carved lines on bamboo or wood were said to represent the words of Heaven.

In answer to the question of who created these lines on bamboo or wood, the scholar answered that no one knew. Some said it was a historical emperor, others said Fu Xi, others said Cang Jie 倉頡, others said an official of the Yellow Emperor, but no one really knew. As to the origin of the lines on bamboo or wood, Prémare cited the historian Luo Bi to say that they emerged from the cosmological Yellow River Chart and the Luo River Diagram (*Hetu Luoshu* 河圖落書) (see figures 3.2 and 3.3).[74] This was the famous diagram in which the nonary chart appeared on the back of a horse wading in the Yellow River (*Hetu*) and another nonary diagram appeared on a tortoise shell emerging from the Yellow River (*Luoshu*). Since words were given to the ancient kings by Heavenly Spirits or Angels (*Tianshen* 天神), this indicated that words were not human inventions, but rather reflected an inherent meaning.

Prémare said that the differences in the styles of script in which the Chinese characters were written—the Tadpole Script (*ketou* 科头), Ancient Script (*gu wen* 古文), Large and Small Seal Script (*da xiao yuan* 大小篆) and the Official Script (*liwen* 隸文)—were insignificant. However, what was significant were the divisions into the Six Kinds of Characters. These six divisions were first defined in the preface to Xu Shen's *Shuowen jiezi* dictionary.[75] They are described as: (1) indicative or self-explanatory (*zhishi* 指事); (2) pictorial (*xiangxing* 像形); (3) phonetic (*xingsheng* 形聲); (4) suggestive compounds (*huiyi* 會意); (5) deflective (*zhuanzhu* 轉注); and (6) adoptive (*jiajie* 假借).[76]

In the postscript, Prémare introduced a Figurist interpretation of the *Classic of Changes* using the lines of the early script found in the Eight Trigrams (*Bagua* 八卦) and the Great Appendix (*Xizi* 繫紫).[77] He explained the trigram of three unbroken lines in Trinitarian terms with one line representing the Father (*Fu* 父), two lines representing the Son (*Zi* 子), and three lines representing the Holy Spirit (*Shengshen* 聖神). He applied the term *shengren* 聖人 to Jesus (*Shengren Yesu* 聖人耶穌), altering the traditional literati meaning of the term *shengren* from "sage," to "holy man," or "saint."[78] In the *Vestigia*, Prémare later elaborated at length on the importance of this reinterpretation of this term *shengren* from sage to saint. The philological theories would provide a basis for the fundamental Figurist claim that the ancient Chinese texts anticipated Revelation. The claim would be derived from the nature of the characters themselves. Although this nature had been lost by later Chinese interpreters, Prémare believed that the anticipation of Revelation was contained in the nature of the characters in the ancient Chinese texts.[79] The *Liushu shiyi* was never printed. Prémare claimed he could not obtain the needed approbation due to the lack of suitable revisers.[80] However, the fact is that the Figurist interpretation of the *Changes* probably would have prohibited its publication. Consequently, he circulated several copies to scholars like Fourmont.

Although Prémare's *Notitia Linguae Sinicae* was derived from his *Liushu shiyi*, the Figurist elements were deleted. Prémare sent copies of the *Notitia Linguae Sinicae* manuscript to Fourmont and others during his lifetime, but the work was not published until a century later, using a copy made by the French Sinologist Stanislas Julien.[81] The *Notitia Linguae Sinicae* was edited by Elijah Coleman Bridgman and published by the Protestant Anglo-Chinese College in Malacca in 1831. The work is sometimes mistakenly called a Chinese grammar, but it is really a comprehensive textbook of the Chinese language and literature.[82] Because the Figurist theories underlying the work were omitted, it qualified as one of those scholarly works that Gaubil had wished the Figurists had focused on instead of their radical theories.

The first part of the *Notitia Linguae Sinica* deals with colloquial Chinese and the second part turns to classical Chinese, drawing examples from Yuan drama and popular novels. Instead of developing grammatical categories, Prémare used quotations from Chinese texts to make his point. He relied on texts rather than spoken Chinese because in his base in Jiangxi province the Gan 贛 dialect, which differed from the Mandarin dialects of northern China, predominated. Instead of developing grammatical categories, he used quotations from Chinese texts to make his point. Prémare complained that many missionaries did not bother to learn the correct tones of Chinese words.[83] He believed that proficiency in Chinese was best achieved by leaving Macau as soon as possible after arrival and going into the interior of China where the missionary would hear only Chinese spoken.

IDENTIFYING PRÉMARE'S CHINESE COLLABORATORS

Prémare's *Rujiao shiyi* 儒教實義 (The True Meaning of the Literati Teaching) reflects views that are so distinctive of Chinese literati that it was probably composed with the assistance of Chinese collaborators or at least writings by Chinese literati.[84] In 1707 Prémare wrote to Bouvet that his Chinese library had attracted a number of Chinese literati and that he had discussed his interpretations of Chinese literature in his meetings with them.[85] The *Rujiao Shiyi* is a 15,000 character dialogue in Chinese between a "Student from Afar" (*yuan sheng* 遠生) and a "Pure-minded Literatus" (*chun Ru* 醇儒). The latter was a pseudonym or perhaps even a composite creation drawn from literati Prémare knew. He may even have drawn from works by Christian literati because there are striking similarities in certain passages to works by the literati converts Zhang Xingyao (1633–after 1715) and Shang Huqing (ca.

1619–after 1698). In the dialogue, the student poses brief questions about complex topics and the literatus responds at length. The author of the work is identified as Venerable Master Wen (Wen Guzi 溫古子), which is a pseudonym for Prémare, possibly based on the site Wenzhou 溫州 where he took his great vows in 1701.

Although it was customary in their Chinese works for a Jesuit to include a preface or postscript by a Chinese scholar, their absence in *Rujiao shiyi* is notable. The high standards of literary Chinese usually required China missionaries to seek assistance from literati collaborators to acquire suitable sources and to achieve a respectable level of literary polish in their compositions. Early China Jesuits, such as Matteo Ricci, had found it useful for the promotion of Christianity in China to seek out eminent Chinese collaborators and to identify them through their prefaces. But Ricci was far more socially-attuned than Prémare and the cultural and social climate in China in 1600 had been far more open to foreigners and to unorthodox philosophies than a century later when Prémare worked.

The political dynamics of a protracted military conquest made the Manchu conquerors more culturally conservative in the Qing than the native Han emperors had been in the earlier Ming dynasty. The Manchus were more likely to prefer the orthodox Song Neo-Confucian interpreters of the Classics than the creative and challenging interpreters of the late Ming Literati. And yet the Manchus were not Han Chinese. They continued to use their own language along with Chinese. Jesuit missionaries who worked at the Beijing court were obliged to learn Manchu as well as Chinese and they found Manchu easier to learn. All of this seems to have contributed to a more receptive atmosphere toward Christianity during the reigns of the Shunzhi (1644–1661) and Kangxi (1662–1722) emperors. Jesuits like Adam Schall had a very close relationship with the Shunzhi emperor and Bouvet was favored by the Kangxi emperor. Bouvet cultivated contacts with Chinese scholar-officials in Beijing and found receptive minds for his Figurist interpretation of Chinese antiquity. The personality differences of individual missionaries as well as the persuasiveness of their ideas seem to have played an important role in these contacts with Chinese.

On October 25, 1707, at his mission station in Jianchang, Prémare wrote to the Jesuit Father Grimond in Paris, expressing how he and others were attempting to save the China mission from ruin.[86] The Rites Controversy inspired a wave of creative thinking in Prémare. He was driven by the conviction that if China were converted to Christianity, no other nation on earth could rival it. In the process of assembling a fine collection of Chinese books, he seems to have generated contacts with several Chinese scholars who provided valuable information and discussions for his edification. These contacts appear to have played a role in his composition of the *Rujiao Shiyi*.

Prémare's letter of October 25, 1707, to Fr. Grimond referred to the *Rujiao* (Literati Teaching or Confucianism) and indicated his early interest in that teaching.[87] Prémare's *Rujiao Shiyi* was written around the time he was in Beijing. The work's reference to the *Zhouyi zhezhong* 周易折中 (Annotations to the Book of Changes) by Li Guangdi 李光地(1642–1718) which was printed at Beijing in 1715, indicates that it was composed in 1715 or soon afterwards.[88] Bouvet's Figurist numerology appears to have had some influence on this prominent Grand Secretary Li Guangdi.[89] There was some interaction between them in the composition of Li's *Zhouyi zhezhong*.[90] After four years in Beijing (1714–1717) Prémare returned to the remote small cities in Jiangxi province, adding Jiujiang 九江 as one of his mission stations. His return from Beijing marked a significant shift in his scholarship.

The *Rujiao shiyi* is devoid of Figurism and appears to have been written before Prémare did his most intensive research and writing in the *Vestigia*. Its content is more akin to the accommodationism of early China Jesuits like Ricci. The author presents a fairly orthodox explanation of the Confucian tradition as it was viewed in the early eighteenth century. This tradition viewed the Literati Teaching as going into decline after the death of Confucius. In this work Prémare criticized Buddhism and Daoism, in contrast to his Figurist theories which are often positive on Daoism. In the dialogue, the "Pure-minded Literatus" does not dispute the historical basis of the first three dynasties, as Prémare does in the *Vestigia*. Some Song literati are criticized, but the teaching of Zhu Xi is quoted in favorable ways. Prémare's attitude toward Zhu Xi was mixed: sometimes he quoted Zhu Xi as an authoritative figure who contributed to his argument, but at other times, Prémare claimed that the traditional Transmission of the Dao (*Daotong* 道通) through the Song Neo-Confucians and Zhu Xi was flawed. These claims all fell within the parameters of orthodox Confucian debate.

The *Rujiao Shiyi* dialogue may have been based on questions and answers that Prémare (the "Student from Afar") had posed to a literatus (the "Pure-minded Literatus") either orally or in correspondence. This question-and-answer form of composition was as typical of Chinese essays as Socratic dialogues were typical of Greek philosophy. The "Pure-minded Literatus" might have been based on Liu Ning 劉凝 (*Erzhi* 二至). Liu Ning and Prémare seemed to have shared a preference for scholarly isolation. The landscape painting image of a hermit wandering alone on a mountain path was a widespread traditional meme that comes to mind here. Literati often preferred to communicate in writing or with a poem rather than make a personal visit. It is likely that Prémare and Liu had contact, if not in person, then by correspondence prior to Liu's death. It is possible that Prémare published Liu's answers to questions Prémare would pose in the *Rujiao Shiyi* after Liu's death. It is also possible that other un-named literati had supplied answers to Prémare's questions and that the "Pure-minded Literatus" represents a composite figure. But the timing of the appearance of this dialogue remains unexplained.

NOTES

1. Johannes Beckmann, SMB, "Die katholischen Missionare und der Taoismus von 16. Jahrhundert bis zur Gegenwart," *Neue Zeitschrift für Missionswissenschaft* 26 (1970): 11–12.

2. *Vestigia*, f. 45r-v; *Vestiges*, p. 92–94.

3. Witek, p. 219 and Claudia von Collani, Harald Holz, and Konrad Wegmann, *Uroffenbarung und Daoismus: Jesuite Missionshermeneutik des Daoismus* (Bochum: Europäischer Universitätsverlag, 2008) p. 31–33.

4. "Textus undecim ex libro *Tao* 道 *Te* 德 *Kim* 經 excerpti, quibus probatur SS.mae Trinitatis et Dei incarnati mysteria Sinicae genti olim nota fuisse." Collani, Holz, and Wegmann, p. 92–93.

5. Collani, Holz, and Wegmann, p. 31.

6. Jean-Pierre Abel Rémusat, *Mémoire sur la vie et les opinions de Lao-tseu, philosophe chinois du Vie siècle avant notre ère*. *Academie des inscriptions et belles-lettres. Mémoires.* 7 (1824): 1–54.

7. Pan Feng-chuan 潘鳳娟 《不可譯, 不可道之名：雷慕沙與<道德經>翻譯》 中央大學人文學報 61 (2016.04): p. 72–73.

8. Riccardo Fracasso, "*Shanhaijing*" in *Early Chinese Texts: a Bibliographical Guide*. Ed. Michael Loewe (Berkeley: Institute of East Asian Studies, 1993), p. 357–67.

9. Anne Birrell, tr., *The Classic of Mountains and Seas* (London: Penguin, 1999), p xv.

10. *Shanhaijing jiaozhu* 山海經校注, Yuan Ke, ed. (Shanghai: Shanghai guji, 1930; reprinted 1986), p. 47, and *Vestigia*, f. 64r–66v; *Vestiges*, p. 129–33.

11. Anne Birrell, *Chinese Myths* (Austin: University of Texas Press, 2000), p. 59.

12. Joseph Needham, *Science and Civilisation in China*. Volume 3. *Mathematics and the Sciences of the Heavens and the Earth*. (Cambridge, UK: Cambridge University Press, 1959), p. 565–68.

13. *Shanhaijing*, p. 21, 27, and 41 and *Vestigia*, p. 65a-b; *Vestiges*, p. 132.

14. *Shanhaijing*, p. 40, 47, and 51.

15. *Shanhaijing*, p. 31, 37, and 47.

16. *Shanhaijing*, p. 59.

17. *Shanhaijing*, p. 48.

18. *Shanhailing*, p. 40.

19. *Vestigia*, f. 66r–v; *Vestiges*, p. 133.

20. *Shanhaijing*, p. 47; *Vestigia* p. 67a–b; *Vestiges*, p. 134.

21. *Shanhaijing*, p. 294

22. *Shanhaijing*, p. 298. Birrell, p. 140, translates *kaiming shou* as "Openbright animal."

23. Edward L. Shaughnessy, "*Shang shu (Shu ching)*," in *Early Chinese Texts.* Ed. Michael Lowe, p. 376–78 [176–389]

24. *Shujing*, book *Yi Xun*. In Ruan Yuan 阮元, Shisan jing zhu shu 十三經注疏 (Notes and commentary on the Thirteen Classics). Originally published in 1806. 2 vols. (Beijing: Zhonghua Shuju Chuban, 1980) p. 163上. Cf. James Legge, trans. *The Chinese Classics.* 5 vols. (Oxford: Oxford University Press, 1893) IV.ii.2 (p. 193–94).

25. *Vestigia*, f. 68r–70v; *Vestiges*, p. 136–39.

26. Zhuangzi, *Complete Works*, Burton Watson, tr. (New York: Columbia University Press, 2013), p. 59.

27. James Legge, tr., *The I Ching.* in *Sacred Books of the East.* Ed. Max Müller (Oxford: Clarendon Press, 1899) vol. XVI, p. 58. Cf. Z. D. Sung, *The Text of the Yi King* (Shanghai: The China Modern Education Company, 1935.), p. 2.

28. *Vestigia*, f. 71r–v; *Vestiges*, p. 142.

29. Legge, *I Ching*, p. 135.

30. *Vestigia*, f. 71r–v; *Vestiges*, p. 143.

31. *Shanhaijing*, 6/198, 15/372, and 18/466–68.

32. Anne Birrell, *Chinese Myths*, p. 35 and Yuan Ke, *Dragons and Dynasties—An Introduction to Chinese Mythology*. Ed. And tr. Kim Echlin & Nie Zhixiong (London: Penguin, 1993), p. 74–79.

33. *Vestigia*, f. 72r–73r; *Vestiges*, p. 144–45.

34. *Vestigia*, f. 74r–v; *Vestiges*, p. 146.

35. Prémare, "*Discours Preliminaire, ou recherches sur les temps antérieurs a ceux don't parle le Chou-king, and sur la mythologie chinoise*," p. cxi.

36. Yuan, p. 9–13.

37. Prémare, "Discours Prelminiaire," p. cxiii.

38. *Shujing*, Da Yu mo, 136 above. Cf. Legge II.ii.14, p. 60–61.

39. Bouvet, letter of August 30 1697, in Henri Bernard-Maitre, *Sagesse Chinoise et Phiosophie Chrétienne* (Paris: Cathasia, 1935), p. 145–46.

40. Witek, *Controversial Ideas*, p. 149–50.

41. Witek, *Controversial Ideas*, p. 39–40.

42. Witek, *Controversial Ideas*, p. 268.

43. Ann Birrell, *Chinese Myths*, p. 33–35.

44. *Vestigia*, p. 90r–91v; *Vestiges*, p. 167–68.

45. Cf. the description of Chiyou (Ch'ih Yu) in Anne Birrell, *Chinese Mythology: an Introduction* (Baltimore: Johns Hopkins University Press, 1993), p. 50–53.

46. *Vestigia*, f. 74r–75v; *Vestiges*, p. 146–47.

47. *Shujing*, lü, 247下. Cf. translation of Legge, V.xxvii.2, p. 590.

48. Henderson, p. 82–87.

49. *Vestigia*, p. 75r–76v; *Vestiges*, p. 147.

50. *Shanhaijing* 14/359–60.

51. *Vestigia*, f. 76r–v; *Vestiges*, p. 148–49.

52. *Vestigia*, p. 77r–v; *Vestiges*, p. 150.

53. Cf. the translations of *Shijing* Mao 48 in Legge, I.iv.iv (p. 78–80) and Arthur Waley, *Books of Songs* (New York: Grove Press, 1937) ode 23, p. 34.

54. Yuan Ke, *Dragons and Dynasties: An Introduction to Chinese Mythology*, p. 9–12.

55. Liu Shu (Daoyuan), *Zizhi tongjian waiji*, 資治通鑑外紀 (Addition Chronicle to the *Comprehensive Mirror for Aid in Government*) 1078, cited in *Vestigia*, f. 77(3) r–78v; *Vestiges*, p. 152.

56. *Shanhaijing* 8/233; *Vestigia*, f. 79r–v; and *Vestiges*, p. 154.

57. Charles Le Blanc, "Huai nan tzu." In *Early Chinese Texts*. Ed. Michael Loewe. p. 189.

58. *Vestigia*, f. 81r–v; *Vestiges*, p. 156.

59. Zhuangzi, *Jiaozheng Zhuangze jishi* 校正莊子集釋 。Qing Guoqing 清郭慶 collator. 2 vols. (Taipei: World Publishers, 1971) chapter 10, page 359. Cf. Burton Watson, tr., *Complete Works of Zhuangzi* (New York: Columbia University Press, 2013), p. 73.

60. Zhuangzi, *Jiaozheng Zhuangze jishi*, ch. 7, p. 309. Cf. Burton Watson, tr., *Complete Works of Zhuangzi*, p. 59.

61. *Vestigia*, f. 81r–82a-v; *Vestiges*, p. 158.

62. *Vestigia*, p. 85r-86v; *Vestiges*, p. 161.

63. Herbert A. Giles, *Chinese Biographical Dictionary* (1898), p. 704–5.

64. *Vestigia*, p. 82r–87v; *Vestiges*, p. 158–63.

65. The five *Shijing* odes are Mao #218, #304, #264, #188, and #65.

66. The two omitted hexagrams were hexagram number 12 *pi* 否 and hexagram number 18 *gu* 蠱. *Vestigia*, f. 86r–87r; *Vestiges*, p. 163.

67. Legge, *Shujing*, II.ii.III.12 (p. 39–40) claims that San Miao was the name of a country.

68. *Shujing*, Da, 137above. Cf. Legge, II.ii.20 (p. 64).

69. *Vestigia*, f. 87r–88v; *Vestiges*, p. 163–65.

70. Wenguzi [Joseph de Prémare], *Liushu shiyi*. Xujiahui Library. 31 double sheets. There are also two copies of this work in the Biblioteca Vaticana Apostolica, Borgia Cinese 357.10 & Borgia Cinese, 443.3. There are also two copies in the Bibliothèque Nationale France copied in different handwriting. Pfister, p. 522, refers to this work under the title *Liu shu xi yi* 六書析義.

71. Lundbæk, p. 143.

72. The named authors of the preface and postscript were probably fictional, a common practice among Chinese literati.

73. Wenguzi [Prémare], *Liushu shiyi*, p. 1a.

74. Wenguzi [Prémare], *Liushu shiyi*, p. 1b.

75. Xu Shen 許慎, compiler. *Shuowen jiezi duanzhu* 說文解字段注. Annotated by Duan Yucai 段玉裁. (Taipei: Yiwen Yinshuguan , 1967) preface, p.1b.

76. Cf. the translations of the Six Kinds of Characters in Herbert A. Giles, *A Chinese-English Dictionary*. 2nd ed. (Shanghai, 1912) p. 911 and Lundbæk, *Joseph de Prémare*, p 148.

77. Prémare, *Liushu shiyi*, postscript, p. 1b–2a.

78. Prémare, *Liushu shiyi*, postscript, p. 2b.

79. Chen Xinyu, p. 87–88.
80. Prémare letter to Fourmont of August 29, 1731. Lundbæk, p. 146.
81. Louis Pfister, SJ, *Notices Biographiques et Bibliographiques sur les Jésuites de l'ancienne mission de Chine 1552–1773* (Shanghai: Imprimerie de la Mission Catholique, 1932), p. 523.
82. For a detailed summary of the contents of the *Notitia Linguae Sinicae*, see Lundbæk, p. 64–102.
83. Lundbæk, p. 73, and 75.
84. The manuscript of the *Rujiao shiyi* is preserved in the Biblioteca Apostolica Vaticana. Borgia Cinese 316 (20). A facsimile reproduction is found in *Tianzhujiao Dongzhuan wenxian xubian* 天主教儒教東傳續編. Ed. Wu Xiangxiang 吳相湘. 3 vols. (Taipei: Student Bookstore, 1966) III, 1333–411.
85. Prémare to Bouvet (?), December 26, 1707, Bibliotheca Apostolica Vaticana, *Borgia latino 565*, 423 v, cited in Witek, p. 152–53.
86. Prémare to Fr. Grimond, October 25, 107, BNF, Ms. Lat. Nouv. Acq. 156, f. 8–21v.
87. Prémare to Fr. Grimond, October 25, 107, BNF, Ms. Lat. Nouv. Acq. 156, f. 13.
88. Prémare [Wen Guzi], *Rujiao shiyu*, p. 36a (1405).
89. Witek, *Controversial Ideas*, p. 204–6.
90. Han Qi, "Kexue yu zongjian," p. 422–25.

Chapter Five

Earth to Earth, Dust to Dust

Earth is the last of the Five Elements

THE ISOLATED SCHOLAR-PRIEST

The Figurists were driven by creative intellects that made them outliers among China Jesuits. They were not apostates who questioned the fundamentals of their faith, but their ideas challenged the limits of intellectual and religious orthodoxy. Prémare had devoted over half of his life to the China mission, to studying difficult Chinese texts and developing remarkable new theories about China's antiquity. But his creativity and intellectual integrity came at great personal cost and led to the suppression of manuscripts that he had toiled on in the hope that they would save the mission from destruction.

While most Jesuits were intellectual and scholarly, not all of them were gregarious. Prémare was not and chose to live an isolated mission existence in remote areas, combining scholarship with evangelism. But the fact that we know relatively little about his evangelism indicates that he was probably more inclined toward scholarship, which he viewed as a variant form of evangelism. In the manner typical of China Jesuits at that time, he was probably freed to do research and carry on an extensive correspondence by having the assistance of a literate assistant (*xianggong*) who could instruct the neophytes and prepare them for baptism.[1] The Society of Jesus was not a monastic order. It was organized by Ignatius of Loyola in the sixteenth-century to serve Christ by sending its members out into the world. They were trained for service in remote lands by being educated in ways that anticipated the technical needs of the modern world. Some Jesuits, like Adam Schall, came from prominent families and others, like Prémare, from obscure backgrounds, but all had demonstrated an intellectual aptitude as well as spiritual discipline and were highly educated.

Jesuits were given more training than other religious orders in specialized skills (mathematics, natural sciences, law, medicine, and the humanities), in addition to theology. Some of them used their education to achieve positions of importance with access to prominent people and hopefully to make conversions of the powerful, wealthy, and sophisticated. Matteo Ricci, Adam Schall, and Joachim Bouvet were notable examples of this type, but they were not characteristic of all Jesuits. Prémare was different and chose the relatively withdrawn life of a scholar. He was not a hermit, but he preferred the solitude of reading Chinese books or communicating through correspondence to social interaction. He became in many ways the model of a traditional Chinese hermit-scholar. He attempted to apply what he had learned from years of study of Chinese books to advance the true faith in China.

Prémare was prolific in his scholarship. However, his works are difficult to categorize because he wrote them for different audiences. Some of his works sought "to proclaim the Gospel to the Literati of China" (*d'annoncer Evangile aux Lettrés de Chine*), some aimed at popular topics, others were heavily focused on scholarly subjects, and still others were addressed solely to Europeans.[2] His *Liushu shiyi* which dealt with the six classes of Chinese characters was aimed at a Chinese audience while his Latin adaptation of that work, *Notitia Linguae Sinicae*, was aimed at European scholars. His *Vestigia* was a bilingual work with a Latin text and extensive quotations in Chinese. This meant that it was aimed at an extremely select readership even though Prémare viewed it as his most important work. His *Rujiao shiyi* was addressed to Chinese literati. His *Lettre sur le monothéisme de Chinois* was aimed at European philosophes. His drama *Orphan of Zhao* was aimed at a popular audience of theatre-going Europeans.

The atmosphere of that time contributed to Prémare's silence in naming his Chinese collaborators. His reticence is partly attributable to the turmoil Christianity was then undergoing in China. Since the beginning of the mission in 1579, there had been underlying disputes over allowing converts to practice traditional ancestral rites as well as differences about the appropriate terminology to be used for the name of God. These differences broke into open conflict with the embassy of the papal legate Tournon in 1705–1710. The critics of Jesuit accommodationism were highly sensitive to any Chinese influence in matters of theology. This turmoil placed the China Jesuits in a vise, squeezed between conflicting pressures from the Kangxi emperor in Beijing and the papal authorities in Rome. The fate of the mission tottered. Although Tournon had offended the Kangxi emperor, imperial hostility did not peak until the accession of the Yongzheng emperor who exiled most of the missionaries to the southern fringe of China.

GUANGZHOU (CANTON), CITY OF EXILE

The 1724 exile was not the first expulsion of the missionaries to Guangzhou. They had previously been expelled in 1665 in a manner that had many parallels to the later expulsion. The missionaries' 1665 exile had been caused by the effort of disgruntled Muslim members of the Bureau of Astronomy to discredit the Jesuit director of the Bureau, Fr. Adam Schall. The campaign was led by the official Yang Guangxian 楊光先 who in 1664 accused Schall of choosing an inauspicious day in 1658 for the burial of an infant prince.³ He claimed that Schall had acted in order to cast a malign spell on the Empress Xiaoxian 孝獻皇后 and the Shunzhi emperor, which led to their premature deaths in 1660 and 1661. The shamanistically-minded Manchus tended to give credence to such accusations.

The regents then running the government on behalf of the child Kangxi emperor, sentenced Schall and several Chinese astronomers to a lingering death. Although Schall and the missionaries were saved by the occurrence of an earthquake, five Chinese astronomers were executed. Instead of being flogged and exiled, Schall, who had been paralyzed by a stroke, as well as Jesuits Ferdinand Verbiest, Gabriel de Magalhães and Ludovico Buglio were allowed to remain at the Beijing court. All other Christian missionaries were banished along with thirty servants to Guangzhou.⁴ These twenty-five priests included nineteen Jesuits, four Dominicans and one Franciscan. They included the benign Franciscan Antonio Caballero, OFM (Li Andang 利安當) (1602–1669) and the contentious Dominican Friar Domingo Fernández de Navarrete, OP (Min Mingwo 閔明我) (1618–1689) who Schall described as "a trouble-maker with long ears, and a longer tongue."⁵ Navarrete, in turn, blamed Schall for their expulsion by saying "the first Adam got us driven out of Paradise, and this second one, out of China."

These exiles arrived in Guangzhou in March 1666 where they were confined to the cramped Jesuit residence, and subjected to government roll-calls as well as strict surveillance. In 1667 the young Kangxi emperor discharged the regents and took control of the government. He dismissed Yang Guangxian for incompetence and named Verbiest associate-director of the Bureau of Astronomy. Gradually, the restrictions in Guangzhou were eased and in 1668 the priests were allowed to venture outside of the residence. Discouraging news came in 1669 when they were initially told they would not be allowed to return to their mission stations in China. At first they were given the option of going only to Macau, but eventually they were allowed to return to the interior of China.

One of the more notable events of this Guangzhou confinement was a five-week conference (December 1667–January 1668) to debate and resolve controversial theological issues, including the Chinese rites. There were twenty-three participants—one Franciscan, three Dominicans, and nineteen Jesuits.[6] A committee consisting of the Franciscan Caballero, the Dominican Navarrete, and the Jesuit Inácio da Costa were elected to compose a refutation to Yang Guanxian's accusations.[7] However, the differences between the Jesuits and the mendicants could not be overcome and there was an inability on all sides to compromise. Nationalistic differences also surfaced, particularly in the Portuguese Jesuit António Gouvea whose animosity toward Spaniards like Navarrete was intense.[8] When Navarrete discovered the 1623–24 treatise of the Jesuit Father Niccolò Longobardo, SJ (1565–1655) which disagreed with Ricci's accommodating interpretation of Chinese culture, he found reason to become even more entrenched in his opposition.[9] The situation was aggravated by the claustrophobic and oppressive circumstances of so many priests being confined to such a small house. A melancholic mood of depression pervaded the house. Theological differences became personal differences as the Jesuits mocked Navarrete for his poor command of Latin and his abrasive personality.[10] Navarrete's sense of paranoia grew along with the intensity of his invective toward the Jesuits.

A half-century later, the missionaries' second confinement in Guangzhou was less contentious, less constructive and less hopeful. It was marked by dismay and an impending sense of doom. It was constricted by accusations of disobedience and heresy from Rome along with the emperor's criticism of Christianity from Beijing. This claustrophobic atmosphere increased Prémare's sense of isolation, making him more cautious about circulating his works and implicating Chinese collaborators by name. His deteriorating health can be seen as a metaphor for the state of the China mission.

PRÉMARE'S INTERPRETATION OF THE NEO-CONFUCIAN TERM *TAIJI* (GREAT ULTIMATE)

Most Jesuit accommodationists were hostile to both Daoism and Neo-Confucianism. Prémare, by contrast, found a basis for agreement with both Daoism and Neo-Confucianism. In 1725 he devoted a section of his *Vestigia* to the Neo-Confucian term *Taiji* which he explained in terms of Figurism. He referred to *Taiji* as the "great extreme, great terminus, the highest point or culmination" (*magnum extremum, magnum terminum, non plus ultra*).[11] He said that *Taiji* was usually joined with *yin* 陰 and *yang* 陽 in a way that misled the most famous Chinese philosophers into a serious error, an error that he himself had shared for a long time. They followed Zhu Xi who said *Taiji* was "reason" (*ratio*) (*Dao* 道) which surpassed every physical dimension in such a way that it transcended matter. *Yin* and *yang* were said to be material and constituted the seeds that contained reason (*ratio*) (*Taiji shi li; Yin yang shi qi* 太極是理。陰陽是器。). He further cited Zhu Xi to say "it is said in the *Classic of Changes* that *yin* and *yang* are reason (*ratio*), better yet that *yin* and *yang* are the inscrutable spirit" (*Yi yin yi yang zhi wei dao; yin yang bu ce zhi wei shen.* 一陰一陽之謂道。陰陽不測之謂神。).

Prémare claimed that the Chinese struggled to explain the triune unity of *Taiji*, *yin*, and *yang* because they had lost the original meaning of their ancient texts. He said they had retained the notion of a single God, but had lost the meaning of a triune God which remained only as a vestige in these texts.[12] He interpreted the whole (*yang*) and broken (*yin*) lines of the hexagrams of the *Classic of Changes* by assigning three dots to the whole line and two dots to the broken line. When these were added to the single point, symbolizing the source from which *Taiji* emerged, a three-lined figure was generated with the bottom line of three dots, a middle line of two dots and a top line of one dot. Prémare interpreted this figure as representing an equilateral triangle which was a rough representation of the entire *Taiji* as well as one of the hieroglyphs of the Most Holy Trinity.[13] He hastened to add that these were symbolical representations. With the exception of Zhou Dunyi's diagram (see figure 5.1), the Chinese usually did not attempt to illustrate *Taiji*. It was regarded as an essentially ideational and spiritual form, without body or shape, although it manifested itself in physical form. However, Prémare quoted a common Chinese expression to argue that *Taiji* was unified and contained within itself three (persons) *Taiji han san wei yi* 太極含三為一.

The Song philosopher Zhou Dunyi (Lianxi) 周敦頤 （濂溪）(1017–1073) was the founding figure of Song Neo-Confucianism. His "Explanation of the Diagram of the Supreme Ultimate" (*Taiji tushuo* 太極圖說) comprised the opening chapter in the well-known Neo-Confucian anthology, *Xingli jingyi* 性理精義 (1717) (see figure 5.1). The very first statement in Zhou Dunyi's essay explained that the accompanying diagram illustrated "*Wuji er Taiji*" 無極而太極 (Ultimate Nothingness and yet the Great Ultimate).[14] Prémare translated this phrase as "without limit and yet at the same time, the great limit" (*sine termino et inde magnus terminus*).[15]

Zhu Xi claimed that Zhou Dunyi had inserted the particle *er* 而 between *Wuji* and *Taiji* because he did not wish to prioritize one over the other, however Prémare cited the dissent of the Yuan dynasty literatus Wang Shen 王紳 who had written a commentary on the *Classic of Changes*. Wang argued that the particle *er* indicated, not that *Taiji* existed simultaneously with *Wuji*, but that the generating of *Taiji* followed *Wuji* in time. Prémare found Wang Shen's commentary helpful, first, because it offered an argument to prove that Zhu Xi was not, contrary to the beliefs of certain "minor savants" (*contra quosdam sciolos*), an atheist. Secondly, and what was of even greater importance for Prémare, Wang Shen furnished an argument that demonstrated to the Chinese that the visible world had a beginning, and had been made by God who is eternal and unlimited reason (*ratio*). This would shift the *Taiji* from being part of a cyclical process of creation to the *ex nihilo* form of creation found in the book of Genesis. Prémare believed this was confirmed by a passage from the Daoist work Zhuangzi which he translates as: "Reason [*ratione*, i.e., *Dao*] existed a long time before *Taiji* existed." As was his practice, he included the Chinese characters: *Dao zai Taiji zhi xian.* 道在太極之先.[16] The term *Taiji* appears only once in the *Zhuangzi*.[17] The noted translator Burton Watson translates the *Zhuangzi* passage in which this phrase appears as follows:

> Before Heaven and earth existed, [the Way] was there, firm from ancient times. It gave spirituality to the spirits and to God; it gave birth to Heaven and to earth. It exists beyond the highest point [*zai Taiji zhi xian*], and yet you cannot call it lofty; it exists beneath the limit of the six directions, and yet you cannot call it deep. It was born before Heaven and earth, and yet you cannot say it has been there for long; it is earlier than the earliest time, and yet you cannot call it old.[18]

Prémare also quoted from the Neo-Confucian cosmologist Shao Yong 邵雍 (Kangjie 康節) (1011–1077) and, even more forcefully, his son Shao Bowen 邵伯溫 (1057–1134) in what appears to be a translation of the same passage from the *Zhuangzi*:

> Taiji existed before the heaven and the earth and nevertheless has nothing before it. It will exist after the heaven and the earth, and nevertheless has nothing afterward. It is placed at the end of the heaven and the earth, and itself has no end. It gives existence to heaven and earth, and itself has no beginning.[19]

LETTRE SUR LE MONOTHÉISME DE CHINOIS

Figurism is largely absent from Prémare's presentation of Neo-Confucian philosophy in his letter on the monotheism of the Chinese of 1728. Neither the presentation of Chinese philosophy in *Rujiao shiyi* nor the *Lettre sur le monothéisme de Chinois* contains any direct elaboration of Figurism. In fact, the *Rujiao shiyi* and the *Lettre sur le monothéisme de Chinois* seem like collateral pieces. The first was written for a Chinese audience. The second was written for a European audience to counter a misinterpretation promoted by certain philosophes of the European Enlightenment.

Prémare's motive for writing the *Lettre sur le monothéisme de Chinois* was to combat the "libertines of Europe" (i.e. philosophes of the Enlightenment) who argued that "atheism is therefore not at all such a detestable monster, since the wisest and most ancient nation in the world makes a pubic profession [of it]."[20] In composing the essay, Prémare duplicated the same style of careful scholarship used in the *Vestigia* of including the Chinese characters for the numerous textual references.[21] However practical difficulties of reproducing the characters forced the editor of the published version, Pauthier, to eliminate many of these Chinese characters.

Prémare divided his essay into two parts. The first part examined the physical system of several modern Chinese (*quelques Chinois modernes*), although by "modern" he meant post-ancient and mainly from the eleventh and twelfth centuries of the Song dynasty. His aim was to rebut those unnamed "two or three missionaries" who believed that the physical system of the modern Chinese represented Spinozism (pantheism). He summarized their argument in the following way:

> Zhu Xi and his disciples say of *Taiji* 太極 [Supreme Ultimate] all that the ancient *Jing* have said of *Tian* [Heaven], of *Shangdi* [Lord-Above], etc. But it is clear that *Taiji* is none other than the atheistic *Li* 理 of the Chinese. Therefore *Tian, Shangdi*, etc. are likewise only the atheistic *Li* of the Chinese.[22]

Matteo Ricci's accommodation approach to introducing Christianity in China was first elucidated in his *Tianzhu shiyi* 天主實義 (The True Meaning of the Lord of Heaven) (1603) which took the form of a dialogue between a "Chinese scholar" (Zhongshi 中士) and a "Western scholar" (Xishi 西士).[23] The Chinese scholar represented a Confucian literatus and the Western scholar was the voice of Ricci. The prefaces by Feng Yingjing 馮應京 (1601) and Li Zhizao 利之澡 (1607) and the epilogue by Wang Ruchun 汪汝淳 (1607) reflected the collaborative nature of the work's composition and the attempt to create a Confucian-Christian synthesis by "repairing Confucianism and displacing Buddhism" (*bu Ru yi Fo* 補儒易佛).

Prémare's approach differed from Ricci's accommodationism in two important ways. First, although Ricci believed that the ancient Chinese texts revealed a Chinese belief in a monotheistic God—*Shangdi* (Lord-Above)—he did not believe (as Prémare did) that these ancient Chinese texts contained a knowledge of Revelation.[24] Secondly, Ricci was critical of the Neo-Confucian concepts *Taiji* and *li* and claimed that they were not present in Chinese antiquity.[25] Rather, he regarded Neo-Confucian concepts, like Buddhist concepts, as being products of intellectual degeneration. Prémare had a better understanding of both ancient Chinese and Neo-Confucian texts than Ricci and his interpretation was more nuanced. In the *Essai sur le monothéisme de Chinois*, Prémare interpreted *li* as *Raison* (Reason) by which he seems to mean an independent, free-standing, rational organizing principle. However, in the Chinese context, *li* almost always appears in conjunction with *qi* (material force).

In the second part of his essay on monotheism, Prémare cited from a number of documents in order to counter the widespread assumption that all modern literati after Zhu Xi were atheists.[26] He quoted passages from a large number of texts by these modern Chinese to show that they had the same notions of the divinity as monotheistic Europeans. First, he noted that not all modern literati followed Zhu Xi's philosophy. Although Zhu's commentaries were dominant in the school curriculum and in the academic path to a literary degree, leading literati often abandoned and refuted his works. Zhu Xi's influence on the interpretation of the Four Books was far greater than his influence on interpreting the *Jing* (Five Classics). As the Confucian scholar Tu Wei-ming noted, Zhu Xi reconstituted the Confucian tradition by selecting two chapters from the *Classic of Rites* (Liji 禮記)—the *Great Learning* and the *Doctrine of the Mean*—by writing commentaries on them, and then by grouping them together with the Confucian *Analects* and the *Mencius* to create the new category of the Four Books.[27] Zhu published his commentaries on the Four Books as the *Si zi* 四子 (The Four Masters) in 1190.[28] More commonly known as the *Sishu jizhu* 四書集注 (Collected Commentaries on the Four Books), his commentaries became the basic texts in the scholar-official examinations from 1313 to 1905. He wrote commentaries on three of the five Jing—the *Classic of Changes*, The *Classic of History*, and the *Classic of Odes*.[29] However, Zhu showed far less interest in the Five Classics than the Four Books. Moreover, his skeptical attitude toward the *Jing* undermined their traditional authority.[30] He was criticized for disparaging twenty-four of the 305 odes from the *Classic of Odes* as love songs and he was also criticized in the Kangxi emperor's commentaries in the *Zhouyi zhezhong* (Annotations to the Book of Changes) by Li Guangdi 李光地 (1642–1718).

THE EVOLUTION OF THE TERM *LI* (PRINCIPLE)

The term *li* 理 does not appear in most of the *Jing*, but it underwent a long evolution to culminate in the twelfth century as one of the primary terms of Neo-Confucianism.[31] The earliest occurrence appears to have been in the *Classic of Odes* (Mao number 210), where it means division of the fields or a pattern. It appears in a spurious part of the *Classic of History* (chapter 22) where it means harmonizing and ordering *yin* and *yang*. It appears several times in the commentary, but not in the text, of the *Classic of Changes*, where it means putting things in order, a pattern, and has the sense of principle. The Daoist book of *Zhuangzi* uses *li* thirty-eight times where it usually means pattern and putting things in order, but it is also coupled with *dao* for the first time to form *daoli* 道理 (the right way). The Neo-Confucian scholar Wing-tsit Chan believed Zhuangzi's coupling of *li* with *tian* (heaven) was very important because the idea of *tianli* as the Principle of Nature eventually became the ultimate expression of *li* in Neo-Confucianism.

In its evolution, *li* acquired a moral significance that became very prominent in the moral principle of *daoli*. The early meaning of *li* as "to put in order" was gradually superceded by the meaning of "principle."[32] In the Han dynasty (206 BC–AD 220), the meaning of *li* became associated with polishing jade (*zhiyu* 治玉) which involved determining the stone's pattern of venation in order to make a proper cut of the stone. In this context, the eminent Sinologist Peter Boodberg translated *li* as "infrastructure" as opposed to superstructure. The *Shuowen* dictionary defined *li* as polishing jade.[33]

In the period between the Han dynasty and the Song dynasty (960–1279), Buddhism played the major role in the development of *li*. The Buddhist monk Facang (643–712) 法藏 of the Huayan school is said to have been called by Empress Wu Zetian in 704 to explain the *Huayan Sutra*. To illustrate the complex teaching of the sutra, he pointed to a statue of a golden lion and used an explanation that he later incorporated into the famous *Essay on the Golden Lion* (*Jin shizi zhang* 金師子章). In this essay, the gold is used to represent *li* as principle or noumenon while the lion represents *shi* 事 or phenomena.[34] The Huayan school taught that reality was ultimately ideational and so the material force of *qi* was de-emphasized.

Confucianism revived the interest in *li* with the emergence of Neo-Confucianism in the eleventh century in the works of Shao Yong, Zhang Zai, the brothers Cheng Hao and Cheng Yi and finally culminating in Zhu Xi (1130–1200). There was general agreement that the meaning of *li* as principle required it to be linked with *qi* 氣 as material force. There were subtle differences among Neo-Confucians in treating the relationship between *li* and *qi*. Cheng Hao, tended to view their relationship as monistic (inseparable) while others, such as Cheng Yi, saw their relationship as more dualistic (separable).[35] Zhu Xi attempted to harmonize the two trends. Prémare diverged from this tradition in emphasizing *li* (principle) and de-emphasizing *qi*, which he translated in a more static form as "matter" rather than matter-energy or material force. In interpreting Zhou Dunyi's "Diagram of the Supreme Ultimate" which is an explanation of creation in the world, Prémare translated *taiji* as "matter still in chaos" (*Matière encore dans le chaos*) and *wuji* as "eternal Reason" (*Reason eternal*).[36] In explaining *taiji* and *wuji*, Prémare cited passages from the influential anthology *Xingli daquan* 性理大全 (Great Collection of Neo-Confucianism) (1405).[37] This seems to have reflected his Christian priority of spirit over matter. And yet, as the above account of the historical evolution of the meaning of *li* shows, the Chinese literati themselves engaged in extensive debate over the exact relationship between principle and material force.

RIVALRIES BETWEEN THE EUROPEAN GATEKEEPERS OF SINOLOGY

In 1861, 133 years after its composition, Prémare's essay on the monotheism of the Chinese was published with extensive editing and notations by Guillaume Pauthier (1801–1872). Pauthier was an Orientalist, poet and active member of the Société Asiatique. He had published a work on the AD 781 Nestorian Monument which had been discovered in Xi'anfu in 1625.[38] His interest in Confucianism was shown in his translation of the Confucian Four Books published in 1841.[39] Pauthier's Sinological work was competent, but not particularly noteworthy. His fame derives more from one of the most bitter rivalries in European Sinology. The story reflects the fact that personal ambitions and professional rivalries were not confined to the eighteenth century and to Etienne Fourmont's dealings with Prémare, but rather continued among the European gatekeepers of nineteenth-century Sinology.

Pauthier and Stanislas Julien (1797–1873) had both been students of the Sinologist Abel Rémusat, but it was Julien and not Pauthier who became Rémusat's successor and occupied the Sinological chair at the Collège de France from 1854 to 1873. The French Sinologist Paul Demiéville said that Julien "was incontestably the master of European sinology in the middle of the nineteenth-century. He had a character as abominable as his science was irreproachable. Jealous, choleric, quarrelsome, he monopolized posts and dismissed all rivals."[40] In their public disputes, Pauthier became Julien's "whipping boy" (*têtes de turc*).

Julien and Pauthier were representative of a group of *sinologues du chambre*.[41] Neither had lived in China nor had direct contact with Chinese speakers or with Chinese culture. Their Sinological work was done entirely within the confines of European libraries. Although they made limited use of the Chinese commentarial tradition, a scholar like Julien even prided himself in not seeking assistance from contemporary Chinese scholars in his search for the meaning of a text. They were trained as specialists in classical European scholarship and comparative philology. Philology dominated Sinological study throughout the nineteenth century and well into the twentieth century until the death of Paul Pelliot in 1945 and the emergence of post-World War II area studies.

The culmination of this famous rivalry came with their near-simultaneous deaths—Pauthier in 1872 and Julien in 1873. In his report to the annual meeting of the Société Asiatique on June 29, 1873, Ernest Renan eulogized their relationship by praising Julien's achievements while lamenting the consequences of their dispute for Pauthier. He wrote: "The caprice of death obliges us in fairness to reconcile M. Julien with the man who seems destined to have been his rival, and the regrettable animosities that separated him."[42] Renan conceded that Julien had an unmatched facility in translating Chinese, but he said that Pauthier had a greater comparative knowledge. Pauthier never received an appropriate position and suffered the unjust deprecation of his works by Julien. Renan wrote: "This is a lesson, gentlemen, from which we should learn. The freedom to criticize is the fundamental condition of scholarship. . . . But all personal remarks should be severely banished. Take care that rivalry henceforth does not degenerate into hatred."[43]

The publication of Prémare's essay on the monotheism of the Chinese in 1861 occurred in a very different intellectual climate than when Prémare sent the essay to Fourmont in 1730. Fourmont had belonged to the category of proto-Sinologists who had no formal training in Sinology and were self-taught. Pauthier, by contrast, had been trained in Sinology by Rémusat, but belonged to the category of *sinologues du chambre* who were philologists rather than Sinologists. Most of the Chinese texts they relied on had been selected and sent to Europe by missionaries like Foucquet and Prémare a century earlier. When the Jesuit-Sinologists were eliminated by the dissolution of the Society of Jesus in 1773, a temporary vacuum was created that was partially filled by Protestant missionary-scholars like James Legge.

In his introduction, Pauthier said Prémare's essay on monotheism could contribute to the then-current debate over whether the idea of God and souls in China had been present among the Chinese since antiquity. Pauthier noted that in spite of Prémare's lack of impartiality in the debate, he had an understanding of Chinese texts that was difficult at that time in Europe to surpass.[44] Pauthier recognized the growing European sense of self-absorption in the age of colonialism. He noted that European interest in these questions,

> which at the time of Leibniz so impassioned interest in the philosophical world and religious world, today attract scarcely any attention of the intellectual elite. These peoples, who we always treat as barbarians, and who had already become a very advanced civilization centuries before the age when our ancestors still lived in the forests of Gaul and of Germany, inspire in us today only a profound disdain![45]

The stimulus for publishing Prémare's essay came from an article by Ernest Renan that appeared in the *Journal Asiatique* in 1859. Renan juxtaposed the tendency toward monotheism (Judaism, Christianity and Islam) found in Semitic peoples with an absence of monotheism in other societies. Pauthier published Prémare's essay to argue, on the contrary, that monotheism existed in the non-Semitic culture of China. Pauthier admitted that several China missionaries, such as, Niccolò Longobardo, SJ and Domingo Navarrete, OP, had disagreed, but he also noted that two prominent Protestant missionaries, Walter Henry Medhurst (1796–1857) and James Legge (1815–1897), wrote essays arguing for the presence of monotheism among the Chinese.[46] The Figurist claim that ancient Chinese works contained Revelation played no role in this debate.

Like his Chinese essay *Rujiao shiyi* (The true meaning of the Literati Teaching), Prémare's *Essai sur le monothéisme de Chinois* makes only slight reference to his work on Figurism. There is some overlap with Figurist sources, such as the *Classic of History*, the *Classic of Odes*, and Luo Bi's history, but his main focus is upon Song dynasty Neo-Confucian texts. Zhu Xi is emphasized because his works were the main source of the claims by Europeans that the Chinese were atheistic.

At the end of his essay, Prémare summarized his argument that the attribution of atheism to the Chinese had no substance and that *Tian* (Heaven) and *Shangdi* (Lord-Above) signified the same God that Christians believe in. He also said that the principal object of the *Jing* was to focus on the Man-God (*l'Homme-Dieu*) of the world. The reference to the Man-God (i.e., Jesus Christ) introduced an element of Figurism. He concluded by saying that the aim of proving this argument:

> is what drives me to devote myself to the mysteries of the savoir Lord which I have recovered from these *Jing*, the most obscure and perhaps the most ancient monuments which may have come down to us. And although I am sixty-four years old, I hope not to die until I have achieved a work that is glorious to Jesus-Christ and to his Church.[47]

It is worth noting that Pauthier, like Prémare's fellow China missionaries a century before, rejected his Figurist theories. Pauthier wrote in a footnote to the above conclusion by Prémare: "We are unnable to stop ourselves from remarking here, that in our view, it is a great error to believe like Fr. Prémare, that the Man-God is the principal object of the Chinese *Jing*."[48]

THE YONGZHENG EMPEROR'S ENMITY TOWARD CHRISTIANITY

In January of 1724 the Yongzheng emperor endorsed the Board of Rites' proposal and issued an edict requiring that all missionaries, except for those at the Beijing court, be expelled to Macau and that Christian churches be converted to public places.[49] The missionaries were temporarily allowed to reside in Guangzhou from 1724 to 1733 until they were sent to Macau. Another edict was issued on May 28, 1727, that accused the Westerners (Xiyang ren 西洋人) of attempting to plant an alien teaching (Christianity) in China and stated "what followed in the wake of this religion was poison, confusion, lunacy, and ignorance. This is the false teaching (yiduan 異端) of the West."[50] The term yiduan was very harsh and was typically reserved by the literati for the most insidious and unorthodox teachings in China.

While the Kangxi emperor had attempted to accommodate the missionaries' teachings with Chinese culture, he had been frustrated in his effort by the Papal Legate Tournon who was acting on instructions from Rome. In comparison with his father the Kangxi emperor, the Yongzheng emperor expressed a far less open-minded point of view. The 1727 edict states: "China has the religion of China and the West has the religion of the West. The teaching of the Westerners is not necessarily able to work in China, nor would the religion of China be able to work in the West." This is not an attempt to define the religion of Europe as merely different. There was an explicit xenophobic element in the Yongzheng emperor's edict. We know that he had been trained in Buddhist literature in his youth and this edict was far more favorable to Buddhism than to Christianity.[51] In any case, this edict is as much a political as a religious document.

The enmity of the Yongzheng emperor toward the missionaries dated back to the time of his succession to the throne when several missionaries, such as Fr. João Mourão, SJ, joined with the Sunu family and some high officials, many of whom were either converts or sympathetic to Christianity, to support opposing candidates, particularly Yinti and Yintang.[52] When the heir apparent Yinreng 胤礽 was deposed by the Kangxi emperor because of unstable behavior, the remaining sons contended to displace him. Yinti 胤禵 was favored by the emperor, but he was serving as a military commander in far-away Gansu province when his father suddenly died at the Summer Palace near Bejing and his brother Yinzhen 胤禛 took the throne as the Yongzheng emperor.[53] Discrepancies in the official accounts have given rise to claims that

Yinzhen murdered his father to advance over his brothers and subsequently had the official records altered with the assistance of the powerful military commander of Beijing, Lungkodo.⁵⁴

SCHOLARLY FRUSTRATION, DECLINING HEALTH, AND DEATH

By 1720 Prémare was becoming trapped. The results of his research and his Figurist theories were banned from being disseminated by his vows of obedience to religious superiors. The Rites Controversy had aroused clerical suspicion of Jesuit accommodation with Chinese culture and this helped to make Figurism a casualty in the open dissemination of ideas. And yet, as a Jesuit trained in the subtleties of thinking, he saw that he was torn between two religious vows—a vow of obedience to his religious superiors and a vow of his conscience to bring the teachings of Christ to China. He believed the key to realizing both vows was found in the unrecognized revelation of Christ in the ancient texts of the Chinese. He sought a way out of this trap by writing works that tamped down suspicions of his writings. These writings included the *Lettre sur le monothéisme de Chinois* and *Orphan of Zhao*. Given the attempts by some in Rome to have him recalled from China, he had good reason to try and appease their suspicions. And yet he did not relinquish his effort to present his Figurist ideas, but rather sought the assistance of sympathetic European scholars who might help disseminate Prémare's Figurist research while not revealing his name as the author.

In a letter to Fourmont of August 27, 1731, Prémare referred with resignation to himself as an old man of 65 and Fourmont as a much younger man of 46. He hoped that Fourmont would complete the work that he had begun in China. After suffering two strokes early in 1731, Prémare realized that his declining health would prevent him from seeing his work through to publication. He probably prayed for a solution. One month before suffering a third and more debilitating stroke, he made his decision. In desperation, he included with that letter to Fourmont the only copy of his monumental 329-double sheet *Vestigia* manuscript that he had toiled over for thirteen years, completing it in 1725 in Guangzhou. Given the vicissitudes of shipments between China and Europe, this amounted to an act of faith.

In addition, he had sent the first half of his history of the ancient Chinese to Fourmont in his letter of November 10, 1730, but he wrote that he was too ill to send the entire essay. Actually, he sent several important manuscripts to Fourmont, but Fourmont often did not even acknowledge receiving them. It is true that Fourmont disagreed with the Figurist interpretations in some of these manuscripts and it is highly likely that he used the rationalizations of an intellectual gatekeeper to justify his failure to disseminate them. However, it is hard to deny that another probable reason for Fourmont's failure to disseminate Prémare's works was his own personal ambition. Prémare's works were so much more sophisticated than Fourmont's proto-Sinological efforts that revealing them would have been embarrassing. Fourmont was far more committed to building his own reputation as a scholar than he was to serving scholarship or saving Chinese souls. Eventually Prémare realized that his hopes for assistance from Fourmont were futile, but he was too old and too sick to find another scholar to help him. And yet he was not prone to bitterness. Although his relationship with Bouvet had turned sour, when Bouvet died in 1730, Prémare praised the erudition of the man who had once been his teacher.[55]

Gradually Prémare's Figurist writings came to the attention of more and more unsympathetic readers who denounced him to Propaganda in Rome. Seven months after completing his *Vestigia*, Prémare had written to Foucquet in Rome on December 24, 1725, and mentioned some refinements he had made to his Figurist views.[56] One year later a French priest named F. Rouillard who was a chaplain on a French ship that docked at Macau, visited the house where Prémare was staying and obtained a copy of an unsigned document with extracts from the *Vestigia*.[57] This copy eventually was forwarded by a circuitous path to Propaganda in Rome, which found the contents heretical. Propaganda requested Foucquet, who was residing in Rome, to identify the author of the document.[58] Foucquet tried to avoid Prémare's recall by being ambivalent, saying that the document was comparable in some ways to Prémare's original writings, but not clearly attributable to Prémare. On October 18, 1727, Propaganda ordered the Jesuit Father General Michel Angelo Tamburini to recall Prémare.[59] However, Prémare's advanced age and record of obedience to the Jesuit Order caused Tamburini to suspend the recall order.

In February 1728 the Holy Congregation commuted the recall order with the demand that Prémare either disavow the contents of the document obtained by Rouillard as not being his views or else submit a clear retraction of those views. Meanwhile the Chinese Rites Controversy continued to churn in Rome. On October 5, 1736 the order for Prémare's recall was renewed, but never implemented. Prémare had died at Macau in September.[60]

Prémare's first two strokes had each lasted for several hours.[61] When in September 1731 he suffered from a more serious stroke that lasted for an entire day, he prepared for his demise. In a note written on October 6, 1733, he spoke of a large box of 217 books, including the Thirteen Classics and the Kangxi dictionary, that he was sending to Abbé Bignon for the French royal library.[62] He spent his last days in such poverty in Macau, that he was forced to ask Bignon for alms.

And so our chapter-by-chapter cycle of the Five Elements that began with water ends with earth. As a priest Prémare had said the words many times to parishioners: "dust thou art, and to dust thou shalt return."[63] For a man who sought to practice such painstaking accuracy in his scholarship, it is ironic that the exact date of his death in 1736—September 7 or the 17—is uncertain.[64] In any case, it was his faith, not the reception of his scholarship, that consoled him at his death.

NOTES

1. Prémare to Bouvet (?), December 26, 1707, BAV, *Borgia latino, 565*, 423v, cited in Witek, *Controversial Ideas*, p. 152–53.
2. Prémare, *Lettre inédite du P. Prémare sur le Monothéisme des Chinois*. Edited by G. Pauthier (Paris: Benjamin Duprat, 1861), p. 4.
3. Fang Chao-yiing, "Yang Kuang-hsien," in *Eminent Chinese of the Ch'ing Period (1644–1912)*, Arthur Hummel, ed. (Washington, D.C.: United States Government Printing Office, 1943), p. 890–91.
4. J. S. Cummins, *A Question of Rites: Friar Domingo Nararrete and the Jesuits in China* (Aldershot, England: Scolar Press, 1993), p. 142.
5. Cummins, p. 140.
6. Standaert, ed., *Handbook of Christianity in China. Volume* One, p. 313.
7. Cummins, p. 146.
8. Cummins, p. 155.
9. Fr. Caballero had an incomplete copy of Longobardi's manuscript that he showed to Navarrete. Cummins, p. 159.
10. Cummins, p. 153.
11. *Vestigia*, f. 51r; *Vestiges*, p. 104.
12. *Vestigia*, f. 51r-v; *Vestiges*, p. 105.
13. *Vestigia*, f. 53r-v; *Vestiges*, p. 106.
14. *Xingli jingyi* 性理精義. Sibu beiyao collection, 1717. *juan* 1.
15. *Vestigia*, f. 55r-v; *Vestiges*, p. 108.
16. *Vestigia*, f. 56r; *Vestiges* p. 109.
17. Zhuangzi, *Jiaozheng Zhuangzi jishi* 校正莊子集釋 (Revised collected commentary on the Zhuangzi) 2 vols. (Taipei: Shijie Shuju, 1971) *juan* 6 大宗師, 1:247.
18. Zhuangzi, *The Complete Works of Zhuangzi*. Translated by Burton Watson. (New York: Columbia University Press, 2013), p. 45.
19. *Vestigia*, f 58r-v; *Vestiges*, p. 110–11.
20. Prémare, *Lettre*, p. 4–5.
21. Prémare, *Lettre*, p. 4, fn. 2.
22. Prémare, *Lettre*, p. 9.
23. Matteo Ricci [Li Madou 利馬竇], *Tianzhu shiyi* 天主實義。In Li Zhizao 李之藻, ed. *Tianxue chuhan* 天學初函. 6 卷。(Taipei台北: Taiwan Xuesheng Shuju 台灣學生書局, 1965) 1: 351–635.

24. Li Madou (Ricci), 1: 404–5. Cf. the translation in Matteo Ricci, SJ, *The True Meaning of the Lord of Heaven*. Douglas Lancashire and Peter Hu Kuo-chen, SJ, trs. (St. Louis, MO: Institute of Jesuit Sources, 1985), p. 106–7.

25. Li Madou (Ricci), 1: 405–11.

26. Prémare, *Lettre*, p. 25–26.

27. Tu Wei-ming, "Reconstituting the Confucian Tradition," *Journal of Asian Studies* 33 (1974): 452.

28. Chan, "Chu Hsi's Completion of Neo-Confucianism," p. 81–82.

29. Zhu Xi's commentaries on the Five Classics include: *Zhouyibenyi* 周易本義 (The original meaning of the Classic of Changes) 12 *juan* (1177); *Shiji zhuan* 詩集傳 (Collection of Commentaries on the Classic of Odes) 8 *juan* (1177); and *Shu shuo* 書說 (Explanation of the Book of History) 30 *juan* which was compiled by his pupils under his order.

30. Chan, "Chu Hsi's Completion of Neo-Confucianism," p. 83–84.

31. Wing-tsit Chan, "The Evolution of the Neo-Confucan Concept *li* 理 as Principle," *Tsing Hua Journal of Chinese Studies.* new series IV, no. 1. (February 1964): 123–24.

32. Chan, p. 128

33. Chan, p. 129.

34. Kenneth K. S. Ch'en, *Buddhism in China: a Historical Survey* (Princeton: Princeton University Press, 1964) p. 316–18.

35. Chan, p. 142.

36. Prémare, *Lettre*, p. 10–11.

37. Prémare cited the *Xingli daquan* 1:16b, 1:17b, 26:2b, and 26:31.

38. G. Pauthier, *L'Inscription syro-chinoise de Si-ngan-fou*. 1858.

39. G. Pauthier, *Doctrine de Confucius ou le Quatre Livres de Philosophie Morale et Politique de la China* (Paris: Librairie Garnier Frères, 1841).

40. Paul Demiéville, "Aperçu historique des études sinologiques en France," *Acta Asiatica* 11 (1966): 81.

41. David B. Honey, *Incense at the Altar: Pioneering Sinologists and the Development of Classical Chinese Philology* (New Haven, CN: American Oriental Society, 2001), p. 326–27.

42. Ernest Renan, "Rapport sur les travaux du conseil de la Société Asiatique pendant l'annee 1872–1873 fait à la séance annuelle de la Société, le 29 Juin 1873," *Journal Asiatique.* Seventh series, vol. II (Paris) 1873. p. 16.

43. Renan, p. 17.

44. G. Pauthier, *Lettre*, p. 1.

45. Pauthier, *Lettre*, p. 1–2.

46. Pauthier, *Lettre*, p. 2–3.

47. Prémare, *Lettre*, p. 54.

48. Prémare, *Lettre*, p. 54, fn. 1.

49. Antonio Sisto Rosso, OFM, *Apostolic Legations to China of the Eighteenth Century* (South Pasadena: Perkins, 1948), p. 227.

50. A copy of this edict is preserved in the Roman Archives of the Society of Jesus, *Japonica-Sinica* 168, f. 186–87.

51. Fang Chao-ying, "Yin-chên," in *Eminent Chinese of the Ch'ing Period (1644–1912)* Ed. Arthur W. Hummel (Washington, D.C.: Government Printing Office, 1943), p. 916.

52. Rosso, p. 213–14.

53. Matteo Ripa, *Storia della Fondazione dell Congregazione e del Collegio de cinesi*. 3 vols. (Napoli: Tipographia Mandfredi, 1832) II, 94.

54. Fang, p. 916. See also Evelyn S. Rawski, *The Last Emperors: A Social History of Qing Imperial Institutions* (Berkeley: University of California Press, 1998) p. 102 & 331, fn 22.

55. Lundbæk, p. 118.

56. Witek, *Controversial Ideas*, p. 301, cites Prémare's letter to Foucquet of December 24, 1725. BNF, *Mss. Fr.* 12209, 39–40.

57. "Extraits d'une dissertation sur les caractères chinois et les livres anciens, ou précis d'une lettre au R. P. de Briga, Archivum S. Congregationis de Propaganda Fide, Rome, *SOCP* (1727–1728), vol. 33, 248–49v.

58. For a detailed account of these recall proceedings, see Witek, *Controversial Ideas*, p. 300–5.

59. Pfister, p. 521.

60. Pfister, p. 210.

61. Lundbæk, p. 57.

62. Lundbæk, p. 62.

63. *Genesis* 3:19.

64. Dehergne, p. 210.

Bibliography

Appleton, William W. *A Cycle of Cathay: the Chinese Vogue in England during the Seventeenth and Eighteenth Century*. New York: Columbia University Press, 1951.

Beckmann, Johannes, SMB, "Die katholischen Missionare und der Taoismus von 16. Jahrhundert bis zur Gegenwart," *Neue Zeitschrift für Missionswissenschaft* 26 (1970): 1–17.

Bernard-Maitre, Henri. *Sagesse Chinoise et Philosophie Chrétienne*. Paris: Cathasia, 1935.

Bertuccioli, Giuliano. "Two Previously Unknown Prefaces of Ricci's *Jiaoyou Lun* and Martini's *Qiuyou Pian* by Liu Ning and Shen Guangyu." In *Western Humanistic Culture Presented to China by Jesuit Missionaries (XVII–XVIII Centuries)*. Edited by Federico Masini. Rome: Institutum Historicum S.I., 1996. p. 101–18.

Birrell, Anne. *Chinese Mythology: An Introduction*. Baltimore: The Johns Hopkins University Press, 1993.

———. *Chinese Myths*. Austin: University of Texas Press, 2000.

Bonnetty, A. "Analyse d'un Ouvrage Inédit du P. Prémare," second article. *Annales de Philosophie Chrétienne* XV (July 31, 1837), p. 134–54.

———. "Notice sur la Vie et les Ouvrages de M. l'abbé Sionnet," *Annales de Philosophie Chrétienne* XIII, no. 52 (1856), p. 440–54.

Bouvet, Joachim., SJ. *Caelestis disciplina vera notitia* (An examination of the True Teaching of Heaven). Biblioteca Capitolare Fabroniana, Pistoia, Ms. 53. Translation of *Gujin jing Tian jian Tianxue benyi* (An Examination of the Ancient and Modern cult of Heaven; the Original Meaning of the Heavenly Teaching) by J. de Prémare. Before 1706.

———. *De cultu celesti Sinarum veterum et modernorum* (An examination of the ancient and modern cult of Heaven). Translation of *Gujin jing Tian jian Tianxue benyi* by J. de Prémare & J. Hervieu. 1706. Bibliothèque nationale France MS. Nouvelles acquisitions latines 155.

———. *Gujin jing Tian jian* 古今敬天鑑. Bibliothèque Nationale France, Chinois 7161.

———. *Gujin jing Tian jian Tianxue benyi* 古今敬天鑑 天學本義 (An Examination of the original meaning of the Heavenly Teaching in the ancient and modern expression "revere Heaven"). Xujiahui Library, Shanghai.

———. *Tianxue benyi* 天學本義 (The Original Meaning of the Heavenly Teaching). Bibliothèque Nationale France, Chinois 7160.

———. *Tianxue benyi.* Bibliothèque Nationale France, Chinois 7162.

Boxer, C. R., ed. & trans. *Seventeenth Century Macau in Contemporary Documents and Illustrations.* Hong Kong: Heinemann (Asia), 1984.

Brevis Relatio eorum quae spectant ad declarationem Sinarum Imperatoris KamHi circa Caeli, Confucii et avorum cultum, datum anno 1700 . . . Augsburg-Dillingen, 1703.

Brou, A., SJ, "Les Jésuites sinologues de Pékin et leurs éditeurs de Paris," *Revue d'histoire des Missions* 11 (1934): 551–66.

Catholic Encyclopedia. Edited by Charles George Herbermann. Volume 2. New York: Encyclopedia Press, 1913.

Chan, Wing-tsit. "Chu Hsi's Completion of Neo-Confucianism." In *Etudes Song—Sung Studies. In Memoriam Etienne Balazs.* Edited by Francoise Aubin. Ser. II, #1, 1973. p. 59–90.

———. "The Evolution of the Neo-Confucan Concept li 理 as Principle," *Tsing Hua Journal of Chinese Studies.* new series IV, no. 1. (February 1964): 123–48.

———. "The Study of Chu Hsi in the West," *Journal of Asian Studies* 35 (1976): 555–77.

Ch'en Shou-yi, "The Chinese Orphan: a Yuan Play. Its Influence on European Drama of the Eighteenth Century," *Tien Hsia Monthly* III (2) (1936): 89–115.

Ch'en, Kenneth K. S. *Buddhism in China: a Historical Survey.* Princeton: Princeton University Press, 1964.

Chen Xinyu 陳欣雨, "Lizu yu Wenzixue de Ma Ruose de Yijing Yanjiu: Zhouyi Lishu yu Taiji Lueshuo" 立足于文字學的馬若瑟的《易經》研究：以《周易理數》與《太極略說》為例 (Establishing a Foothold on the Philology of Joseph de Prémare's Research on the Classic of Changes: a Study of the Yijing Numerology and The Abridged Discourse on the Great Ultimate), *Aomen ligong xuebao* 1 (2017): 85–92.

Cheng, Yinghong. "'Is Peking Man Still Our Ancestor?'—Genetics, Anthropology, and the Politics of Racial Nationalism in China," *Journal of Asian Studies* 76 (2017): 575–602.

Cibot, Pierre Martial, SJ "Essai sur la langue et les caractères des Chinois," in *Mémoires concernant l'histoire, les sciences, les arts, les moeurs, les usages, etc. des Chinois, par les Missionnaries de Pékin.* 17 vols. Paris: Chez Nyon, Libraire, 1776–1814. vol. VIII, p. 133–266 & vol. IX, p. 282–430.

Collani, Claudia von. "Tianxue benyi—Joachim Bouvets Forschungen zum Monotheismus in China," *China Mission Studies (1550–1800) Bulletin X* (1988): 9–33.

———. *Eine Wissenschaftliche Akademie für China. Studia Leibnitiana* Sonderheft 18. Stuttgart: Franz Steiner Verlag, 1989.

———. "Jesus of the Figurists," in *The Chinese Face of Jesus Christ.* Edited by Roman Malek, SVD. vol 2. Nettetal, Germany: Steyler Verlag, 2003), p. 553–82.

Collani, Claudia von. *P. Joachim Bouvet, SJ Sein Leben und sein Werk* Nettetal: Steyler Verlag, 1985.

Collani, Claudia von, Harald Holz, Konrad Wegmann, Eds. *Uroffenbarung und Daoismus. Jesuitische Missionshermeneutik des Daoismus.* Series Daodejing Research vol. 1. Berlin: Europäischer Universitätsverlag GmbH, 2008.

Cordier, Henri. *Bibliotheca Sinica.* 5 vols. Paris: Librairie Oriéntale & Americaine, 1906–1907.

———. "Les études chinoises sous la Révolution et l'Empire," *T'oung Pao.* Second series. 19 (2) (May 1918–May 1919): 59–103.

———. *L'imprimerie sino-européenne en Chine.* Paris: Imprimerie Nationale, 1891.

Couplet, Philip, SJ et al, *Confucius Sinarum Philosophus.* Paris: Daniel Horthemels 1687.

Cummins, J. S. *A Question of Rites: Friar Domingo Nararrete and the Jesuits in China.* Aldershot, England: Scolar Press, 1993.

Dehergne, Joseph, SJ. *Répertoire des Jésuites de Chine de 1552 à 1800.* Rome: Institutum Historicum S.I., 1973.

Demiéville, Paul. "Aperçu historique des études sinologiques en France," *Acta Asiatica* 11 (1966): 56–110.

Dictionnaire de biographie française, edited by M. Prevost & Roman D'Amat. Paris: Librairie Letouzey et Ané, 1954–1976.

Dong, Yu. *Catalogo delle opere cinesi missionarie della Biblioteca Apostolica Vaticana (XVI–XVIII Sec.).* Vatican: Biblioteca Apostolica Vaticana, 1996.

Drouin, Jean-Claude. "Un Esprit original du XIX° siècle: Le Chevalier de Paravey (1787–1871)," *Revue historique de Bordeaux et du département de la Gironde* (1970): 65–78.

Dudink, Adrian. "The Chinese Christian Texts in the Zikawei 徐家匯 Collection in Shanghai: a Preliminary and Partial List," *Sino-Western Cultural Relations Journal* 33 (2011): 1–41.

Dudink, Ad. "The Chinese Christian Books of the Former Beitang Library," *Sino-Western Cultural Relations Journal* 26 (2004): 46–59.

———. "The Rediscovery of a Seventeenth-Century Collection of Chinese Christian Texts: the Manuscript *Tianxue jijie*," *Sino-Western Cultural Relations Journal* 15 (1993): 1–26.

Elisseeff, Danielle. *Moi Arcade interprete chinois du Roi-Soleil.* Paris: Les Éditions Arthaud, 1985.

Ellman, Benjamin. *From Philosophy to Philology: Intellectual and Social Aspects of Change in Late Imperial China.* Cambridge, MA: Harvard University Press, 1984.

Fourmont, Etienne. *Meditationes sinicae.* 4 parts. Paris: Bullot, 1737.

Froger, François. *Relation du premier voyage des François à la Chine fait en 1688, 1689 et 1700 sur le vaisseau l'Amphitrite.* Edited by E. A. Voretzsch. Leipzig 1926.

Gaubil, Antoine, SJ, *Correspondence de Pékin 1722–1759.* Edited by Renée Simon. Geneva: Librarie Droz, 1970.

Giles, Herbert A. *A Chinese-English Dictionary.* 2nd ed. Shanghai, 1912.

Goodrich, L. Carrington, and Chaoying Fang, eds. *Dictionary of Ming Biography 1368–1644.* 2 vols. New York: Columbia University Press, 1976.

Guignes, Joseph de. *Mémoire dans lequel on prouve que les Chinois sont une colonie égyptienne*. Paris: Desaint & Saillant, 1759.

Han, Qi 韓琦. "Bai Jin de 'Yijing' yanjiu he Kangxi shidai de 'Xixue zhong yuan' shuo" 白晉的《易經》研究和康熙時代的'西學中源'說。(Joachim Bouvet's Study of the *Yijing* and the theory of the 'Chinese Origin of Western Learning' during the Kangxi period), *Hanxue Yanjiu* 漢學研究 16:1 (1998): 185–201.

———. "Kexue yu zongjian *de jian*: Yesuhui shi Bai Jin de *Yijing* yanjiu" 科學與宗教之間：耶穌會士白晉的《易經》研究 (The space between natural science and religion: The Jesuit Joachim Bouvet's study of the *Yijing*). In: 東亞基督教再詮釋 (A reinterpretation of East Asian Christianity). Edited by Tao Feiya 陶飛亞 and Liang Yuansheng 梁元生。 Hong Kong: 香港中文大學崇基學院宗教與中國社會研究中心, 2004. p. 413–34.

Han Yu-shan 韓玉珊, *Elements of Chinese Historiography*. W. M. Hawley: Hollywood, CA, 1955.

Henderson, John B. *The Development and Decline of Chinese Cosmology*. New York: Columbia University Press, 1984.

Herbert A. Giles, *Chinese Biographical Dictionary*. 1898.

Hervouet, Yves & Etienne Balazs. *A Sung Bibliography (Bibliographie des Sung)*. Hong Kong: Chinese University Press, 1978.

Ho Ping-ti. "The Chinese Civilization: A Search for the Roots of Its Longevity," *Journal of Asian Studies* 35 (1976): 547–54.

———. *The Cradle of the East: An Inquiry into the Indigenous Origins of Techniques and Ideas of Neolithic and Early Historic China, 5000–1000 B.C.* Hong Kong: Chinese University of Hong Kong Press; Chicago: University of Chicago Press, 1975.

Honey, David B. *Incense at the Altar: Pioneering Sinologists and the Development of Classical Chinese Philology*. New Haven, CT: American Oriental Society, 2001.

Hucker, Charles O. *A Dictionary of Official Titles in Imperial China*. Taipei: Southern Materials Center, Inc., 1986.

Hummel, Arthur, ed. *Eminent Chinese of the Ch'ing Period*. Washington, D.C.: United State Government Printing Office, 1943.

Idema, W. L. "The Orphan of Zhao: Self-Sacrifice, Tragic Choice and Revenge and the Confucianization of Mongol Drama at the Miing Court," *Cina. No. 21, XXXth European Conference of Chinese Studies Proceedings* (1988) p. 159–90.

Julien, Stanislas. *Tchao-Chi-Kou-Eul, ou l'Orphelin de la Chine*. Paris: Moutardier, 1834.

Kangxi zidian 康熙字典 (Kangxi dictionary). Compiled by Zhang Yushu 張玉書, Chen Tingjing 陳庭敬, et al. 1716

Karlgren, Bernhard. *The Book of Documents*. In *Bulletin of the Museum of Far Eastern Antiquities (Stockholm)*, number 22 (1950). The glosses appear in BMFEA 20 (1948): 39–315 & 21 (1949): 63–206.

———. *The Book of Odes: Chinese Text, Transcription, and Translation*. Stockholm: Museum of Far Eastern Antiquities, 1950. Originally published in *Bulletin of the Museum of Far Eastern Antiquities* (BMFEA) 16 (1945 and 17 (1946). The glosses appear in BMFEA 14(1942): 71–247, 16 (1944): 55–169, and 18 (1946): 1–198.

Reprinted in 1 vol. as *Glosses on the Book of Odes*. Stockholm: Museum of Far Eastern Antiquities, 1964.

Keightley, David N. "Ping-ti Ho and the Origins of Chinese Civilization," *Harvard Journal of Asiatic Studies* 37 (1977): 381–411.

Lackner, Michael. "A Figurist at Work: the Vestigia of Joseph de Prémare S.J." In: *L'Europe en Chine: interactions scientifiques, religieuses et culturelles aux XVIIe et XVIIIe siècles*. Acts du colloque de la Foundation Hugot, 14–17 October 1991. Catherine Jami & Hubert Delahaye, eds. Collège de France. Institut des hautes études chinoises, 1993. p. 23–56.

———. "Jesuit Figurism." In *China and Europe: Images and Influences in Sixteenth to Eighteenth Centuries*. Thomas H. C. Lee, ed. Hong Kong: Chinese University Press, 1991. p. 129–49.

Lai Qutang 來瞿唐, *Yijing tujie* 易經圖解 (Explanations of the Diagrams associated with the Classic of Changes). Taipei: Guangtian chuban she, 1975.

Legge, James, trans. *The Chinese Classics*. 5 vols. Oxford: Oxford University Press, 1893.

———. *The I Ching*. 2nd ed. New York: Dover Publications, 1963. Originally published as F. Max Müller, ed., *The Sacred Books of the East*, vol. XVI (1899).

Leibniz, Gottfried Wilhelm. *Der Briefwechsel mit den Jesuiten in China (1689–1714)*. Edited by Rita Widmaier. Transcribed and translated by Malte-Ludolf Babin. Hamburg: Felix Meiner Verlag, 2006.

Lettres édifiantes et curieuses, écrites des missions étrangères. Mémoires de la Chine. Vol. 9. Lyon: J. Vernarel, Libraire, 1819.

Leung, Cécile. *Etienne Fourmont (1683–1745) Oriental and Chinese Languages in Eighteenth-Century France*. Leuven, Belgium: Leuven University Press, 2002.

Li Guangdi. *Zhouyi zhezhong* (Annotations to the Book of Changes). 22 juan. 1715.

Li Zhen 李真. "Shilun Ming-Qing zhi ji lai Hua Yesuhuishi yu Rujia Jidutu zhi xueshu jiaowang" 试沦明清之 际來华耶稣会士与儒家基督徒之学术交往：以马若瑟与刘凝为中心 (An Examination of the Ming-Qing Scholarly Contact between a Jesuit Scholar who Came to China and a Christian Literatus—with a Focus on Ma Ruose [Joseph de Prémare] and Liu Ning), *Beijing Xingzheng Xueyuan xuebao* 《北京行政学院学报》 2015 (2): 123–28.

Liu Shu (Liv Daoyuan) 劉恕 (劉道原), *Zizhi tongjian waiji* 資治通鑑外紀 (Additional Chronicle to the Comprehensive Mirror for Aid in Government) 10 juan. 1078. In *Siku quanshu*, vol. 312, p. 527–838.

Liu Wu-chi, "The Original Orphan of China," *Comparative Literature* 5 (3) (Summer 1953): 193–212.

Lowe, Michael, Ed. *Early Chinese Texts: a Bibliographical Guide*. Berkeley: Institute of East Asian Studies, University of California, 1993.

Lundbæk, Knud. *Joseph de Prémare (1666–1736), SJ: Chinese Philology and Figurism*. Aarhus, Denmark: Aarhus University Press, 1991.

———. "Pierre Martial Cibot (1727–1780)—The Last China Figurst," *Sino-Western Cultural Relations Journal* XV (1993): 52–59.

Luo Bi 羅泌, ed. *Lu shi* 路史 (Grand History), 47 juan. In *Siku quanshu*, vol. 312, pp. 527–838.

Malatesta, Edward J., SJ, "A Fatal Clash of Wills: The Condemnation of the Chinese Rites by the Papal Legate Carlo Tommaso Maillard de Tournon," in *The Chinese Rites Controversy: Its History and Meaning*. Edited by D. E. Mungello. Monumenta Serica Monograph Series XXXIII. Nettetal, Germany: Steyler Verlag, 1994, p. 211–246.

Martini, Martino, SJ. *De bello tartarico historia*. Milan: Gio. Battista Bidelli, 1654.

Mayers, William Frederick. *Chinese Reader's Manual*. Shanghai: American Presbyterian Mission Press, 1874.

Mencius. D. C. Lau, trans. Middlesex, England: Penguin, 1970.

Min Tan, *The Poetics of Difference and Displacement*. Hong Kong: Hong Kong University Press, 2008.

Mungello, D. E., Ed. *The Chinese Rites Controversy: Its History and Meaning*. Monumenta Serica Monograph Series XXXIII. Nettetal, Germany: Steyler Verlag, 1994.

Mungello, D. E. *Curious Land: Jesuit Accommodation and the Origins of Sinology*. Stuttgart: Franz Steiner Verlag, 1985.

———. *The Forgotten Christians of Hangzhou*. Honolulu: University of Hawaii Press, 1994.

———. "The Seventeenth-Century Jesuit Translation Project of the Confucian Four Books. In *East meets West: the Jesuits in China, 1582–1773*. Edited by Charles E. Ronan, SJ and Bonnie B. C. Oh. Chicago: Loyola University Press, 1988. p. 252–72.

———. *The Spirit and the Flesh in Shandong, 1650–1785*. Lanham, MD: Rowman & Littlefield, 2001.

———. "Unearthing the Manuscripts of Bouvet's *Gujin* after Nearly Three Centuries," *China Mission Studies (1550–1800) Bulletin* X (1988): 34–61.

Needham, Joseph. *Science and Civilisation in China*. Volume 3. *Mathematics and the Sciences of the Heavens and the Earth*. Cambridge, UK: Cambridge University Press, 1959.

Pan Feng-chuan 潘鳳娟《不可譯，不可道之名：雷慕沙與<道德經>翻譯》(The Ineffable Trigrammaton: Jean Pierre Abel-Rémusat's Translation of the *Daodejing*) 中央大學人文學報 number 61 (2016.04): 55–115.

———.《翻译"圣人"：马若瑟与十字的索隐回转》 (Translating the Saint: Joseph de Prémare's Figurist Torque of Chinese from Decem to Crucem), 国际比较文学 *International Comparative Literature* I (2018): 76–96.

———. "Translating the Saint: Joseph Prémare's Figurist Torque of Chinese from Decem to Crucem," in *Leibniz and the European Encounter with China: 300 Years of Discours sur la théologie naturelle des Chinois*. Edited by Wenchao Li. Stuttgart: Franz Steiner Verlag, 2017. p. 105–28.

Pauthier, G. *Doctrine de Confucius ou le Quatre Livres de Philosophie Morale et Politique de la China*. Paris: Librairie Garnier Frères, 1841.

———. *L'Inscription syro-chinoise de Si-ngan-fou*. 1858.

Pelliot, P. "La Brevis Relatio," *T'oung Pao* 23 (1924): 355–72.

Pelliot, Paul. *Inventaire sommaire des Manuscrits et Imprimés chinois de la Bibliothèque Vaticane*. Revised and edited by TAKATA Tokio. Kyoto: Italian School of East Asian Studies (ISEAS), 1995.

———. "Melanges sur quelques manuscrits sinologiques conservés en Russie," *T'oung Pao* 29 (1932): 104–11.

Pfister, Louis, SJ, *Notices Biographiques et Bibliographiques sur les Jésuites de l'ancienne mission de Chine 1552–1773*. Shanghai: Imprimerie de la Mission Catholique, 1932.

Pinot, Virgile, ed. *Documents inédits relatifs a la Connaissance de la Chine en France de 1685 a 1740*. Edited by Virgile Pinot. Paris: Librairie Orientaliste Paul Geunther, 1932.

Pons, Philippe. *Macao*. Translated by Sarah Adams. London: Reaktion Books 2002.

Prémare, Joseph de, SJ. "Discours Preliminaire." In *Le Chou-king, un des livres sacrés des Chinois*. Paris: N. M. Tilliard, 1770. p. xliv–cxxix.

———. *Lettre sur le monothéisme de Chinois*. Edited by G. Pauthier. Paris: Benjamin Duprat, 1861

———. Ma Ruose. *Jingchuan yilun* 經傳議論 (A Discussion of the Classics and their Commentaries). 1710. Bibliothèque Nationale France, Chinois 7164.

———. *Notitia Linguae Sinicae* (A report on the Chinese language). Edited by Elijah Coleman Bridgman Malacca: Anglo-Chinese College, 1831.

———. Wenguzi. *Liushu shiyi* 六書實義 [The true meaning of the six kinds of Chinese characters]. 1720–1721. Xujiahui Library, Shanghai. Bibliotheca Apostolica Vaticana. Borgia Cinese 357(10) and Borg., Cinese 443(3).

———. *Meng meidu ji* 夢美土記 (Dream of a Pilgrim). 1709.

———. "Le petit orphelin de la maison de Tchao." Bibliothèque Nationale France, Paris, Manuscrit BNF, Fonds français 25510. Published in Jean-Baptiste Du Halde, SJ, *Description géographique, historique, chronologique, politique, et physique de l'empire de la Chine et de la Tartarie chinoise*. 4 vols. Paris: P. G. Lemercier, 1735. III, 339–78.

———. Wenguzi. *Rujiao shiyi* 儒教實義 (The True Meaning of Confucianism). 1715–1718. Biblioteca Apostolica Vaticana. Borgia Cinese 316 (20); facsimile reproduction in *Tianzhujiao Dongzhuan wenxian xubian*. Ed. Wu Xiangxiang 吳相湘. 3 vols. Taipei: Student Bookstore, 1966. III, 1333–411.

———. *Ru jiao xin* 儒交信 (Literati Correspondence) 1729?.

———. *Selecta quaedam Vestigia praecipuorum Christianae relligionis dogmatum ex antiquis Sinarum Libris Eruta*. Canton, 1725. Bibliothèque Nationale France, Chinois 9248.

[Prémare, Joseph-Maria de, SJ]. *Sheng Ruose zhuan* 聖若瑟傳 (Life of St. Joseph, husband of the Holy Virgin. B.A.V. Raccolta Generale—Oriente—III. 203.

[Prémare, Joseph de, SJ]. *Tianxue zonglun* 天學總論 (Introduction to the Heavenly Teaching). 1710.

———. *Vestiges des principaux dogmes chrétiens tirés des anciens livres chinois*. Edited and translated by Augustin Bonnetty & Paul Perny. Paris: Bureau des Annales de Philosophie Chrétienne, 1878.

―――― [?]. *Zhouyi yuanzhi tan mulu* 周易原旨探目錄 (Table from Zhouyi yuanzhi tan). [A work on the *Yijing* by a Jesuit. perhaps by Fr. de Prémare]. Borgia Cinese 317.1.

Pulleyblank, E. G. Review of Ho Ping-ti's Cradle of the East, *Journal of Asian Studies* 36 (1977): 715–17.

Rawski, Evelyn S. *The Last Emperors: A Social History of Qing Imperial Institutions.* Berkeley: University of California Press, 1998.

Reichwein, Adolf. *China and Europe: Intellectual and Artistic Contacts in the Eighteenth Century.* Translated by J. C. Jowell. London: Kegan Paul, 1925.

Reil, Sebald. *Kilian Stumpf 1655–1720. Ein Würzburger Jesuit am Kaiserhof zu Peking.* Münster Westfalen: Aschendorff, 1978.

Rémusat, Abel. "Joseph Henry Prémare, Missionnaire a la Chine. China," *Nouveaux Mélanges Asiatiques.* Vol. 2. (Paris: Schubart & Heideloff, 1829), p. 262–76.

Rémusat, Jean-Pierre Abel. "Mémoire sur la vie et les opinions de Lao-tseu, philosophe chinois du Vie siècle avant notre ère." *Academie des inscriptions et belleslettres. Mémoires.* 7 (1824): 1–54.

Renan, Ernest. "Rapport sur les travaux du conseil de la Société Asiatique pendant l'annee 1872–1873 fait à la séance annuelle de la Société, le 29 Juin 1873, " *Journal Asiatique.* Seventh series, vol. II (Paris) 1873. p. 11–19.

[Ricci, Matteo, SJ]. Li Madou, *Tianzhu shiyi* [The True Meaning of the Lord of Heaven]. In *Tianxue chuhan*. 6 juan. Taipei: Taiwan Xuesheng Shuju, 1965) 1: 351–635.

――――. *The True Meaning of the Lord of Heaven*. Translated by Douglas Lancashire and Peter Hu Kuo-chen, SJ St. Louis, MO: Institute of Jesuit Sources, 1985.

Ripa, Matteo. *Storia della Fondazione dell Congregazione e del Collegio de cinesi.* 3 vols. Napoli: Tipographia Mandfredi, 1832.

Rosso, Antonio Sisto, OFM *Apostolic Legations to China of the Eighteenth Century.* South Pasadena, CA: Perkins, 1948.

Ruan Yuan 阮元, ed. *Shisan jing zhu shu* 十三經注疏校勘紀 (Notes and Commentary on the Thirteen Classics). 2 vols. Beijing: Zhonghua Shuju Chuban, 1806; reprinted 1980.

Rule, Paul A. *K'ung-tzu or Confucius: The Jesuit Interpretation of Confucianism.* Sydney, Australia: Allen & Unwin, 1986.

Sebes, Joseph, SJ *The Jesuits and the Sino-Russian Treaty of Nerchinsk (1689).* Rome: Institutum Historicum S.I. 1961.

Shanhaijing jiaozhu 山海經校注 (Annotated edition of the Classic of Mountains and Seas). Yuan Ke 遠珂, ed. Shanghai: Shanghai guji, 1930; reprinted 1986.

Shang Huqing. *Bu Ru wengao* 補儒文告 (A Warning to Repair the Deficiencies of the Literati). 1664. Xujiahui Library, Shanghai.

Sionnet, A. "Analyse d'un Ouvrage Inédit du P. Prémare, sur les Vestiges des Principaux Dogmes chrétiens que l'on retrove dans les livres chinois," first article, *Annales de Philosophie Chrétienne.* Vol. XV (July 31, 1837), p. 7–24; & "Analyse d'un Ouvrage Inédit du P. Prémare," third article, p. 325–36.

Sommervogel, Carlos, SJ. *Bibliothèque de la Compagnie de Jésus.* 12 vols. Brussels: Schepens & Paris: Picard, 1890–1932.

Spence, Jonathan D. "The Paris Years of Arcadio Huang," in *Chinese Roundabout: Essays in History and Culture*. New York: W. W. Norton, 1992.

Standaert, Nicolas, ed. *Handbook of Christianity in China*. Volume One: 635–1800. Leiden: Brill, 2001.

Standaert, Nicolas. *The Intercultural Weaving of Historical Texts: Chinese and European Stories about Emperor Ku and His Concubines*. Leiden: Brill, 2016.

———. Yang Tingyun, *Confucian and Christian in late Ming China*. Leiden: Brill, 1988.

Stumpf, Kilian, SJ, *Acta Pekinensia or Historical Records of the Maillard de Tournon Legation*. Edited by Paul Rule & Claudia von Collani. Vol. I December 1705–August 1706. Rome: Institutum Historicum Societatis Iesu, 2015.

Sung, Z. D. *The Text of the Yi King*. Shanghai: The China Modern Education Company, 1935.

Tu Wei-ming, "Reconstituting the Confucian Tradition," *Journal of Asian Studies* 33 (1974): 441–54.

Verhaeren, H., CM *Catalogue de la Bibliothèque du Pé-t'ang*. Beijing: Imprimerie des Lazaristes, 1949.

Waley, Arthur, trans., *Book of Songs*. New York: Grove Press, 1937.

Wilhelm, Hellmut. *Change: Eight Lectures on the I Ching*. Translated by Cary F. Baynes. New York: Harper & Row, 1960.

Witek, John W., SJ, *Controversial Ideas in China and in Europe: a Biography of Jean-François Foucquet, S J (1665–1741)*. Rome: Institutum Historicum S.I., 1982.

———. "Jean-François Foucquet: un Controversiste Jésuite en Chine et en Europe," in *Actes de Colloque de Sinologie: La Mission Française de Pékin aux XVIIe et XVIII Siècles*. Paris: Les Belles Lettres, 1976. P. 115–35.

Wu, Min 吳旻 & Han Qi 韓琦, "Liyi zhi zheng yu Zhongguo Tianzhujiao tu: yi Fujian jiaotu he Yan Dang de chongtu wei li," 禮儀之爭與中國天主教徒：以福建教徒和顏璫的冲突為例 (The Chinese Rites Controversy and Chinese Catholics: the case of the conflict between the Fujian Christians and Bishop Charles Maigrot). *Lishi yanjiu* 歷史研究 2004 (6): 83–91.

Xiao Qinghe 肖清和. "Qing chu Rujia Jidutu Liu Ming Shengping Shiji" 清初儒家基督徒刘凝生平事跡" (The Life and Deeds of the Early Qing Christian Literatus Liu Ning), *Zhongguo Dianji Yu Wenhua* 《中国典籍与文化》, No. 4, 2012 (总第83期), p. 42–54

———. Suoyin Tianxue: Ma Ruose de Suoyin Shenxue tixi yanjiu"索隐天学：马若瑟的索隐神学体系研究" (Christian Figurism: Research on the Figurist Theology of Joseph de Prémare), *Xueshu Yuekan* 《学术月刊 / Academic Monthly》 48 (01) (January 2016), p. 156–68.

Xingli daquan 性理大全 (The Great Collection of Song Neo-Confucian Philosophers). Edited by Hu Guang 胡廣. 70 juan. 1405.

Xingli jingyi 性理精義 (Essentials of Neo-Confucianism). 12 juan. 1717.

Xu Shen 許慎, compiler. *Shuowen jiezi duanzhu* 說文解字段注 (Shuowen dictionary with commentary). Annotated by Duan Yucai 段玉裁. Taipei: Yiwen Yinshuguan, 1967.

Yuan Ke, Dragons and Dynasties: *An Introduction to Chinese Mythology*. Selected and translated by Kim Echlin & Nie Zhixiong. London: Penguin Books, 1993.

Zhang Xingyao 張星耀. *Tianzhujiao Rujiao tongyi kao* 天主教儒教同異考 (An examination of the similarities and differences between the Heavenly Teaching and the Literati Teaching), 3 juan. 1672–1715. Xujiahui Library Shanghai and Bibliothèque nationale France, Paris.

Zhouyi gujing jinzhu 周易古經今注 (The ancient text and modern commentary on the Book of Changes). Gao Xiang 高享, ed. Hong Kong: China Book Company, Hong Kong Branch, 1963.

Zhu Xi. *Sishu jizhu* 四書集註 (Collected Commentary on the Four Books) (1177). Taipei: Yiwen Yinshu, 1969.

———. *Zhouyi benyi* 周易本義 (The original meaning of the Classic of Changes) 12 juan. 1177.

———. "Zhongyong zhangju xu" 中庸章句序 (Commentary on the Doctrine of the Mean) preface (1194). In *Zhuzi daquan* 朱子大全 (Great Collection of Master Zhu). 76/21a–23a.

Zhuangzi, *Complete Works*, Burton Watson, tr. New York: Columbia University Press, 2013.

———. *Jiaozheng Zhuangzi jishi* 校正莊子集釋 (Revised collected commentary on the Zhuangzi). Collated by Guo Qingfan 郭慶藩. 2 vols. Taipei: Shijie Shuju, 1971.

Index

abandoned girls, 13–14
Académie des Inscriptions et Belles-Lettres, 11, 31, 37
Académie des Sciences (Paris), 10–11
accommodation, Jesuit, 3, 17, 46, 50, 90
    See also Matteo Ricci
Adam, 6, 36, 46, 70, 73, 75, 76, 89
Ambassador's Route, *map 1*
Amiot, Joseph-Marie, SJ, 12
Amphitrite, 7
ancient literati (*gu ru*), 46
Ancient Script (*gu wen*), 78
Ancient Theology (*prisca theologia*), 2
angels, 78
Annales de Philosophie Chrétienne, 55, 58
annalistic style of history (*biannian*), 33
antiquity of China debate, 1–4
Appiani, Luigi Antonio, CM, 18
    as politically astute, 10–11
Association for Asian Studies, 1
atheism of Zhu Xi, 92–94, 98

Bacon, Francis, 39
bamboo or wood, lines on, 77, 78
Bao Si, 76
Baopuzi, 69

Beijing, 9, 72
Beitang Library, 17
Benevente, Álvaro de, OESA, 17
Bernard-Maitre, Henri, SJ, 25
Bertuccioli, Giuliano, 21n20
Bible, 2, 56, 58, 68
Bignon, Jean-Paul, 11, 12, 37, 61, 101
binary system, 59
Board of Rites (*Li Bu*), 17
Bocarro, António, 5
Bonnetty Augustin, 55–59, *fig. 3.4*
Boodberg, Peter, 95
Book of Changes. See Yijing
books, Chinese, 38, 101
Bouvet, Joachim, SJ, 2, 7, 12, 14–20, 36, 45–48, 52, 54, 62, 72–73, 80, 88, *fig. 3.1*
Brevis Relatio, 15
Bridgeman, Elijah Coleman, 79
Briga, Melchior della, SJ, 37
Bu Ru wengao, 47
bu Ru yi Fo, 16, 47, 93
Buddhism, 34, 46, 47, 49, 51, 56, 81, 93, 95, 99
Buddhist wheel-maps, 69, *fig. 4.2*
Buglio, Ludovico, SJ, 89
Bureau of Astronomy, 48, 89
Buzhou Mountain, 69, 71, 74, *fig. 4.2*

Caballero, Antonio, OFM, 89–90
calendrical science, 59
Cang Jie, 78
catechist. See xianggong
celestial paradise, 46, *fig. 4.2*
Chan Wing-tsit, 95
Chang Chun-shu, 41n31
Characters, Six Kinds of, 78, *fig. 4.3*, *fig. 4.4*
Charmot, Nicholas, M.E.P., 14
chauvinism, 1–2
Cheng Bo, 28
Cheng Hao, 51, 95
Cheng Tang. See Tang
Cheng Yi, 51, 95
Chinese character fonts, 56
Chinese grammars, dispute over, 38–39
Chinese Rites Controversy, 14–17, 29, 80, 100–1
Chinoiserie, 27, 29, 50, *fig. 2.1*
Chiyou 6, 35, 60, 70–71, 73, 75
Christ, 36, 46, 54, 60, 61, 68, 71–72, 73
Christianity, 40
Chunqiu (*Spring and Autumn Annals*), 8, 49
Cibot, Pierre Martial, SJ, 54
cinnabar, 69
Classic of Changes. See *Yijing*
Classic of History. See *Shujing*
Classic of Mountains and Seas. See *Shanhaijing*
Classic of Odes. See *Shijing*
Clavis Sinica, 39
Clement XI, Pope, 14
collaborators, Chinese, 79–80
    of Prémare, 88
colonialism, 97
Comédie Française, 30
commentaries on the *Jing*, 50
composite style of history (*jichuan*), 33
concubines, 75–76
Confucian-Christian synthesis, 47
Confucianism, 36
Confucius Sinarum Philosophus, 46

Confucius, 49, 51
Cordier, Henri, 24n81, 31, 39
creation, cyclical versus *ex nihilo*, 92, *fig. 5.1*
Creator, 53
Croquer (Croker), Thomas, OP, 18
crows (nine), 70

Dao, 53
Daodejing, 49, 67–68
Daoism, 3, 9, 34, 47, 49, 51, 53, 54, 56, 69, 81, 90
Dayi, 76
deism, 30
Demiéville, Paul, 25
Demon, 60
descriptio mundi, 68
dialogue form, 81
Diku (Noah), 58, 61
Diluvian tradition, 58
Discours Preliminaire. See *Histoire de vieux temps*
disseminationist theory, 56, 58–59
Dominicans, 6, 89–90
Dong Zhongshu, 61
dragon. See *long*
Du Halde, Jean Baptiste, SJ, 29
dust, 102
Dynastic Histories, 8, 21n16

earth, 87, 102
Eastern Zhou, 13, 27, 32, *fig. 2.2*
Edict of Toleration (1692), 17
Egyptian colony (China), 58
Eight Trigrams (*Bagua*), 78
    See also trigrams
Empress Wu Zetian, 95
Empress Xiaoxian, 89
Enlightenment, 29–30, 93, *fig. 2.1*
Enoch. See Hennoch
Erya, 49
Essay on the Golden Lion, 95
etymological analysis, 57
Eucharist, 48

Eurocentrism, 17–20
European intellectuals. *See* gatekeepers
Eve, 74, 75
expulsion edicts. *See* Guangzhou exile

Facang, 95
faith of Prémare, 102
fall from grace, 46, 70
false teaching (*yiduan*), 99
Feng Yingjing, 93
Figurism, 2, 11–13
figuriste, 47
filial piety, 28
Five Classics (*Wu Jing*), 3, 9, 10, 11, 46–47, 52, 94
Five Elements (*Wu Xing*), x, 5, 25, 45, 67, 87, 102
Five Emperors (*Wudi*), 13, 58, 61
flood myths, 36–37, 58, 60, 71–73
Foucquet, Jean-François, SJ, 11, 12, 19, 38, 47, 48, 72, 97, 101
fountain of immortality, 69, *fig. 4.1*, *fig. 4.2*
Four Books (*Sishu*), 46–47, 52, 94
Fourmont, Etienne, 26, 29, 31, 38–40, 71, 96, 100–1
Franciscans, 89–90
Fréret, Nicholas, 12, 47
Fu Xi, 19, 32, 35, 52, 53, 54, 61, 72, 78

Gan dialect, 79
Gan River, 7, 9
gangjian style of history, 33–34
Garden of Eden, 68, 69, 70, *fig. 4.1*
gatekeepers, European, 3, 12, 27, 32, 47, 62, 96–98
Gaubil, Antoine, SJ, 12, 25–26, 31–32, 47–48, 58, 79, *fig. 2.2*
genealogical table of Chinese antiquity, 57–58, *fig. 3.5*
Genesis, 69, 70, *fig. 4.1*
Genghis Khan, 30
geometry, 9, 10, 11
Gerbillon, Jean-Francois, SJ, 14
Gernet, Jacques, 25

God, 46, 62, 67, 72, 91
Goethe, Johann Wolfgang von, 30
Gollet, Jean-Alexis de, SJ, 9, 22n42, 48, 72
Gonggong, 6, 36, 60, 70–71, 72, 74, 75
Gouvea, António de, SJ, 90
Grammont, Jean-Baptist-Joseph, SJ, 22n42
Great Appendix (*Xizi*), 77, 78
Grimond, SJ, 80–81
Guangzhou (Canton) exile, 11, 30–31, 61–62, 67, 76, 89–90, 99
Guanyinzi, 49
Guanzi, 36
Guignes, Joseph de, 31–32, 58
Gujin jing Tian, 15–20, *fig. 1.1*, *fig. 1.2*
Gun, 36–37
Guoyu, 36

Haipian dictionary, 38, 43n66
Han dynasty, 51
Han Qi, 59
Han Tan, 17–18, *fig. 1.1*, *fig. 1.2*
Han Yu, 51
Hatchett, William, 29
hell, 74
Henoch (Enoch), 52, 57
Hermes Trigmegistus, 2
Hervieu, Julien-Placide, SJ, 18–19, *fig. 1.2*
Hetu luoshu. *See* Yellow River Chart and Luo River Diagram
hexagrams (*gua*), 52, 70, 77, 91
hieroglyphs, 11, 12, 53, 58, 70, 71, 72, 73, 76–79
Histoire de vieux temps, 27, 32, 71, *fig. 2.2*
historical versus symbolic interpretations, 12, 22, 25–26, 31–37, *fig. 2.2*
Ho Ping-ti (He Bingdi), 1, 3
Holy Spirit, 78
horse. *See* Yellow River Chart
Hou Ji, 61
Huainanzi, 36, 49, 60, 67, 69, 70, 71, 75

Huang-Lao teaching, 52, 75
  See also Daoism
Huang, Arcadio, 38
Huangdi (Yellow Emperor), 54, 57, 61, 74, *fig. 3.5*
Huayan Sutra, 95
Hundun (Chaos), 70, 75

Ignatius of Loyola, 87
immortality, 69
Intorcetta, Prospero, SJ, 16
isolation of Prémare, 90

Jansenists, 12
Jartoux, Pierre, SJ, 9
Jesus, 78
Jews, 51, 56
Ji Junxiang, 27–28
Jianchang, 7, *map 2*
Jiangxi, 7–8, 9, 62, 81, *map 1*, *map 2*
Jiaoyou lun, 8
Jie, 6
Jin Luxiang, 35
Jing (classics), 46, 48–54, 94, 98
Jing chuan yilun, 8
jing Tian (revere Heaven), 15, 17
Jing zhuan yilun, 8
Jingists, 3
jingtian (well-field system), 59–60, *fig. 3.6*
Jiujiang, 7, 9, 81
Journal Asiatique, 98
Juesi lu, 8
Julien, Stanislas, 55, 79, 96–97

kaiming (animal), 69
Kangxi emperor, 9, 10, 11, 17, 48, 50, 53, 59, 80, 99
Kangxi zidian, 38, 101
Kircher, Athanasius, SJ, 2, 39, 58
Kong Anguo, 49
Kunlun Mountain, 68–69, 74, *fig. 4.1*, *fig. 4.2*

Lackner, Michael, 63
Laozi, 49, 67
later literati (*hou ru*), 46
Le Gobien, Charles, SJ, 14
Legge, James, 97, 98
Leibniz, G. W., 3, 10, 39, 59
Lettre sur le monothéisme de Chinois, 92–94, 100
li (principle), 19, 93–96
li Dao (Supreme Truth), 53
Li Guangdi, 53, 54, 81, 94, *fig. 5.1*
Li Zhizao, 93
libertines, 93
Liezi, 49, 53
Liji (*Record of Rites*), 49, 61, 63, 94
Lionne, Bishop Artus de, MEP, 38
Lishi (Grand History), 33, 52, 53
Liu Ning, 8–9, 21, 77, 81, *map 2*, *fig. 4.3*, *fig. 4.4*
Liu Shu (Liu Daoyuan), 34, 35, 53, 61
Liu shu guai, 77, *fig. 4.3*
Liushu shiyi, 77, *fig 4.3*, *fig. 4.4*
long (dragon), 35, 70
Longobardo, Niccolò, SJ, 90, 98
Louis XIV, 10, 72
Lü Buwei, 49
Lu Ruohan, 9
Lucifer, 46, 70–71, 73
Luo Bi, 34, 41n31, 50, 52, 53, 60, 70, 73, 76, 78, 98
Luo River Diagram (*Luoshu*), 53, 54, 60, 73, 78, *fig. 3.2*, *fig. 3.3*
Lüshi Chunqiu, 49
Lushi, 50, 70, 76, 98

Ma Ruose. *See* Prémare
Macau, 5, 79
Magalhães, Gabriel de, SJ, 89
Maigrot, Bishop Charles, 14, 15
Mailla, Joseph de, SJ, 12
Man-God, 98
Manchu, 15, 80
Mandate of Heaven (*tianming*), 36

Mao Chang, 49
Maria Theresa, Empress, 29
Mariani, Fr. Sabino, 19
Martini, Martino, SJ, 16
mathematics, 9, 59, 72
Medhurst, Walter Henry, 98
Mei Xi, 75
Mei Yingzuo, 38
Mémoires de Trevoux, 37
Mencius (*Mengzi*), 46, 51, 59
Mencius, 49, 51
Mentzel, Christian, 39
metaphorical versus historical texts, 2
Metastasio, Pietro, 29
Miao, King (San Miao), 76
Michael (Archangel), 71, 74
Militant Holy Virgin, 74
millet, 1
Ming Tang diagram, 60
Missions Etrangères de Paris, 56
Mohl, Jules, 57
monotheism of Semitic peoples, 98
moribund children, baptism, 13
Mount Yu (*Yushan*), 36
Mourão, João, SJ, 99
Müller, Andreas, 39
Murphy, Arthur, 30
mythical heroes, 60–61

Nanchang, 7, *map 2*
Nanfeng, 8, *map 2*
nationalistic disputes, 90
natural morality, 50
natural religion, 46
Navarrete, Domingo Fernández de, OP, 89–90, 95
Neo-Confucianism, 46–47, 51–52, 90, 92–93
Neoterici Interpretes, 47
Noachic flood, 58
    See also flood myths
Noah. *See* Diku
Noël, François, SJ, 15
Noëlas, Jean-François, SJ, 22n42, 67–68

nonary cosmography, 59–60, 73–74, *fig. 3.2, fig. 3.3, fig. 3.6*
Notitia Linguae Sinicae, 26, 40, 77–79, *fig. 4.3*

Official Script (*liwen*), 78
Orphan of Zhao (*Zhaoshi gu'er*), 27–30, 100, *fig. 2.1*
Ouyang Xiu, 50, 52, 57

Pan Feng-chuan, 54
Pan Gu, 34
pantheism, 93
Papal Legate. *See* Tournon
Paravey, Le Chavalier de, 58
Parennin, Dominique, SJ, 9
pastoral concerns of Prémare, 13
patronesses, European, 14
Pauthier, Guillaume, 93, 96–98
Pereira, Tomé, SJ, 14
Perny, Paul, MSP, 56, *fig. 3.4*
philological research (*kaocheng*), 8
philology, 8, 59, 72, 77–79, *fig. 4.4*
philosophes, 50, 93
Pinot, Virgil, 25
poor people of China, 13
Poyang, Lake, 7
Prémare, Joseph de, SJ, passim
Primitive Language, 39
Propaganda, 23n51, 101
proto-Sinologists, 3, 4n11, 26, 39, 101

qi (material force), 94–95
Qin book burning, 49
Qin Shi Huangdi, 35

racial nationalism, 4n6
radicals (*bu*), 38–39
Raguet, M. 40
Real Characters, 39
recall of Prémare, 101
reclusiveness of Prémare, 81, 87–88
Rémusat, Abel, 25–26
Renan, Ernest, 98

repairing Confucianism, 47
Revelation, 46, 50, 78, 93
Ricci, Matteo, SJ, 8, 21n20, 88
    accommodation, 2, 3, 46, 50, 51, 81, 90, 93
    Chinese collaborators, 80
    criticism of Daoism, 19
rice, 8, 13
Rouillard, Fr., 101
Royal City diagram, 60, *fig. 3.5*
royal library of France, 37–38, 48
Rujiao shiyi, 79–81, 92

sage to saint transition, 78
saint, 78
Sanhuang ji, 35
San Miao. *See* Miao
San Paulo church, 6
Sanhuang, 54
Satan, 35, 74
Schall, Adam, SJ, 80, 87–88, 89
Seal Script (*da xiao yuan*), 78
Seth, 52
seven apertures, 75
shamanism, 89
Shang dynasty, 2, 3, 58, 61
Shang Huqing, 16, 4779
Shang Tian (Heaven Above), 19
Shangdi (Lord on High), 14, 19, 93
Shanhaijing (*Classic of Mountains and Seas*), 9, 35, 49, 68–69, 70, 74, *fig. 4.1, fig. 4.2*
Shao Bowen, 92
Shao Yong, 92, 95
Shen Nong, 54, 61
Shen, Marquis, 76
sheng ren (sage versus saint), 54
Shiji (*Historical Records*), 28, 34, 70
Shijing (*Classic of Odes*), 26, 33, 42n50, 49, 59, 74, 75, 76, 94, 98
Shujing (*Classic of History*), x, 27, 31, 32, 33, 36, 37, 49, 50, 58, 59, 70, 71, 74, 76, 94, 98, *fig. 2.2*
Shun, 6, 37, 51, 61, 71–72

Shunzhi emperor, 80, 89
Shuowen jiezi, 8, 49, 71, 73, 77, 78, 95
Sibour, Archbishop, 55
Sima Guang, 33, 34
Sima Qian, 28, 33, 34, 35, 49, 57, 70
Sima Zheng (Xiao Sima), 34–35
sinologues du chambre, 96–97
Sinomania, 30
Sionnet, Antoine Matthieu, 55–56
Sishu jizhu, 94
Sishu. *See* Four Books
Sizhi tongjian waiji, 53
Société Asiatique de Paris, 55, 96, 97
society of learning of Bouvet, 10, 11, 46, 48
Son of God. *See* Christ
Son of Man, 72
Song Neo-Confucianism. *See* Neo-Confucianism
Spinozism, 93
Spring and Autumn Annals. *See Chunqiu*
Standaert, Nicolas, 33
strokes of Prémare, 101
Stumpf, Killian, SJ, 18, 48
Su Shi (Dongpo), 49
Sui Huang, 61
Suiren, 61
Sumeria, 1
suns (ten), 70–71
Sunu family, 99
Sunzi, 49
symbolic theologians, 22n42
symbolic versus historical interpretations, 12, 22, 31–37

Tadpole Script (*ketou*), 78
Taiji (Supreme Ultimate), 19, 90–92, *fig. 5.1*
Tamburini, Michel Angelo, SJ, 101
Tang (Shang founder), 6, 51, 61, 75
Tang Xuanzong, 50
Tartre, Pierre de, SJ, 9
Ten Lost Tribes of Israel, 56

Ten Wings (*Shi Yi*), 52
terrestrial paradise, 46, 48, 69, 70, *fig. 4.1, fig. 4.2*
Tetragrammaton YHWH, 68
Thirteen Classics, 8, 101
Three Ancient Dynasties, 2, 32, 57, 58, 61, 75, 81
Three Emperors (*Sanhuang*), 61
Three Sovereigns (*Sanhuang*), 13
Tian (Heaven), 14
Tian Ru tongyi kao, 16–17
Tian Ye (Heavenly Father), 19
Tianjujiao Rujiao tongyi kao, 47
Tianxue benyi, 15
Tianxue jijie, 8
Tianzhu shiyi, 93
Tongzhi, 50
tortoise. *See* Luo River Diagram
Tournon, Cardinal Charles Thomas, 14–15, 17–19, 48, *fig. 1.1, fig. 1.2*
Transmission of the Dao (*daotong*), 51, 81
Treaty of Nerchinsk, 14
tree of knowledge, 75
Trigrammaton IHV, 67–68
Trigrams (*gua*), 52, 53, 77
Trinity, 36, 46, 48, 54, 68, 78, 91
Tu Angu, 28
Tu Weiming, 94

universal language, 39
universal types in myth, 60–61

Vachet, Benigne, MEP, 72
Vatican, 3
vengeance, 28
Verbiest, Ferdinand, SJ, 89
Vestiges, 55–59, *fig. 3.4*
Vestigia, 26, 27, 29, 31, 45–85, *fig. 3.1*
  See also Vestiges
vicar-apostolic, 14, 23n51
virgin mother, 60
Visdelou, Claude de, SJ, 18
Voltaire, 29–30, *fig. 2.1*

Waiji. See Zizhi tongjian waiji
Walpole, Robert, 29
Wang Mang, 60
Wang Ruchun, 93
Wang Shen, 91–92
water of immortality (*dan shui*), 69
water, 5, 74, 102
Wei Lie, King, 35
Wen (Zhou king), 51, 52, 61
Wen Guzi (Prémare), 80
Wenzhou, 7
Western Zhou dynasty, 2, 3, 32, 58
Willow, 74
Woman Wa, 36, 61, 71, 72, 74
women as dangerous, 75–76
  See also concubines
Wu (Zhou founder), 6, 51, 57, 61, 76, *fig. 3.5*
Wuji, 92
Wujing. See Five Classics

xenophobia, 99
Xia dynasty, 2, 3, 58, 61, 70
xianggong (secretary-assistant), 9, 87
Xiao Qinghe, 9
Xiaojing (Classic of *Filial* Piety), 60
Xie, 61
Xingli daquan, 96
Xingli jingyi, 53, 91, *fig. 5.1*
Xu Guangqi, 16
Xu Shen, 8, 49, 77, 78

Yang Guangxian, 89–90
Yangshao culture, 1
Yao, 6, 36–37, 42n50, 50, 58, 61, 70, 71–72
Yellow River Chart (*Hetu*), 52, 54, 60, 73, 78, *fig. 3.2, fig. 3.3*
Yellow River, 69
Yi the Archer, 70–71
Yijing (*Classic of Changes*), 5, 11, 26, 33, 45, 46, 48, 49, 52, 53, 54, 55–56, 59, 60, 70, 72, 76–79, 91, 94, 95
Yili, 49

yin and *yang*, 91, 94
Yinreng, heir apparent, 99
Yintang, Manchu prince, 99
Yinti, Manchu prince, 99
Yinzhen. *See* Yongzheng emperor
Yongzheng emperor, 11, 31, 99–100
You, King, 76
Yu, 6, 36, 51, 71–72, 73, 74, 76
Yuan dramas, 27, 79
Yuan Liaofan, 34
Yuan qu xuan, 28
Yuejing (Classic of Music), 49

Zeng Zi, 51
Zhang Xingyao, 16, 47, 79
Zhang Zai, 51, 95
Zhao Dun, 28
Zheng Qiao, 50
Zhongyong, 51
Zhou Dunyi, 51, 91, 95, *fig. 5.1*

Zhou dynasty, 2, 3, 13, 27, 32, 58, 61
Zhou Gong (Duke of Zhou), 52
Zhouli, 49
Zhouyi zhezhong, 53, 81, 94
Zhu Rong, 71, 74
Zhu Xi, 34, 35, 46, 49, 51, 52, 64n33, 81, 91, 95
    See also atheism
Zhuan Di, 61
Zhuan Xu, 61
Zhuangzi, 49, 53, 67, 70, 75, 92, 95
Zhuxi Quanshu, 53
Zihui dictionary, 38
Zisi, 51
Zizhi tongjian gangmu, 34
Zizhi tongjian qianbian, 35
Zizhi tongjian waiji, 34, 35, 61, 74
Zizhitongjian, 33, 34
Zuoshi (Zuo Qiuming), 49

About the Author

D. E. Mungello, the grandson of Italian and German immigrants, was born in a small town in Pennsylvania in 1943. His fascination with history and with remote cultures drove his search to recapture the past in ten books and numerous articles. At the beginning of his search, he lived and studied in Dallas, Washington, D.C., Copenhagen and Taipei. After completing a doctorate in History at the University of California at Berkeley, he did research in Germany (1978–1980 and 1984), Shanghai (1986), Hangzhou (1989), Jinan (1997), and Rome (1999). He founded a specialized journal dealing with Sino-Western history in 1979 to revive intellectual contacts with mainland Chinese scholars who had become isolated by years of communist rule. His books on Sino-Western history have included the history of Christianity in China as well as sensitive topics, such as, female infanticide in China and Western queers in China. Three of his books have been translated into Chinese and Korean. He has also published articles in VIA (*Voices of Italian Americana*) and the *Gay and Lesbian Review*. Most recently he has published a memoir *Remember This* of his contentious Italian family. He began his teaching career at Lingnan College in Hong Kong (1973), taught Chinese history in German at the University of Düsseldorf (1980 and 1984), and since 1994 taught history at Baylor University in Waco, Texas where he is now professor emeritus.

www.ingramcontent.com/pod-product-compliance
Lightning Source LLC
Chambersburg PA
CBHW061718300426
44115CB00014B/2738